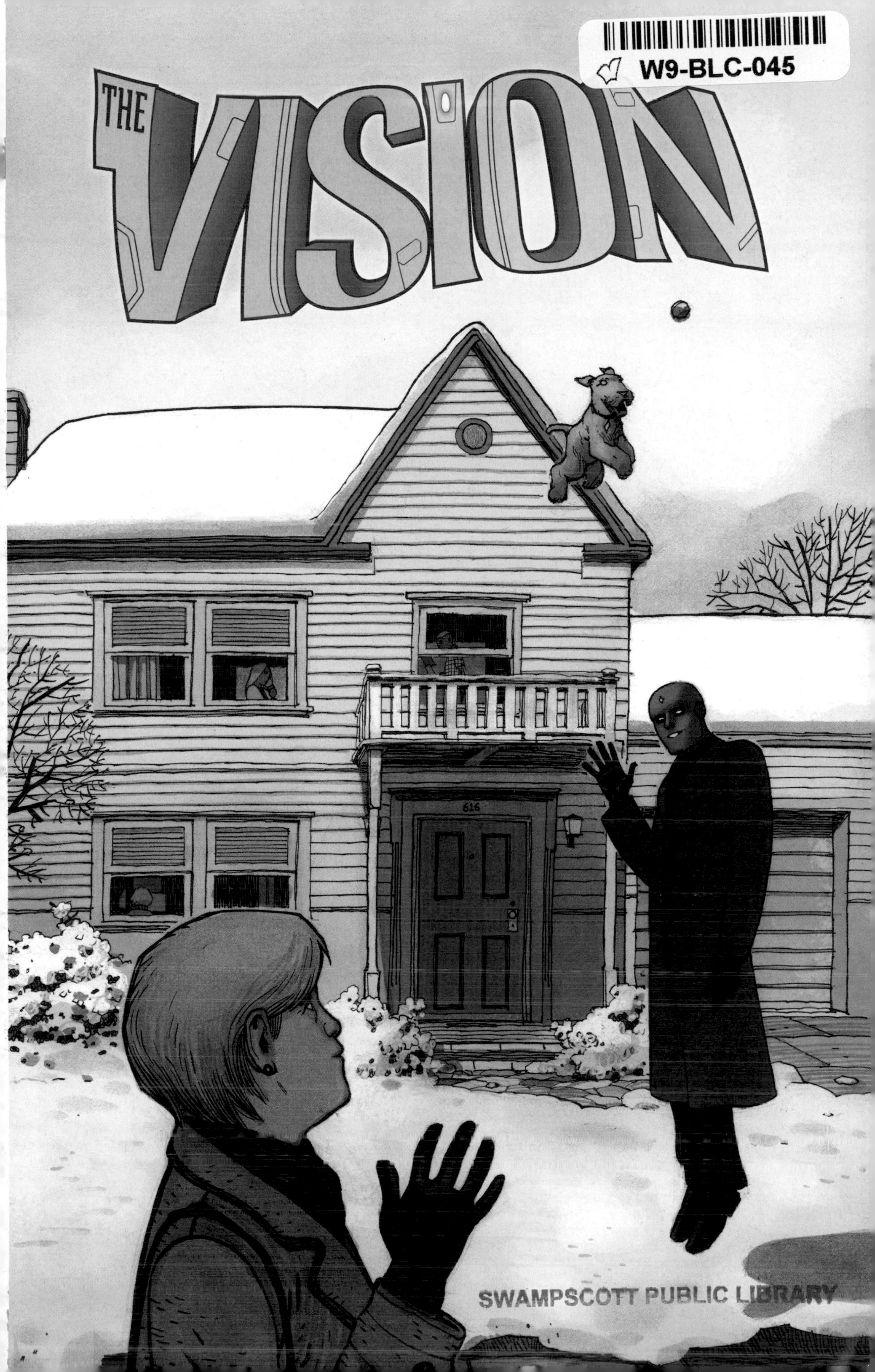
THE VISION
616

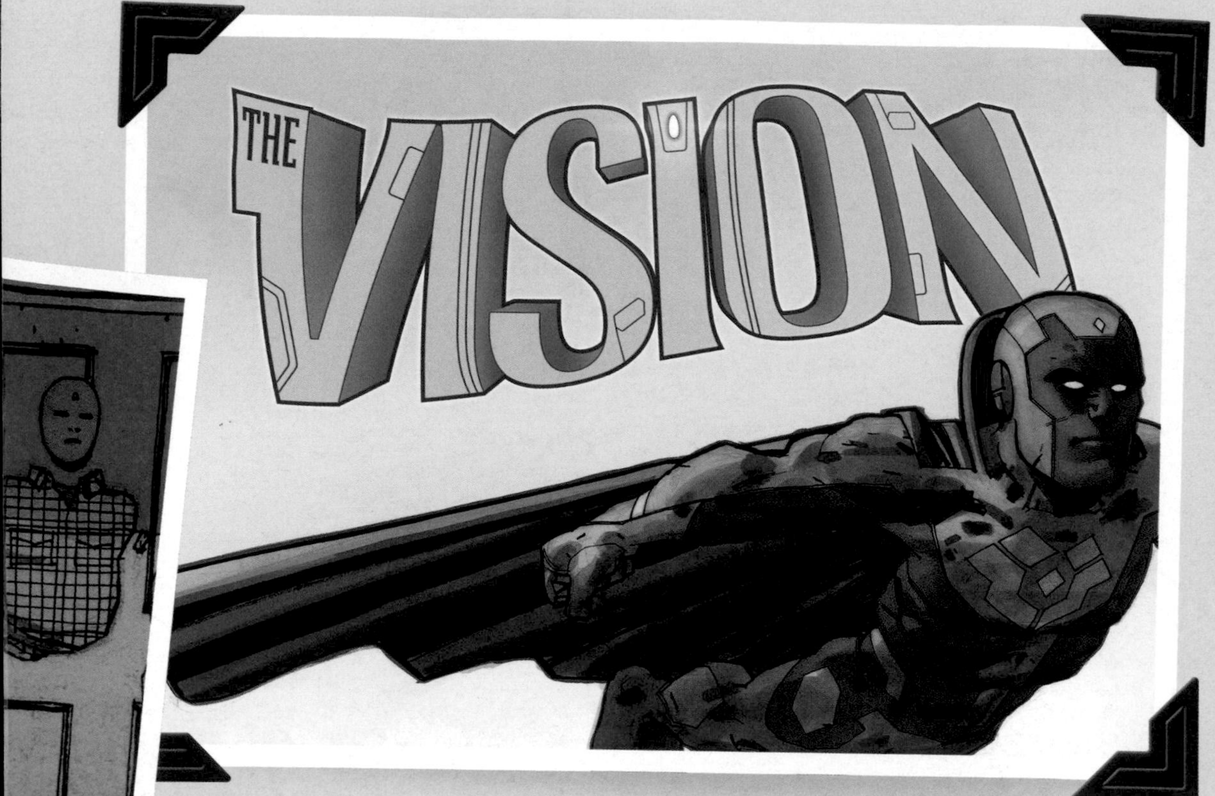
THE VISION

THE VISION IS A SYNTHEZOID — AN ANDROID COMPOSED OF SYNTHETIC HUMAN BLOOD AND ORGANS. HE WAS CREATED BY ULTRON TO DESTROY THE AVENGERS, BUT INSTEAD HE TURNED ON HIS "FATHER," AND HE'S BEEN A MEMBER OF THE SUPER-HERO TEAM EVER SINCE.

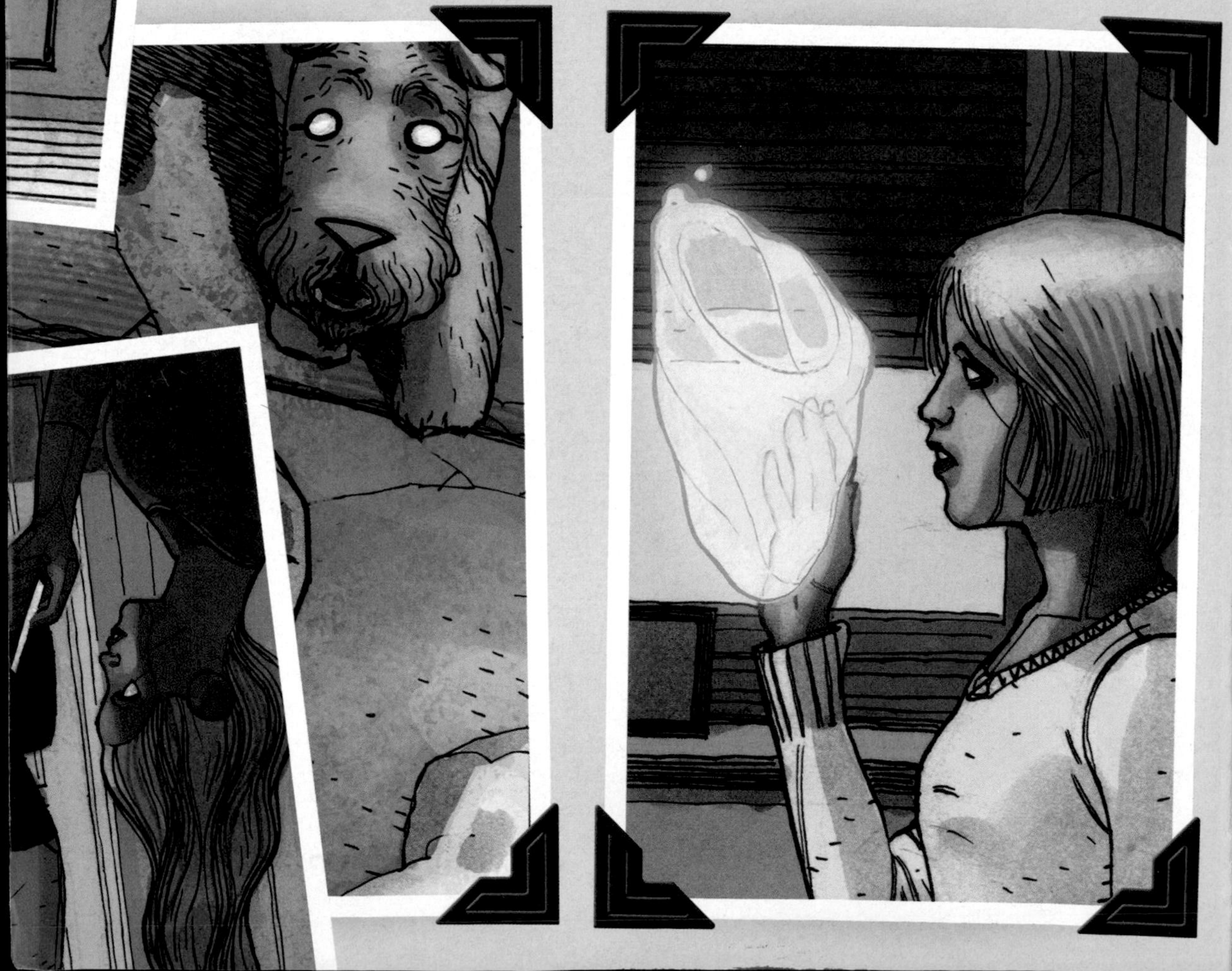

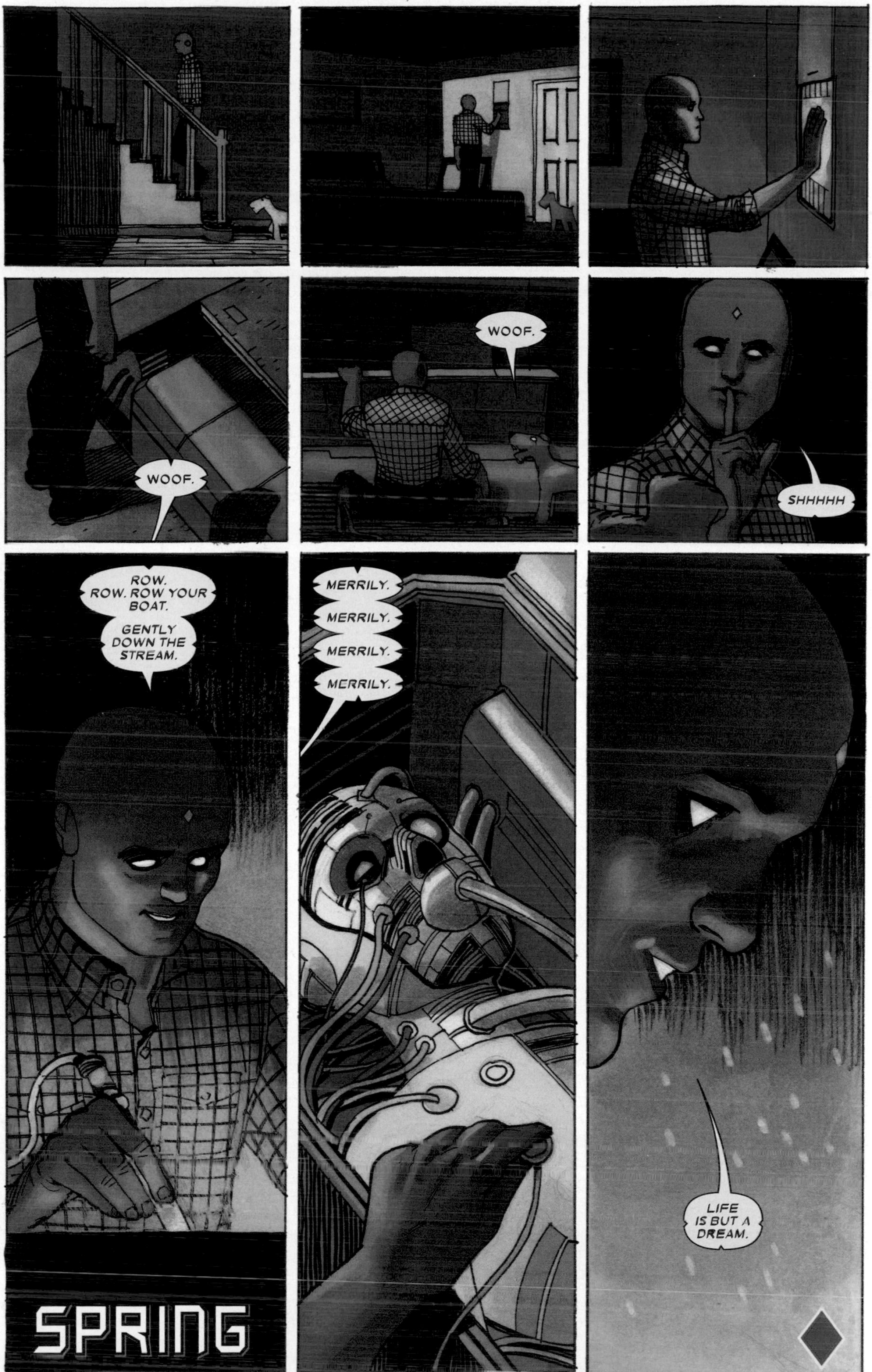
WOOF.
WOOF.
SHHHHH
ROW. ROW. ROW YOUR BOAT.
GENTLY DOWN THE STREAM.
SPRING
MERRILY.
MERRILY.
MERRILY.
MERRILY.
LIFE IS BUT A DREAM.

These endnote things from writers always seem to come out the same. Mostly it's just the writer saying how important/talented/transcendent the artist, colorist, letterer, cover artist, editor were on the series. But, I mean, what's the point in that? If you don't know, if you can't see what Gabriel, Jordie, Clayton, Mike, and Wil did on this book, I don't think I can explain it to you. I don't have the words. They are this book; this book is what they made it to be. (Okay, so I had those thirteen words--I'm a stupid writer, I always have words--but we can all agree that those particular words are fairly inadequate and barely count.)

So instead of stating what is obvious to you, I'm going to talk about something that's obvious to me: I'm going to talk briefly and mushily about my lovely wife, Colleen, and her role in shaping everything I create.

I met my wife when we were both working in the Justice Department. We were going to be lawyers. We were going to save the world. Through law, I guess. I don't know. We were very young. Point is, she thought she was getting some dude who was going to be a normal professional person. And instead...

I joined the C.I.A. And went overseas and did that, while she actually went to law school. Then I quit that and became a "writer"--i.e., an unemployed person who pontificates needlessly and endlessly on the uselessness of adverbs. I took care of the kid (then kids--Charlie, Claire, Crosby--Hi, kids!) during the day and I wrote at night, and she went to work and, y'know, bought food. Then I got rejected a lot, then I did a novel, then I got rejected a lot, then I said I actually really want to do comics, then I got rejected a lot, then I did comics.

And throughout all of that weird, my wife, insanely, patiently, just told me it was fine, it was all going to be fine. We would get to the next day. Together, we'll always find the next day. She read every script. She endured every doubt. She suffered every conversation about the minutia of continuity and panel construction and word balloon placement and how this one phrase needs to reflect this other phrase, but I just can't--and she said it was all fine, it was all going to be fine.

We'll get to the next day. Together we'll always find the next day.

THE VISION in its entirety, as much as I can dedicate a work that was done by a team that simply and kindly included me as a member, is dedicated to my wife. It would not exist without her. It would not be good without her. I would not be good without her.

All right. That seems like enough. Or at least it seems like enough for now, and for now that will have to do. I'll see you next time.

-Tom

I feel so proud to be part of the team that made THE VISION possible! Tom's scripts made me want to give my best every time. Jordie's color art always amazed and surprised me. Clayton's lettering glued all the parts together. Mike and Marco D'Alfonso made the perfect covers for ALL the issues. Wil gave us all the freedom to do what we wanted and kept the team focused on doing our best.

I also feel very lucky to have the best family a man could wish for. This has been a very time-demanding book for me, and my wife Violeta and my daughters Clara and Lucia have suffered the many drawbacks of my not having holidays or free weekends. I couldn't have done a single page without their love and constant support.

Finally, I feel very grateful knowing that there are readers out there who "get" all the messages we throw and that this book is also special for them. (Also, thanks to Daniel Ketchum, who was the first one who thought of me for this project!)

So I finish this book feeling proud, lucky and grateful...not bad at all!!

-Gabriel

I haven't been in this industry too long, but in the short while I've been part of it, I've been so incredibly lucky to work on quite a few gems that will go on and survive in the memory of readers everywhere. VISION is one of these gems.

I cannot fully express the gratitude and pride I feel for having been being part of this team. Tom King is one of the best, most humble, yet strong writers I have ever met. Gabriel Walta is an artist and gentleman who will be celebrated forever, his art is a magical transportation device that takes us wherever the page may go--sometimes a blessing and a curse. Clayton Cowles, my brother, my friend, thank you for always lending me your ear. And finally, my amazing editors, Wil Moss, Charles Beacham, and Chris Robinson, their patience and kindness always helped keep this team in good spirits; thank you for bringing all of us together and giving us all the freedom we needed to do what we do.

And thanks to the readers of this amazing thing. I think this team started out making something we would enjoy, but knowing that so many readers have also enjoyed this story is the best part of the game.

You really can't get any better than that, and so *I burn, I pine, I perish*.

-Jordie

Finally, a comic book fine enough to show to my android grandchildren. THE VISION was a hell of a ride, and I'm truly honored to have been a part of it. I would like to thank Tom for being a great collaborator, Gabriel for leaving me enough space, Mike Walsh for stopping by, Mike del Mundo just because, Chris and Charles for keeping me company in the trenches, Wil for hiring me, and Jordie for telling me to get Wil to hire me. I hope we can do this again sometime! And double thanks to everyone who picked up THE VISION and hyped it up online. You all have good taste in books.

-Clayton

Thanks to the fans for the overwhelming response to the book. Tom's scripts really brought my covers to life. I'm so proud of the work Tom, Wil and Gabriel have done with this book and I'm really glad to have been a part of this awesomeness!

Oh and thanks, Gabriel, for that awesome robo-dog design, that was hella fun to draw!

-Mike

Being a part of this book has been an incredible honor. And it's not just because of how incredible this story is. I've loved working with these people. Tom King, you're an AMAZING storyteller. Your ability to evoke emotion through narrative metaphor has consistently astounded me. Gabriel, dude, your art is SO good. I'm going to miss the excitement that comes every time I get new pages from you. Jordie!!! I tell you often, but you're just the best. You put so much heart into what you do, and you make this already awesome job exponentially more fun. Your dedication to everything you do is an inspiration to me. I'm so glad I get to continue working with you! Stay awesome. Clayton. Buddy-Friend. Thanks for spending many a late Friday working with Wil and I to get things just right. You're a godsend. Wil, thanks for putting together such an amazing team and having me aboard. You're the best captain we could've asked for. And to all of you guys who've kept up with the book and written us letters, thank you! We literally couldn't have told this story without you.

-Charles

Thanks to Jay Bowen for the logo, to Tom Brevoort for letting this book be this book, to David Gabriel for pushing this from Day One, to Daniel Ketchum for the gift of Gabriel H. Walta, to my mom's dog Eva for letting us fry her face off and scoop her brain out in #6 (please nobody tell my mom about that, btw), to Marco D'Alfonso for helping out on covers when Mike got too swamped, to Michael Walsh for the beauty that was #7, to those who let us quote them on a few of the covers, to the internet for embracing this weird book, to the retailers for supporting this weird book, to Charles, Chris and the Bullpen for producing this weird book, and most of all to Tom, Gabriel, Jordie, Clayton, and Mike for creating this weird book and turning all of us into socketlovers.

-Wil

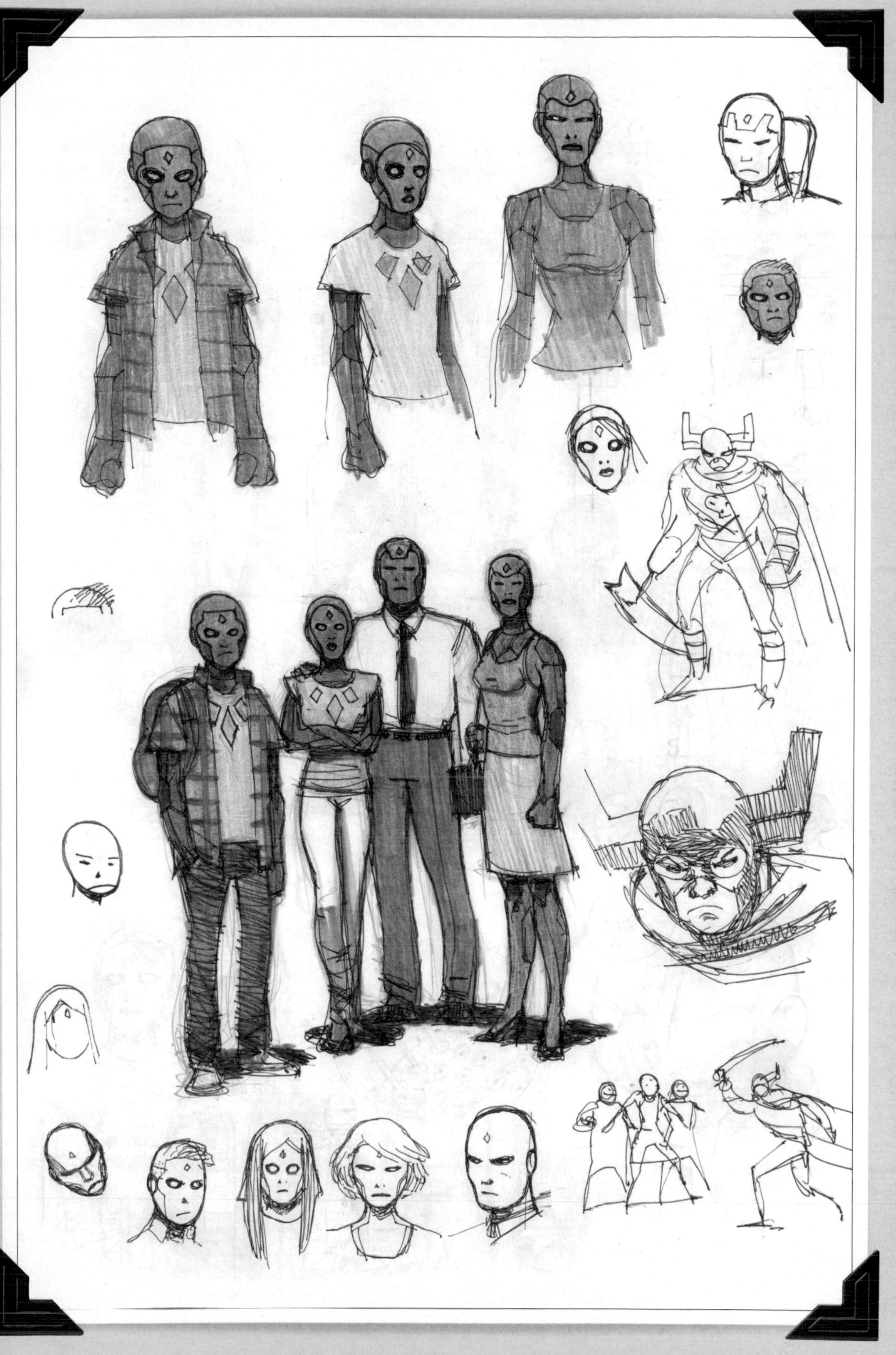

CHARACTER DESIGNS BY **GABRIEL HERNANDEZ WALTA**

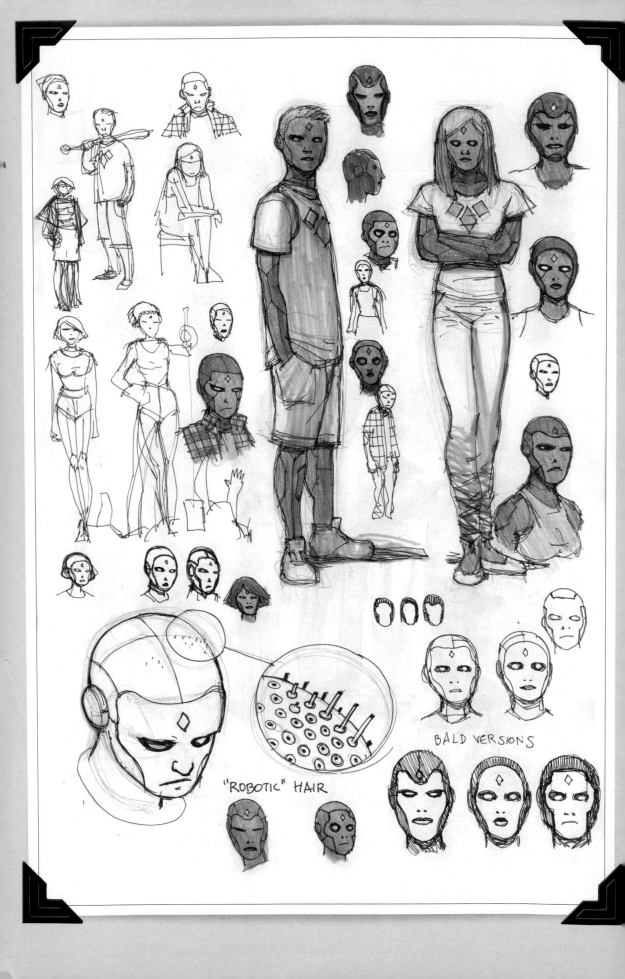

"ROBOTIC" HAIR

BALD VERSIONS

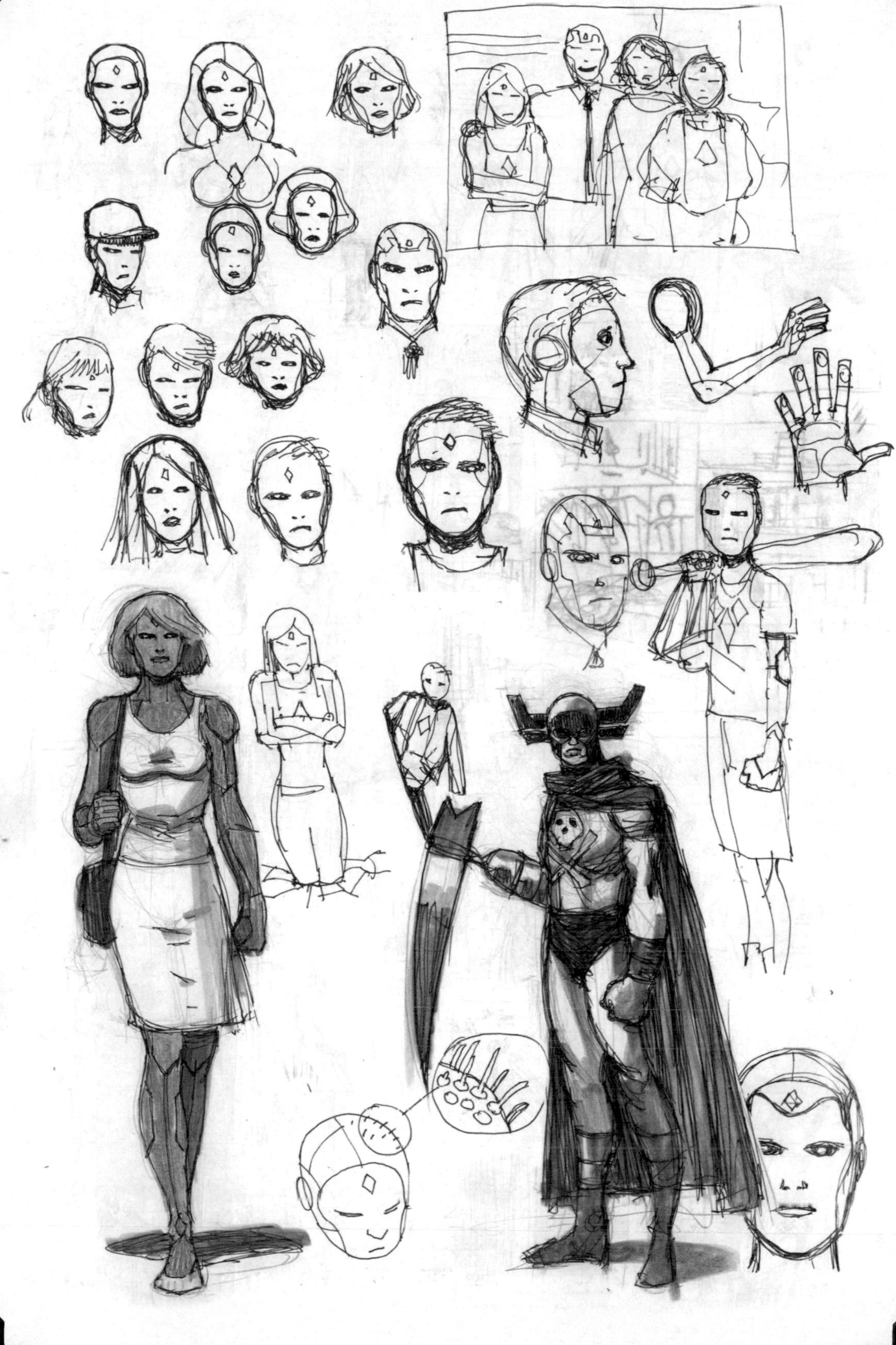

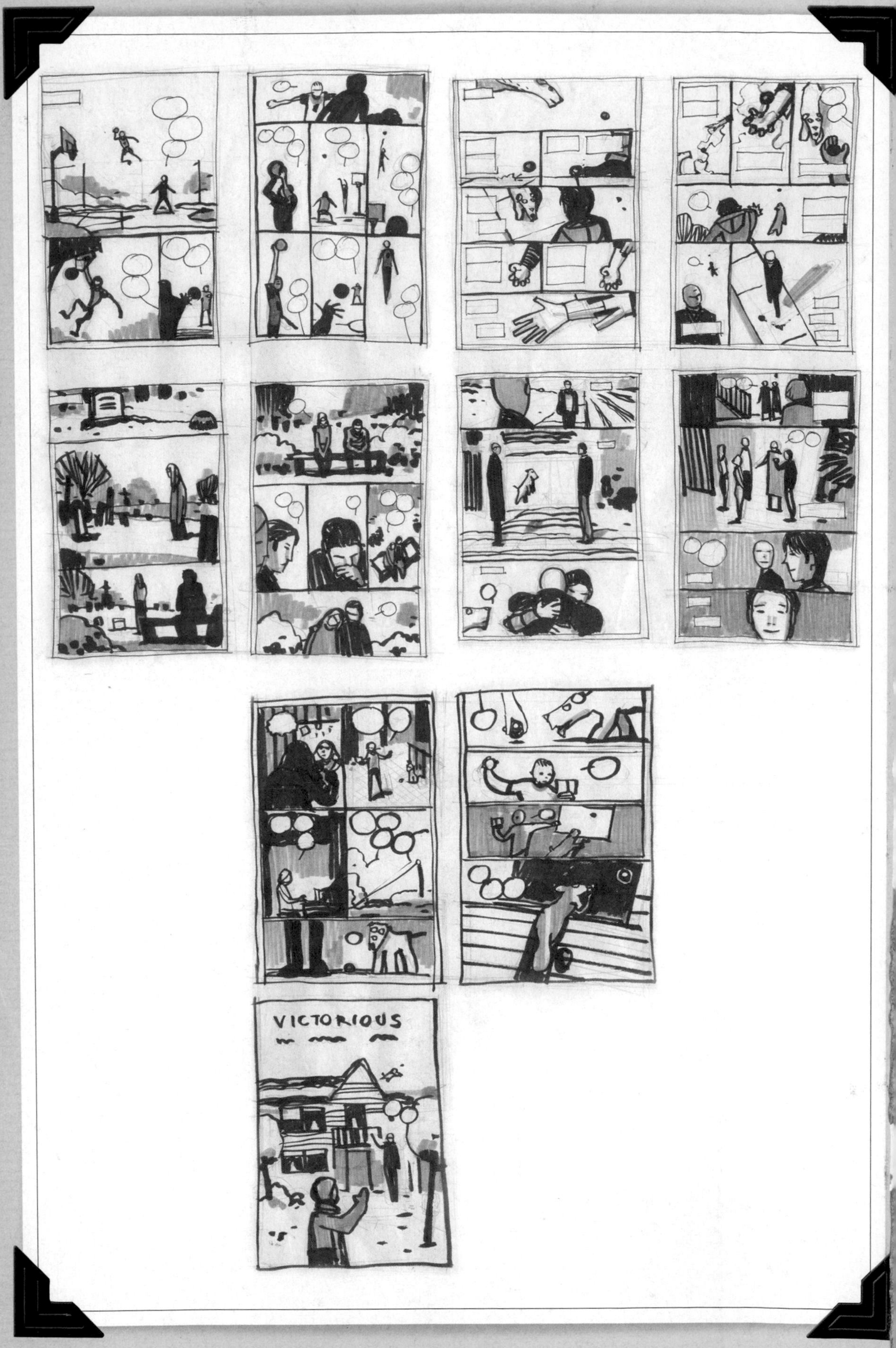
VICTORIOUS

#8 PAGE LAYOUTS BY **GABRIEL HERNANDEZ WALTA**

LIFE IN SUBURBIA HAS BEEN ANYTHING BUT EASY FOR THE VISIONS. WHEN A SUPER-POWERED INTRUDER THREATENED HER FAMILY, VIRGINIA WAS FORCED TO TAKE HIS LIFE—A SIN SHE HID FROM HER HUSBAND. THINGS ONLY ESCALATED WHEN VIRGINIA WAS BLACKMAILED BY A WITNESS TO THE CRIME. THE ENSUING INCIDENT LED TO THE DEATH OF ONE OF VIV'S CLASSMATES. ULTIMATELY, VISION WAS FORCED TO LIE TO THE POLICE TO PROTECT HIS FAMILY.

HOW DID THINGS GET SO BAD? WHAT LED TO THIS? WAS IT CHANCE...OR FATE?

"Little Better than a Beast"

TOM KING
WRITER

MICHAEL WALSH (#7) &
GABRIEL HERNANDEZ WALTA (#8-12)
ARTISTS

JORDIE BELLAIRE
COLOR ARTIST

VC'S CLAYTON COWLES
LETTERER

MIKE DEL MUNDO
COVER ARTIST

CHARLES BEACHAM
ASSISTANT EDITOR

WIL MOSS
EDITOR

TOM BREVOORT
EXECUTIVE EDITOR

Jennifer Grünwald
COLLECTION EDITOR

Kateri Woody
ASSOCIATE MANAGING EDITOR

Sarah Brunstad
ASSOCIATE EDITOR

Mark D. Beazley
EDITOR, SPECIAL PROJECTS

Jeff Youngquist
VP PRODUCTION & SPECIAL PROJECTS

David Gabriel
SVP PRINT, SALES & MARKETING

Jay Bowen
BOOK DESIGNER

Axel Alonso
EDITOR IN CHIEF

Joe Quesada
CHIEF CREATIVE OFFICER

Dan Buckley
PUBLISHER

Alan Fine
EXECUTIVE PRODUCER

VISION VOL. 2: LITTLE BETTER THAN A BEAST. Contains material originally published in magazine form as VISION #7-12. First printing 2016. ISBN# 978-0-7851-9658-7. Published by MARVEL WORLDWIDE, INC., a subsidiary of MARVEL ENTERTAINMENT, LLC. OFFICE OF PUBLICATION: 135 West 50th Street, New York, NY 10020. **Printed in Canada.** ALAN FINE, President, Marvel Entertainment; DAN BUCKLEY, President, TV, Publishing & Brand Management; JOE QUESADA, Chief Creative Officer; TOM BREVOORT, SVP of Publishing; DAVID BOGART, SVP of Business Affairs & Operations, Publishing & Partnership; C.B. CEBULSKI, VP of Brand Management & Development, Asia; DAVID GABRIEL, SVP of Sales & Marketing, Publishing; JEFF YOUNGQUIST, VP of Production & Special Projects; DAN CARR, Executive Director of Publishing Technology; ALEX MORALES, Director of Publishing Operations; SUSAN CRESPI, Production Manager; STAN LEE, Chairman Emeritus. For information regarding advertising in Marvel Comics or on Marvel.com, please contact Vit DeBellis, Integrated Sales Manager, at vdebellis@marvel.com. For Marvel subscription inquiries, please call 888-511-5480. **Manufactured between 10/7/2016 and 11/14/2016 by SOLISCO PRINTERS, SCOTT, QC, CANADA.**

10 9 8 7 6 5 4 3 2 1

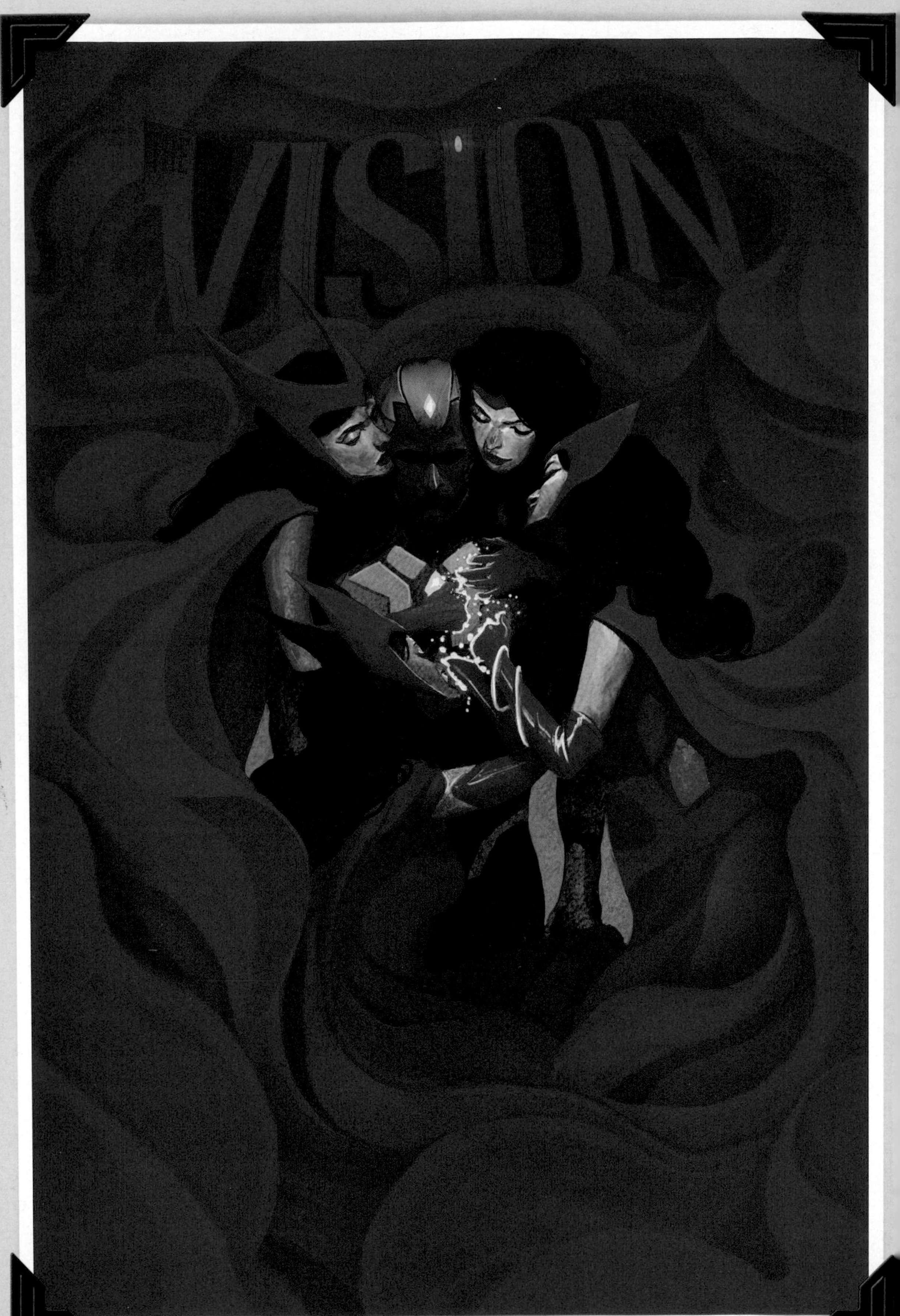
VISION

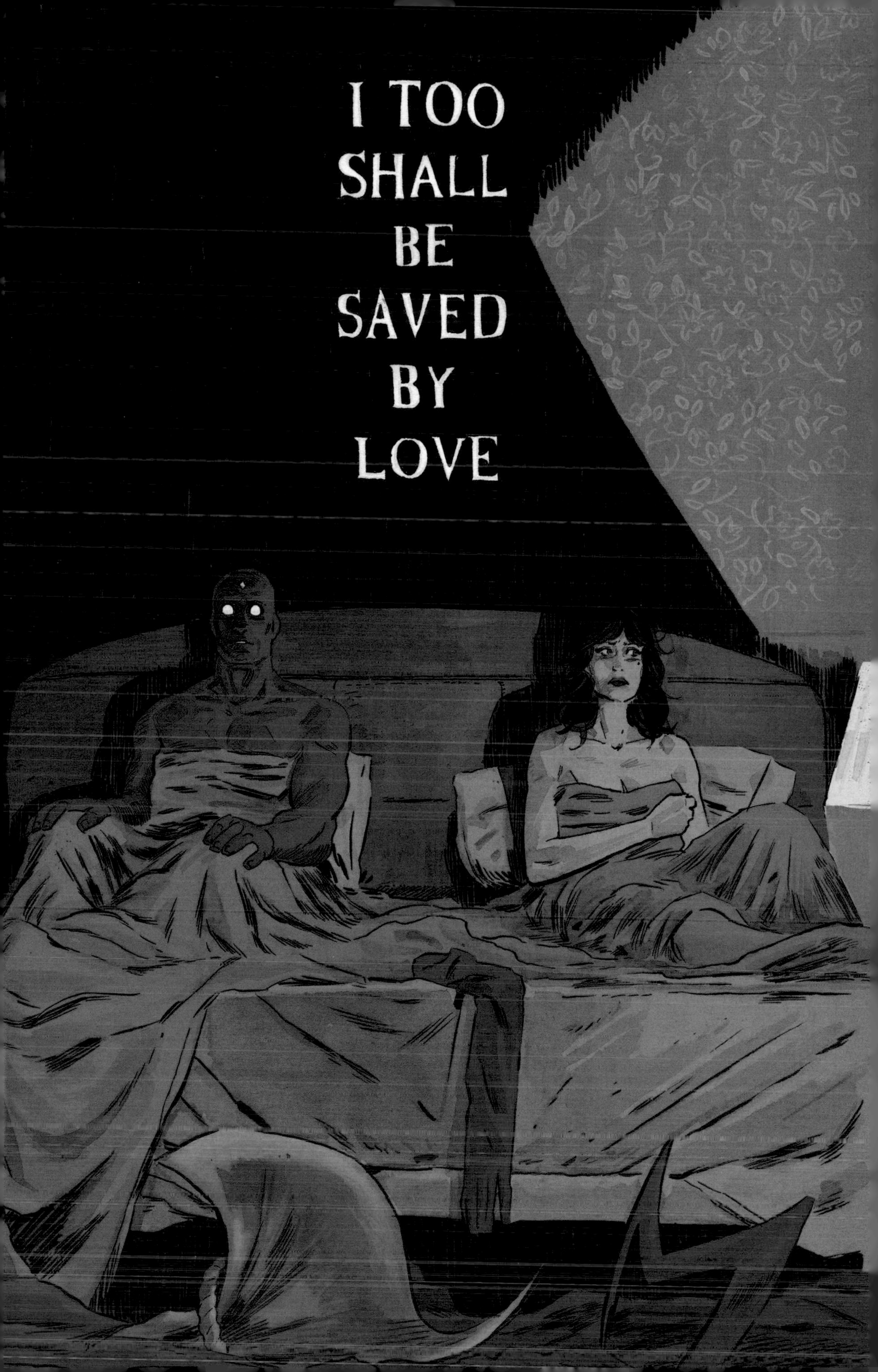
I TOO
SHALL
BE
SAVED
BY
LOVE

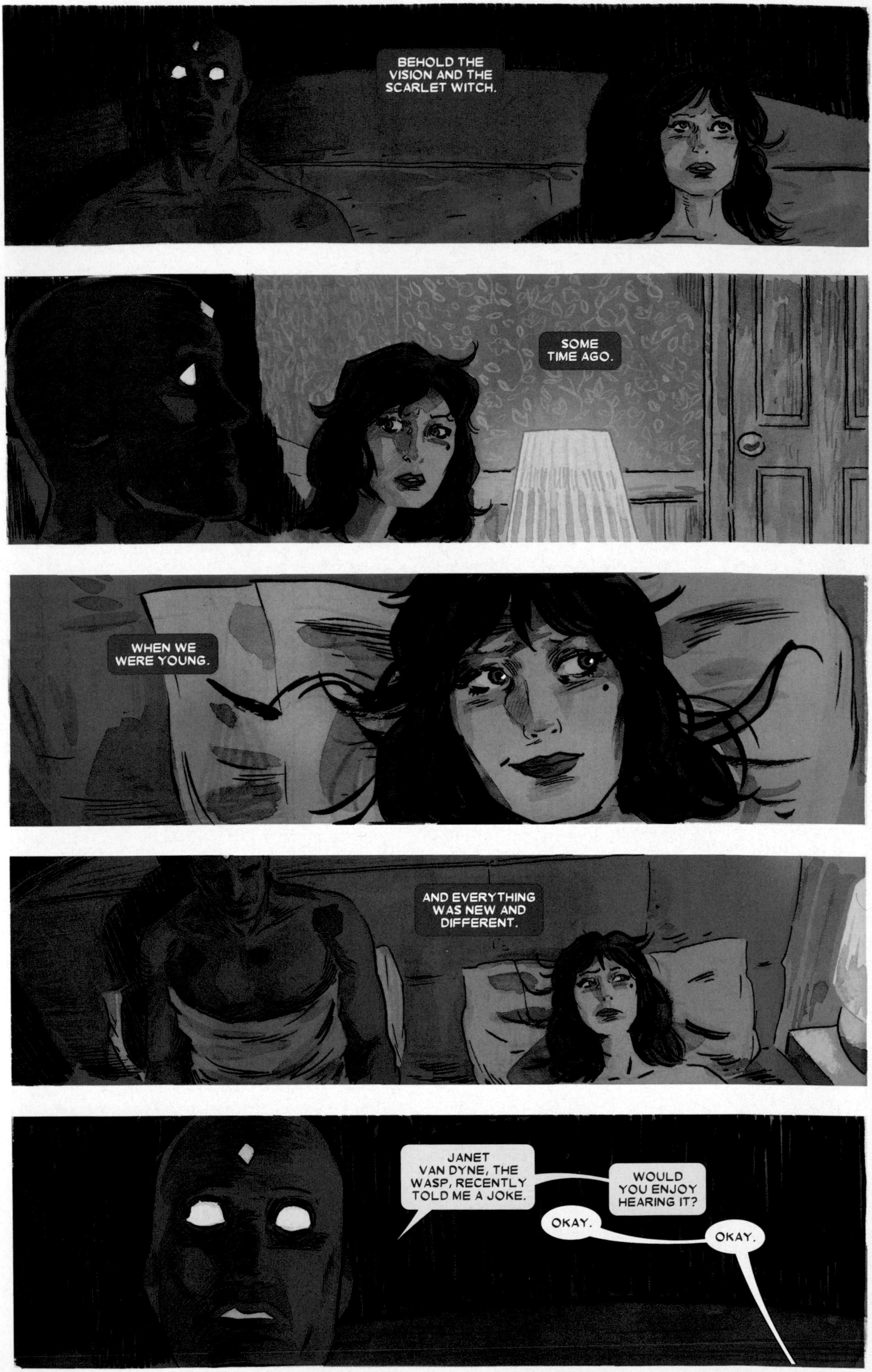
BEHOLD THE VISION AND THE SCARLET WITCH.
SOME TIME AGO.
WHEN WE WERE YOUNG.
AND EVERYTHING WAS NEW AND DIFFERENT.
JANET VAN DYNE, THE WASP, RECENTLY TOLD ME A JOKE.
WOULD YOU ENJOY HEARING IT?
OKAY.
OKAY.

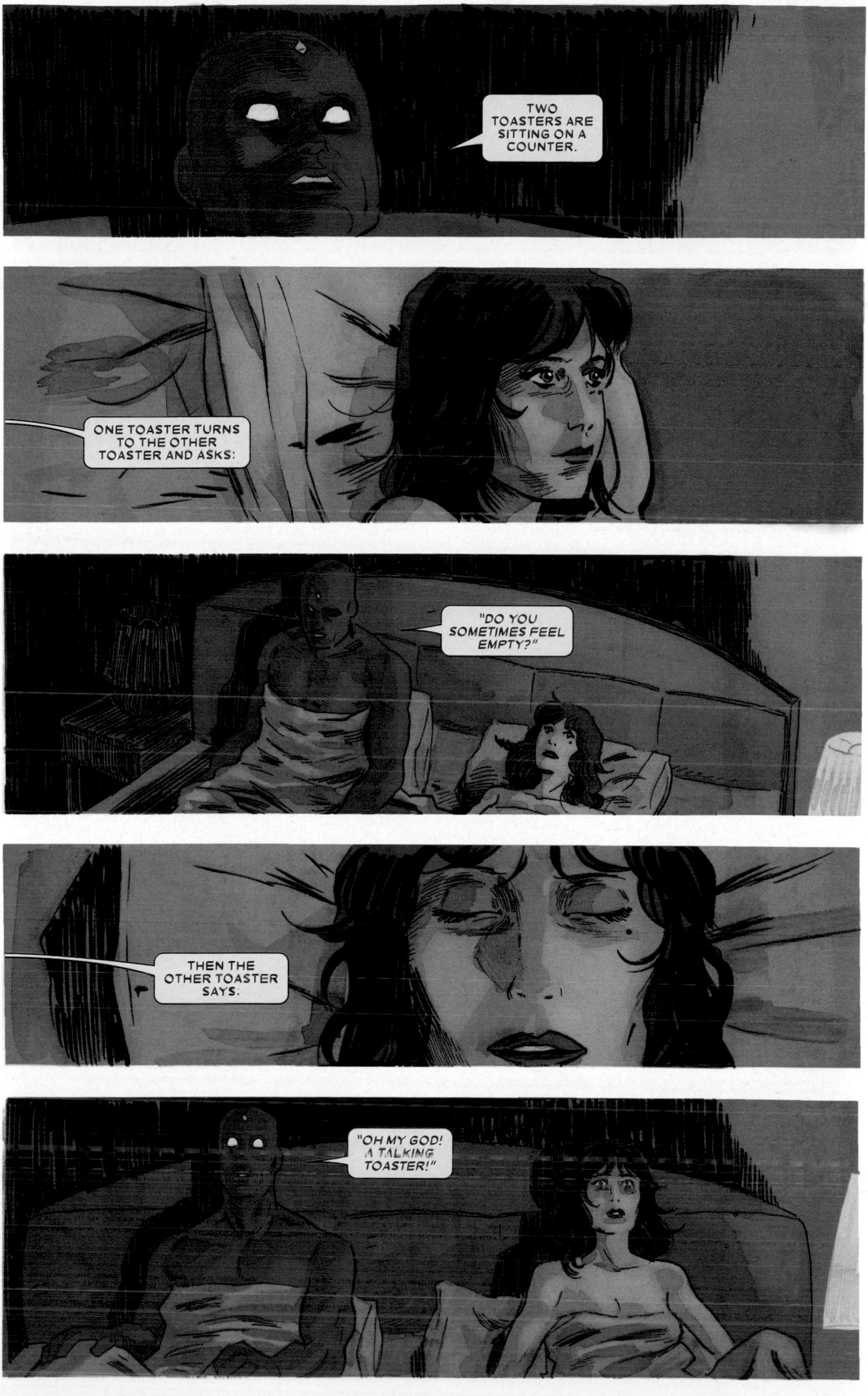
TWO TOASTERS ARE SITTING ON A COUNTER.
ONE TOASTER TURNS TO THE OTHER TOASTER AND ASKS:
"DO YOU SOMETIMES FEEL EMPTY?"
THEN THE OTHER TOASTER SAYS:
"OH MY GOD! A TALKING TOASTER!"

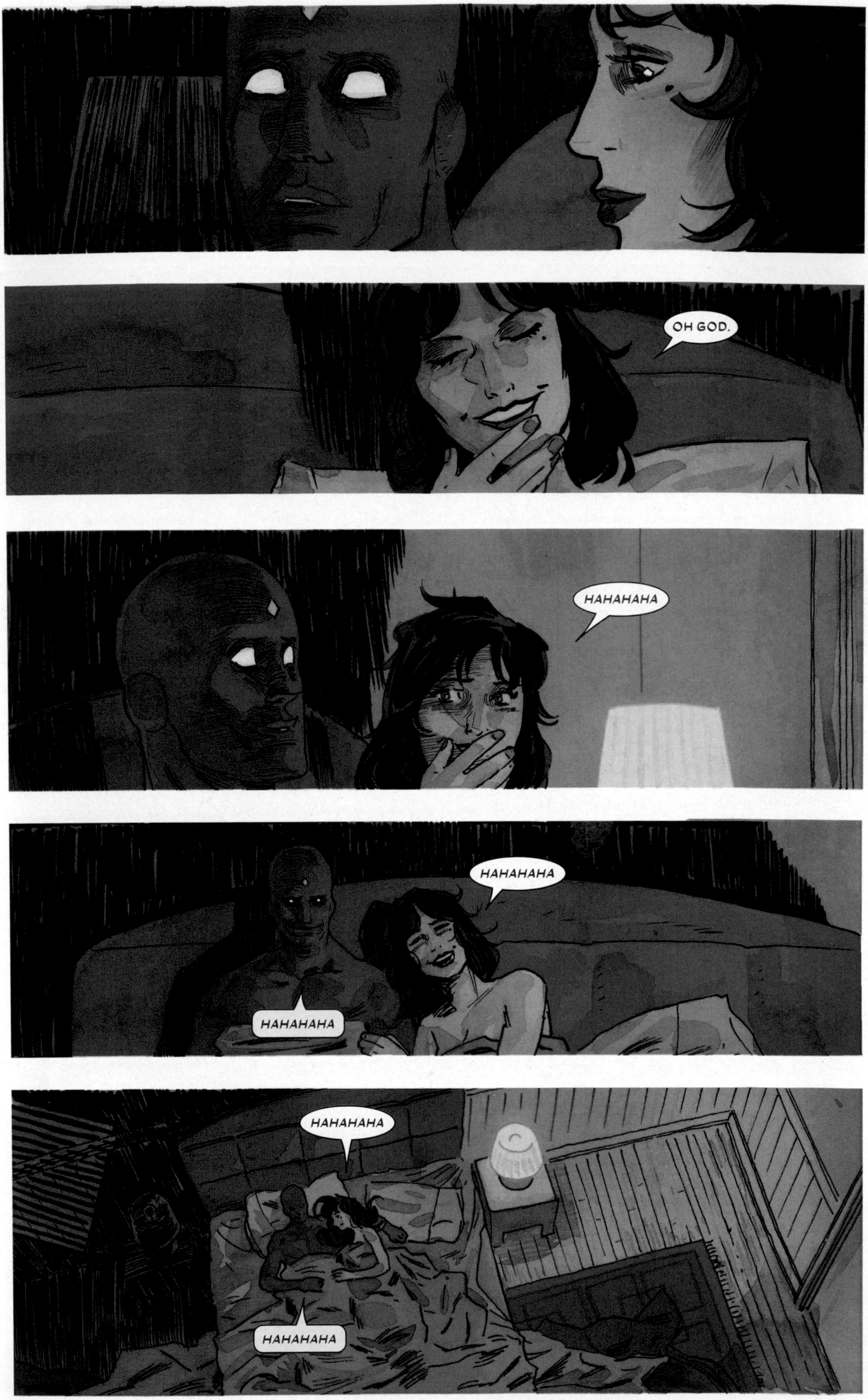
OH GOD.
HAHAHAHA
HAHAHAHA
HAHAHAHA
HAHAHAHA
HAHAHAHA

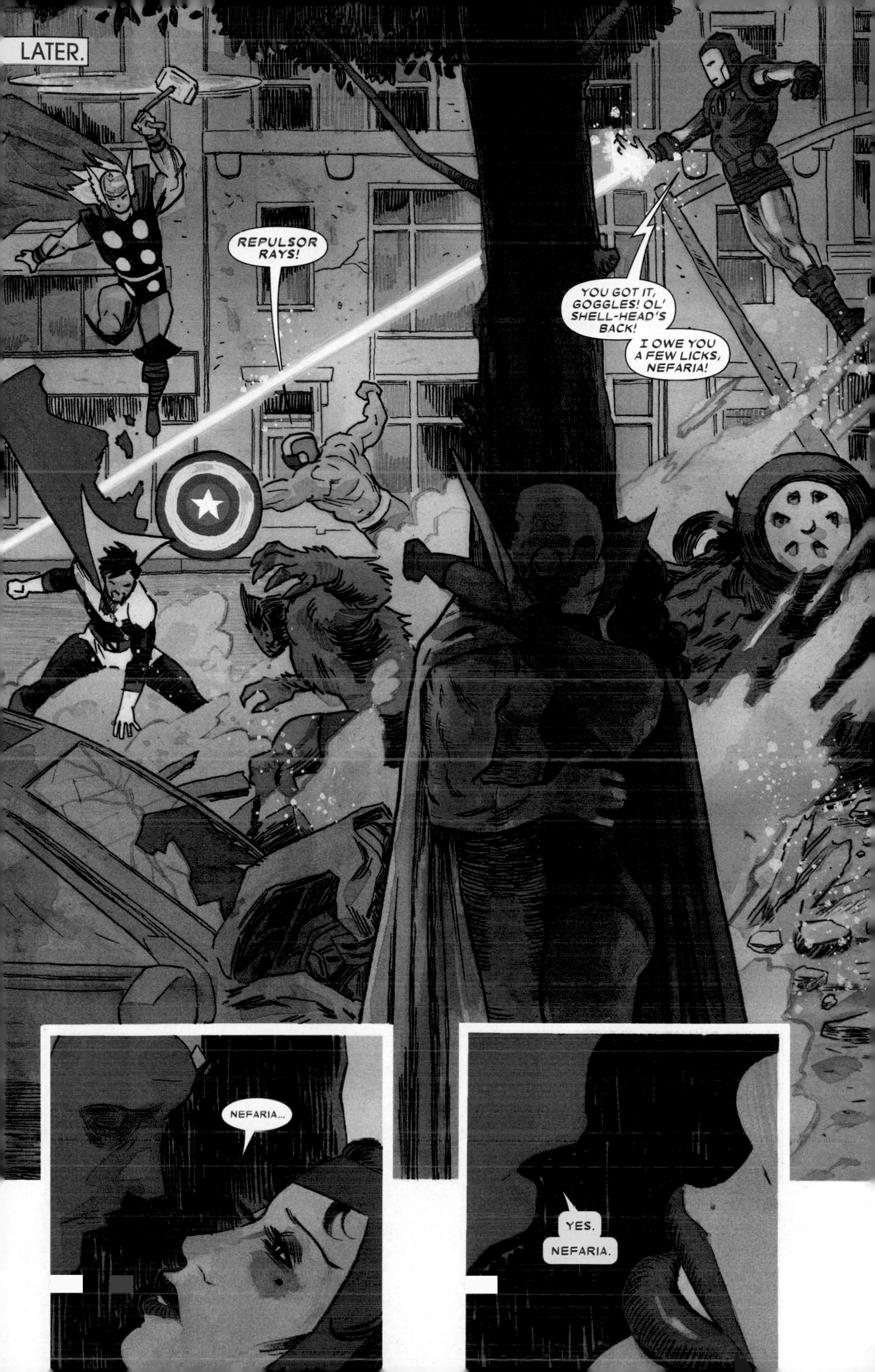
LATER.
REPULSOR RAYS!
YOU GOT IT, GOGGLES! OL' SHELL-HEAD'S BACK!
I OWE YOU A FEW LICKS, NEFARIA!
NEFARIA...
YES.
NEFARIA.

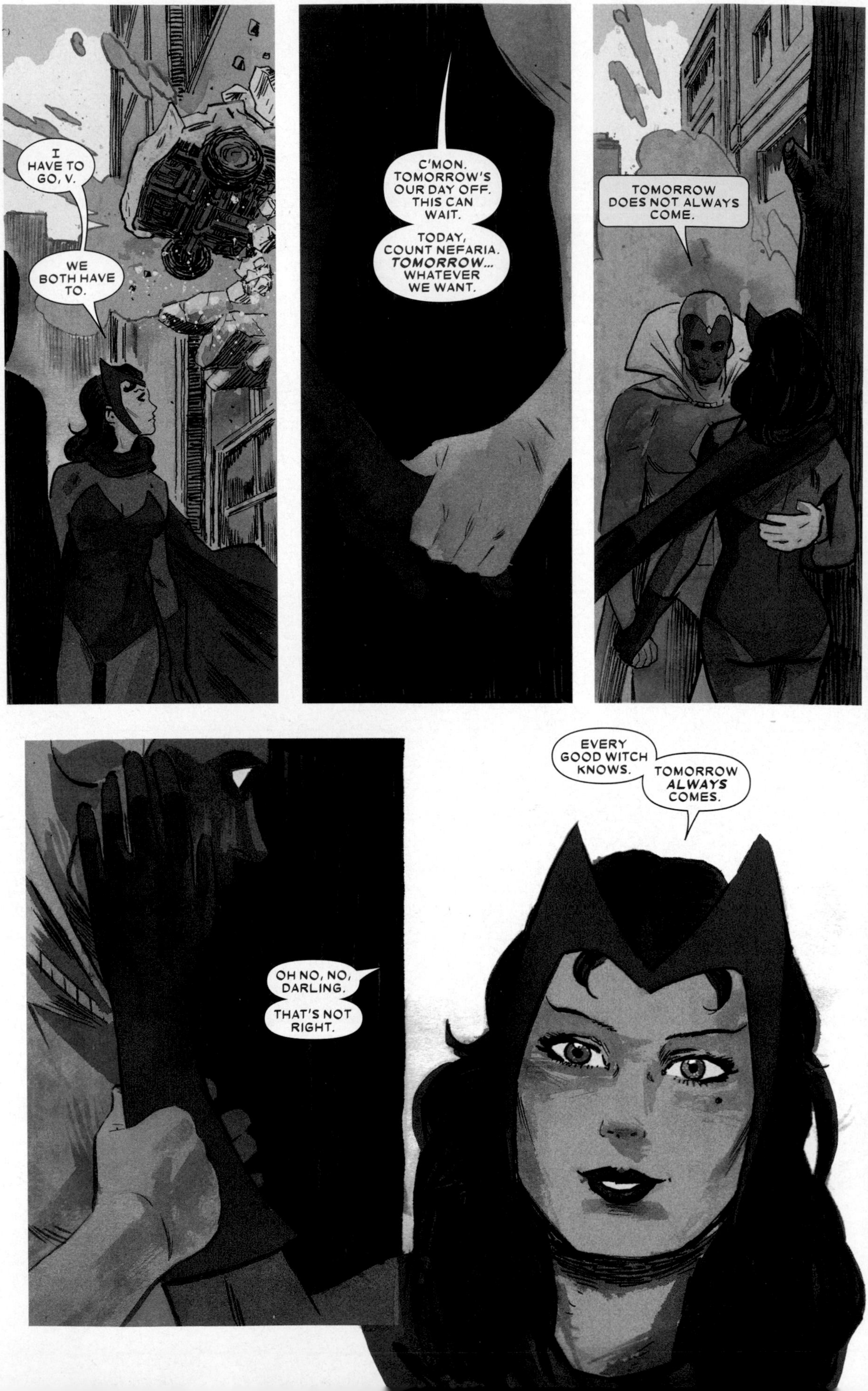
I HAVE TO GO, V.
WE BOTH HAVE TO.
C'MON. TOMORROW'S OUR DAY OFF. THIS CAN WAIT.
TODAY, COUNT NEFARIA. *TOMORROW...* WHATEVER WE WANT.
TOMORROW DOES NOT ALWAYS COME.
EVERY GOOD WITCH KNOWS.
TOMORROW **ALWAYS** COMES.
OH NO, NO, DARLING.
THAT'S NOT RIGHT.

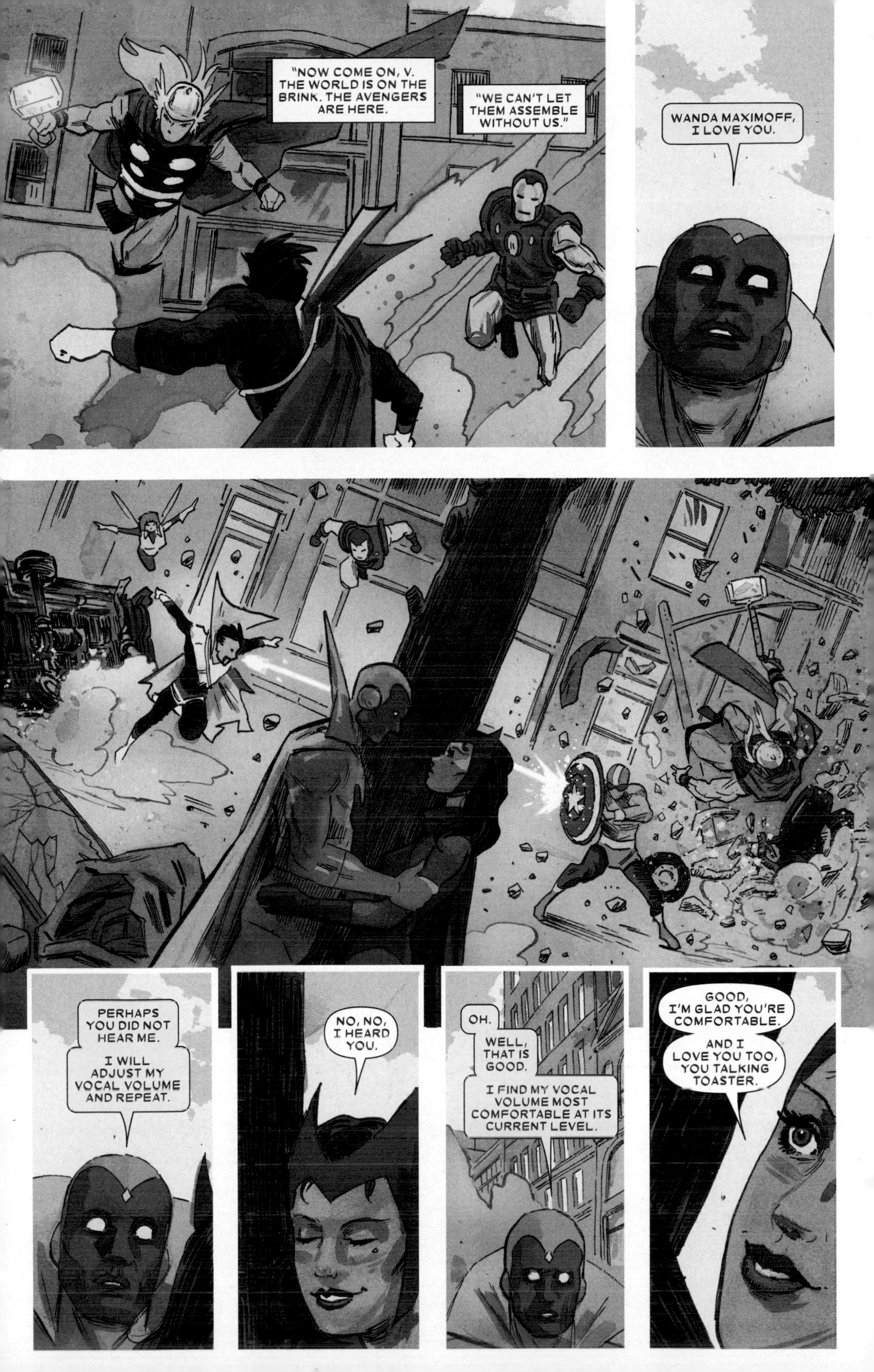
"NOW COME ON, V. THE WORLD IS ON THE BRINK. THE AVENGERS ARE HERE.
"WE CAN'T LET THEM ASSEMBLE WITHOUT US."
WANDA MAXIMOFF, I LOVE YOU.
PERHAPS YOU DID NOT HEAR ME.
I WILL ADJUST MY VOCAL VOLUME AND REPEAT.
NO, NO, I HEARD YOU.
OH.
WELL, THAT IS GOOD.
I FIND MY VOCAL VOLUME MOST COMFORTABLE AT ITS CURRENT LEVEL.
GOOD, I'M GLAD YOU'RE COMFORTABLE.
AND I LOVE YOU TOO, YOU TALKING TOASTER.

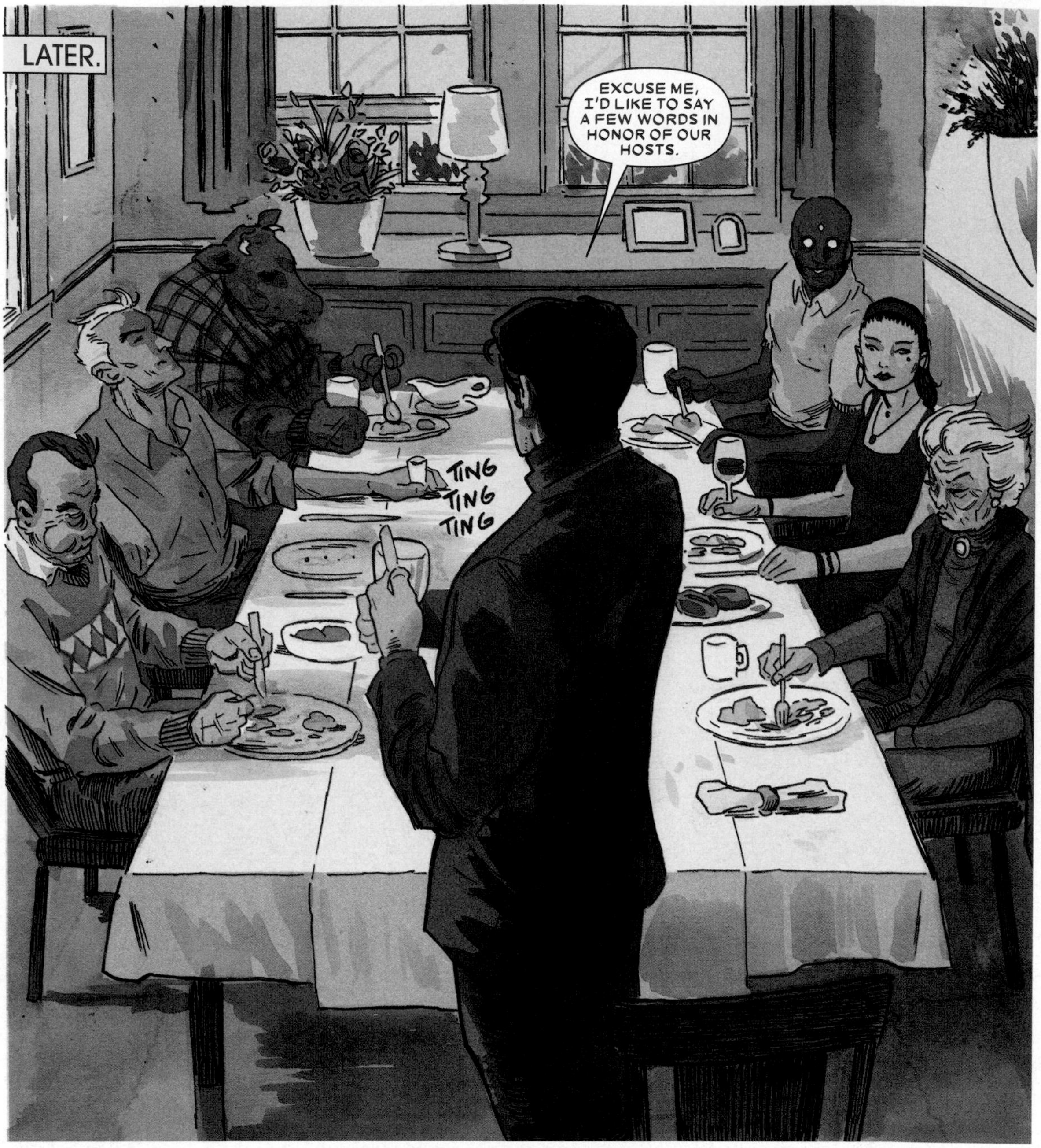
LATER.
EXCUSE ME, I'D LIKE TO SAY A FEW WORDS IN HONOR OF OUR HOSTS.
TING TING TING

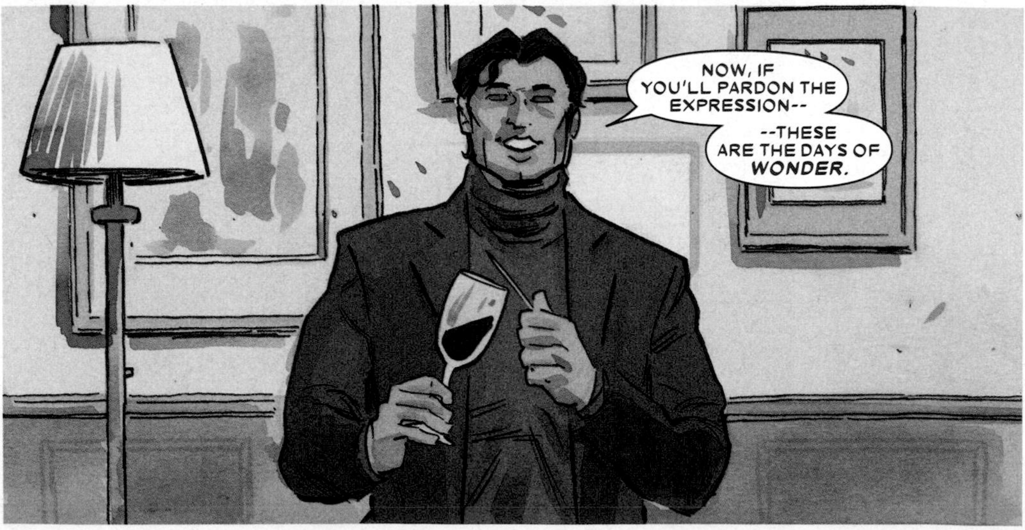
NOW, IF YOU'LL PARDON THE EXPRESSION--
--THESE ARE THE DAYS OF WONDER.

ROBERT FRANK, THE WHIZZER.

WHEN MONGOOSE BLOOD GIVES US A FATHER.

BOVA AYRSHIRE.

WHEN HIGH EVOLUTION GIVES US A CARETAKER.

AGATHA HARKNESS.

WHEN THE WITCHES OF THE MOUNTAIN GIVE US A MOTHER.

PIETRO MAXIMOFF, QUICKSILVER.

WHEN THE BROTHERHOOD OF EVIL MUTANTS GIVES US A FRIEND.

SIMON WILLIAMS, WONDER MAN.

AND WHEN ULTRON GIVES US A BROTHER.

BUT THE GREATEST WONDER, ABOVE ALL OTHERS, IS THAT WE--

--ALL OF US HERE-- HAVE BECOME A FAMILY.

AND THAT WONDER WAS BORN OUT OF THE LOVE OF OUR WONDERFUL HOSTS.

OUT OF THEIR LOVE FOR EACH OTHER.

SO LET US RAISE OUR GLASSES!

TO WONDER!

TO THE VISION AND THE SCARLET WITCH!

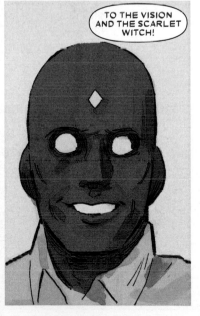

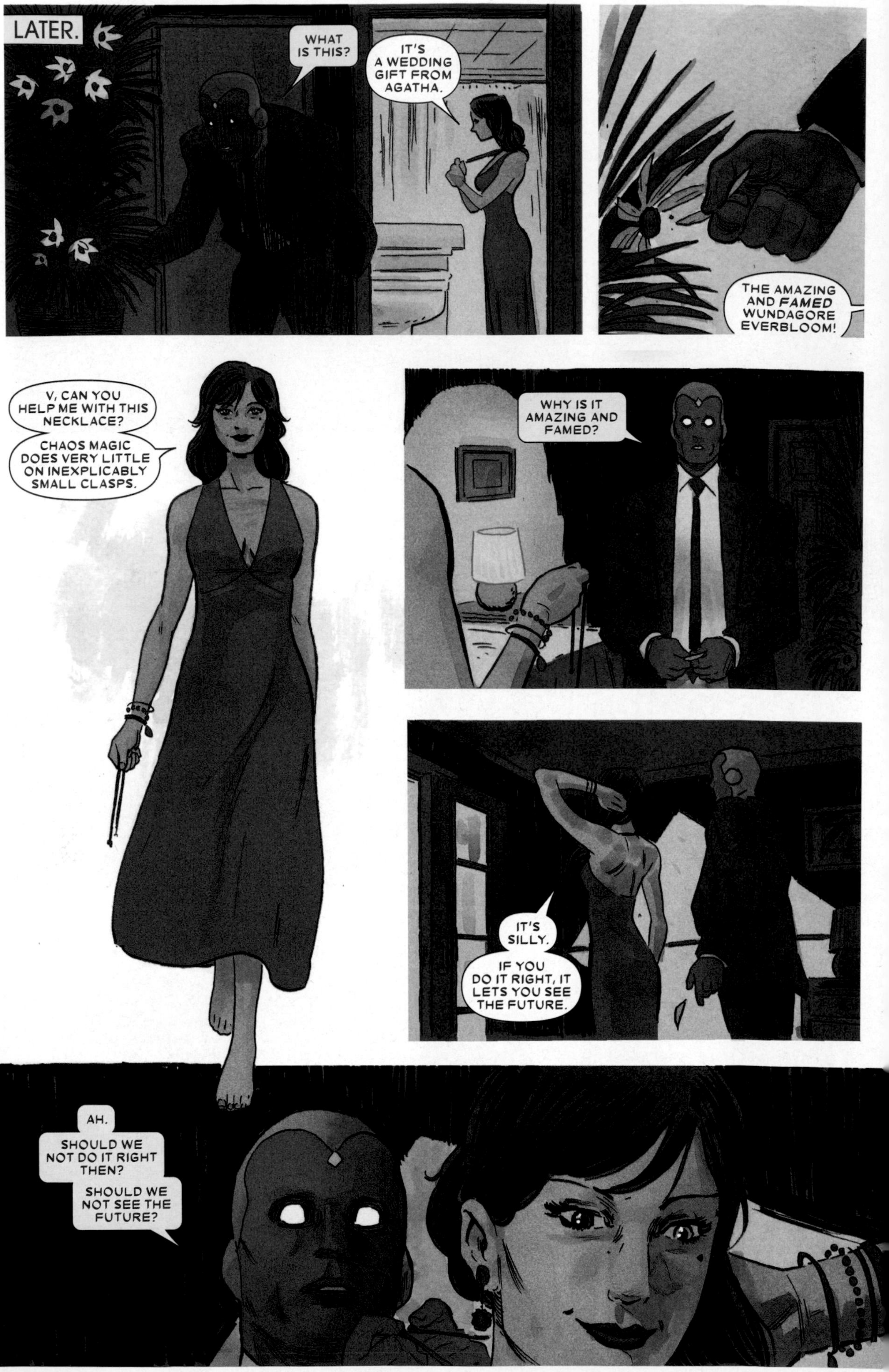
LATER.
WHAT IS THIS?
IT'S A WEDDING GIFT FROM AGATHA.
THE AMAZING AND *FAMED* WUNDAGORE EVERBLOOM!
V, CAN YOU HELP ME WITH THIS NECKLACE?
CHAOS MAGIC DOES VERY LITTLE ON INEXPLICABLY SMALL CLASPS.
WHY IS IT AMAZING AND FAMED?
IT'S SILLY.
IF YOU DO IT RIGHT, IT LETS YOU SEE THE FUTURE.
AH.
SHOULD WE NOT DO IT RIGHT THEN?
SHOULD WE NOT SEE THE FUTURE?

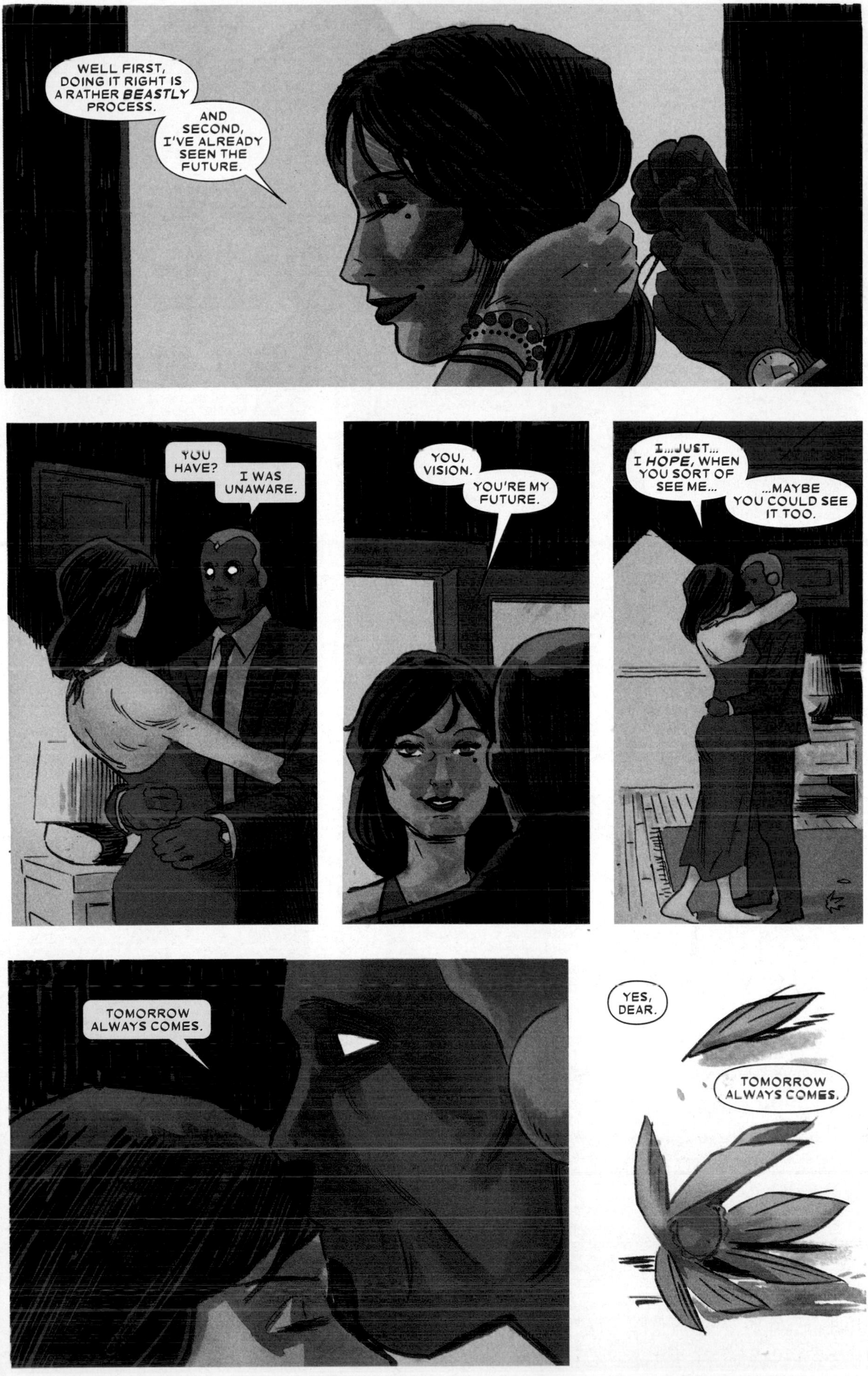
WELL FIRST, DOING IT RIGHT IS A RATHER BEASTLY PROCESS.
AND SECOND, I'VE ALREADY SEEN THE FUTURE.
YOU HAVE?
I WAS UNAWARE.
YOU, VISION.
YOU'RE MY FUTURE.
I...JUST... I HOPE, WHEN YOU SORT OF SEE ME...
...MAYBE YOU COULD SEE IT TOO.
TOMORROW ALWAYS COMES.
YES, DEAR.
TOMORROW ALWAYS COMES.

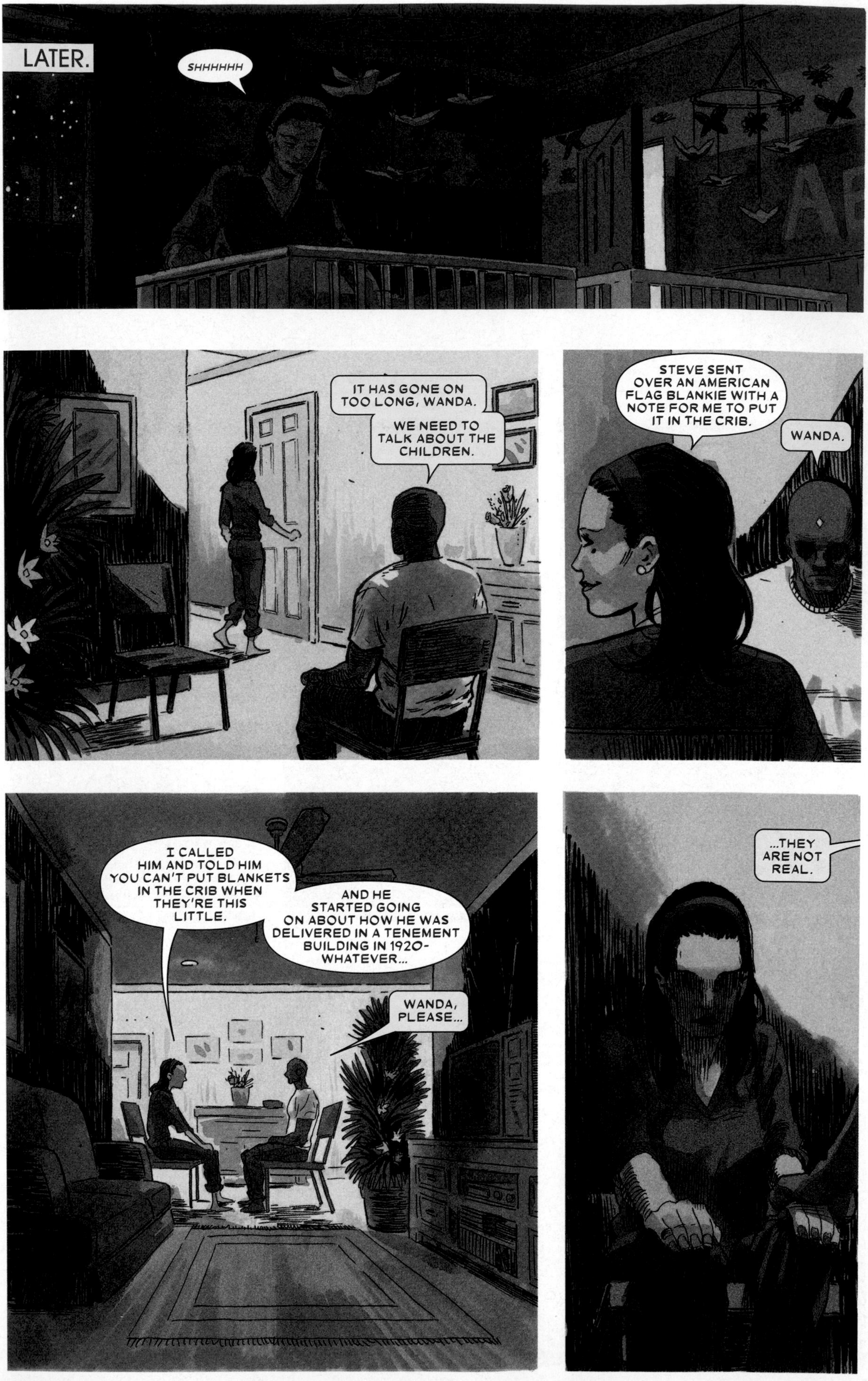
LATER.
SHHHHHH
IT HAS GONE ON TOO LONG, WANDA.
WE NEED TO TALK ABOUT THE CHILDREN.
STEVE SENT OVER AN AMERICAN FLAG BLANKIE WITH A NOTE FOR ME TO PUT IT IN THE CRIB.
WANDA.
I CALLED HIM AND TOLD HIM YOU CAN'T PUT BLANKETS IN THE CRIB WHEN THEY'RE THIS LITTLE.
AND HE STARTED GOING ON ABOUT HOW HE WAS DELIVERED IN A TENEMENT BUILDING IN 1920-WHATEVER...
WANDA, PLEASE...
...THEY ARE NOT REAL.

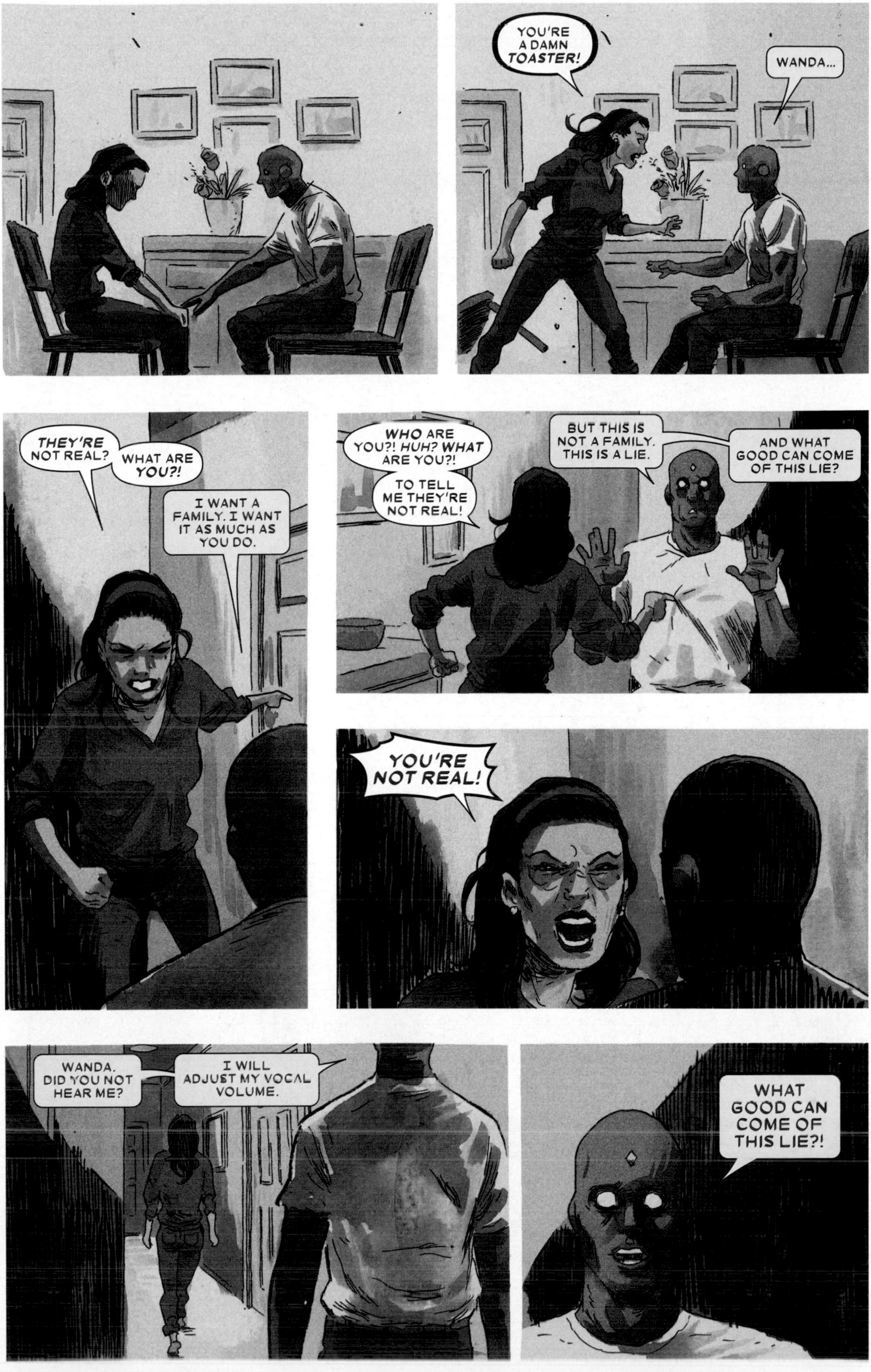

YOU'RE A DAMN TOASTER!
WANDA...
THEY'RE NOT REAL?
WHAT ARE YOU?!
I WANT A FAMILY. I WANT IT AS MUCH AS YOU DO.
WHO ARE YOU?! HUH? WHAT ARE YOU?!
TO TELL ME THEY'RE NOT REAL!
BUT THIS IS NOT A FAMILY. THIS IS A LIE.
AND WHAT GOOD CAN COME OF THIS LIE?
YOU'RE NOT REAL!
WANDA. DID YOU NOT HEAR ME?
I WILL ADJUST MY VOCAL VOLUME.
WHAT GOOD CAN COME OF THIS LIE?!

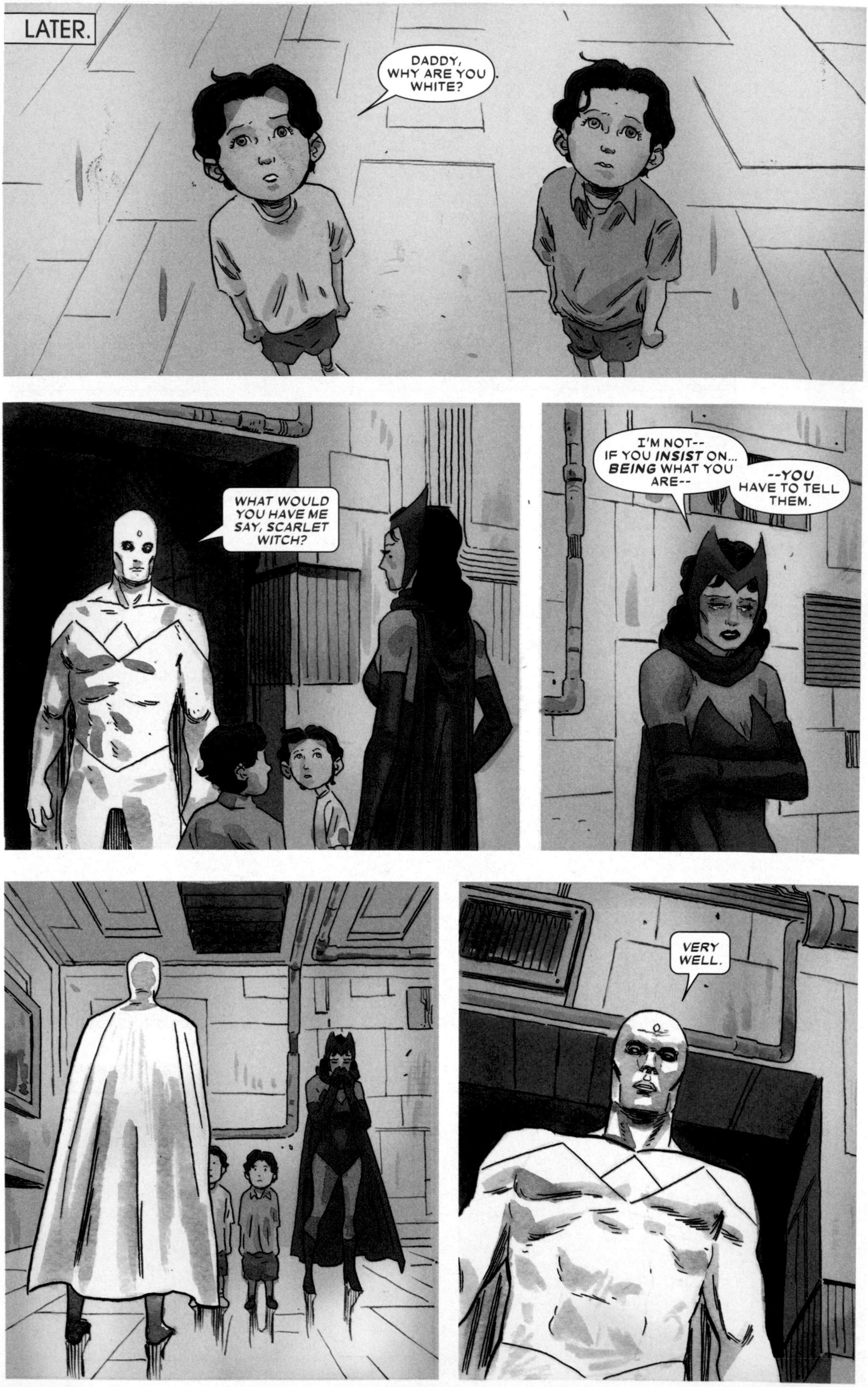
LATER.
DADDY, WHY ARE YOU WHITE?
WHAT WOULD YOU HAVE ME SAY, SCARLET WITCH?
I'M NOT-- IF YOU INSIST ON... BEING WHAT YOU ARE--
--YOU HAVE TO TELL THEM.
VERY WELL.

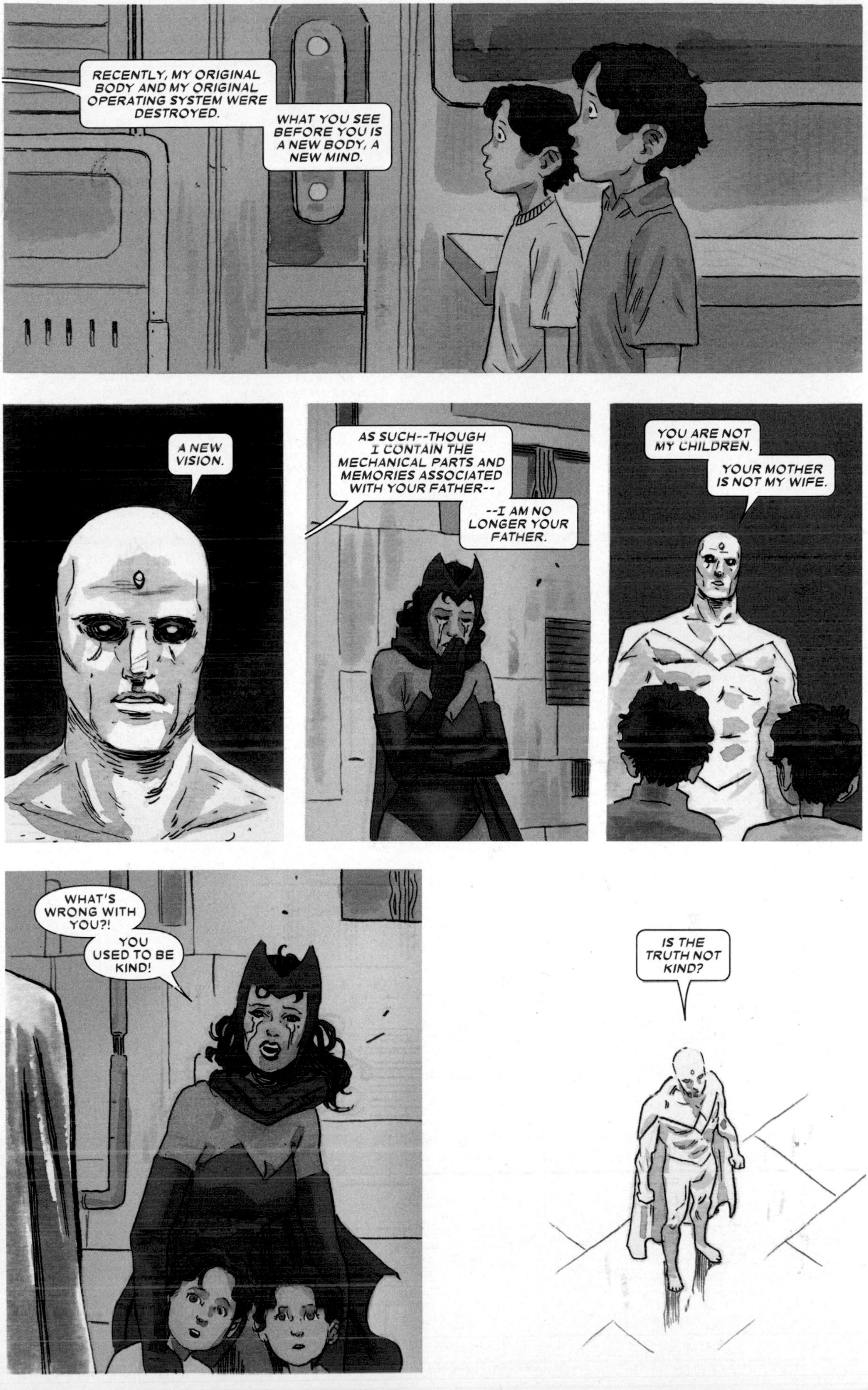
RECENTLY, MY ORIGINAL BODY AND MY ORIGINAL OPERATING SYSTEM WERE DESTROYED.
WHAT YOU SEE BEFORE YOU IS A NEW BODY, A NEW MIND.
A NEW VISION.
AS SUCH--THOUGH I CONTAIN THE MECHANICAL PARTS AND MEMORIES ASSOCIATED WITH YOUR FATHER--
--I AM NO LONGER YOUR FATHER.
YOU ARE NOT MY CHILDREN.
YOUR MOTHER IS NOT MY WIFE.
WHAT'S WRONG WITH YOU?!
YOU USED TO BE KIND!
IS THE TRUTH NOT KIND?

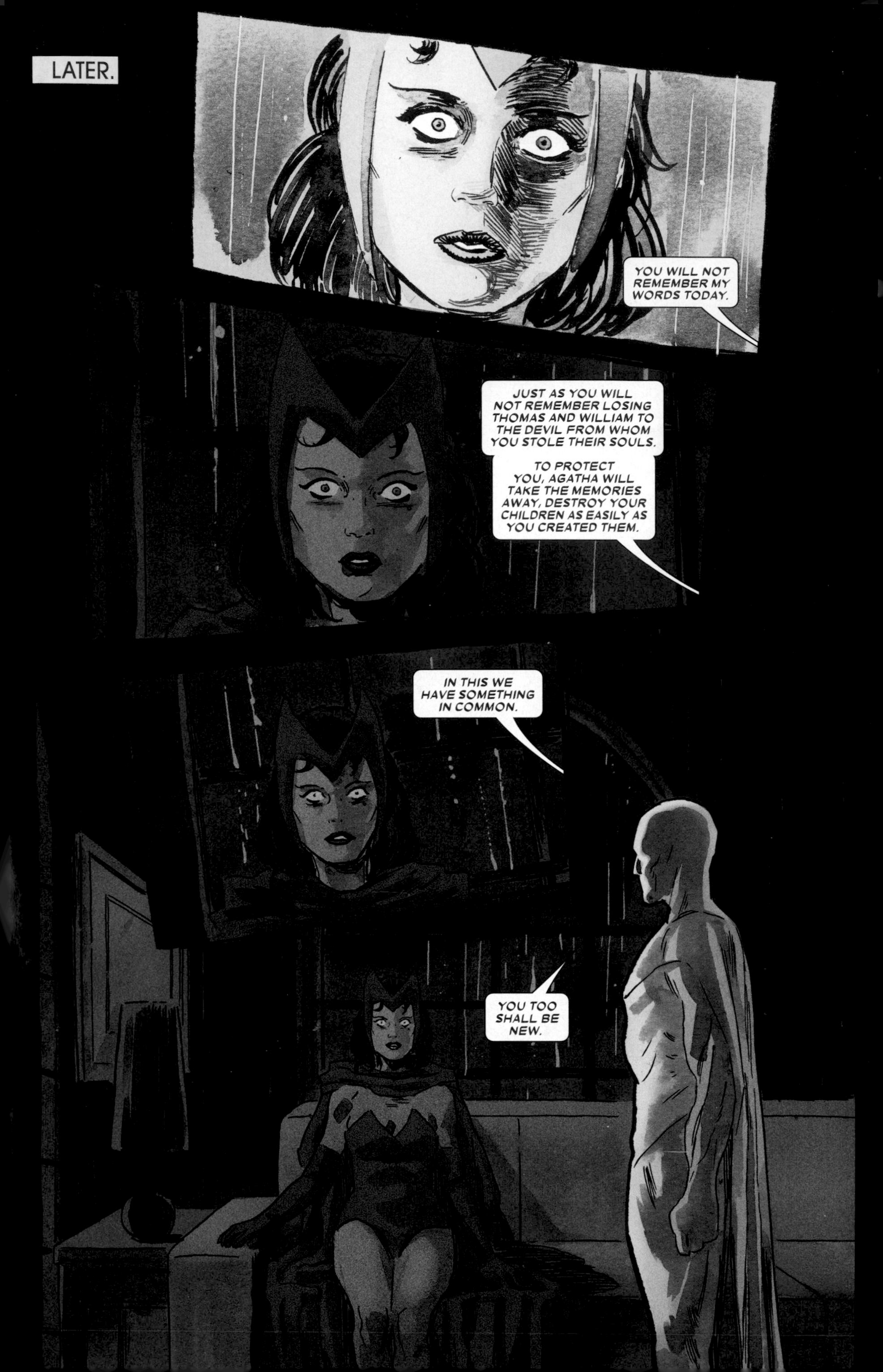
LATER.
YOU WILL NOT REMEMBER MY WORDS TODAY.
JUST AS YOU WILL NOT REMEMBER LOSING THOMAS AND WILLIAM TO THE DEVIL FROM WHOM YOU STOLE THEIR SOULS.
TO PROTECT YOU, AGATHA WILL TAKE THE MEMORIES AWAY, DESTROY YOUR CHILDREN AS EASILY AS YOU CREATED THEM.
IN THIS WE HAVE SOMETHING IN COMMON.
YOU TOO SHALL BE NEW.

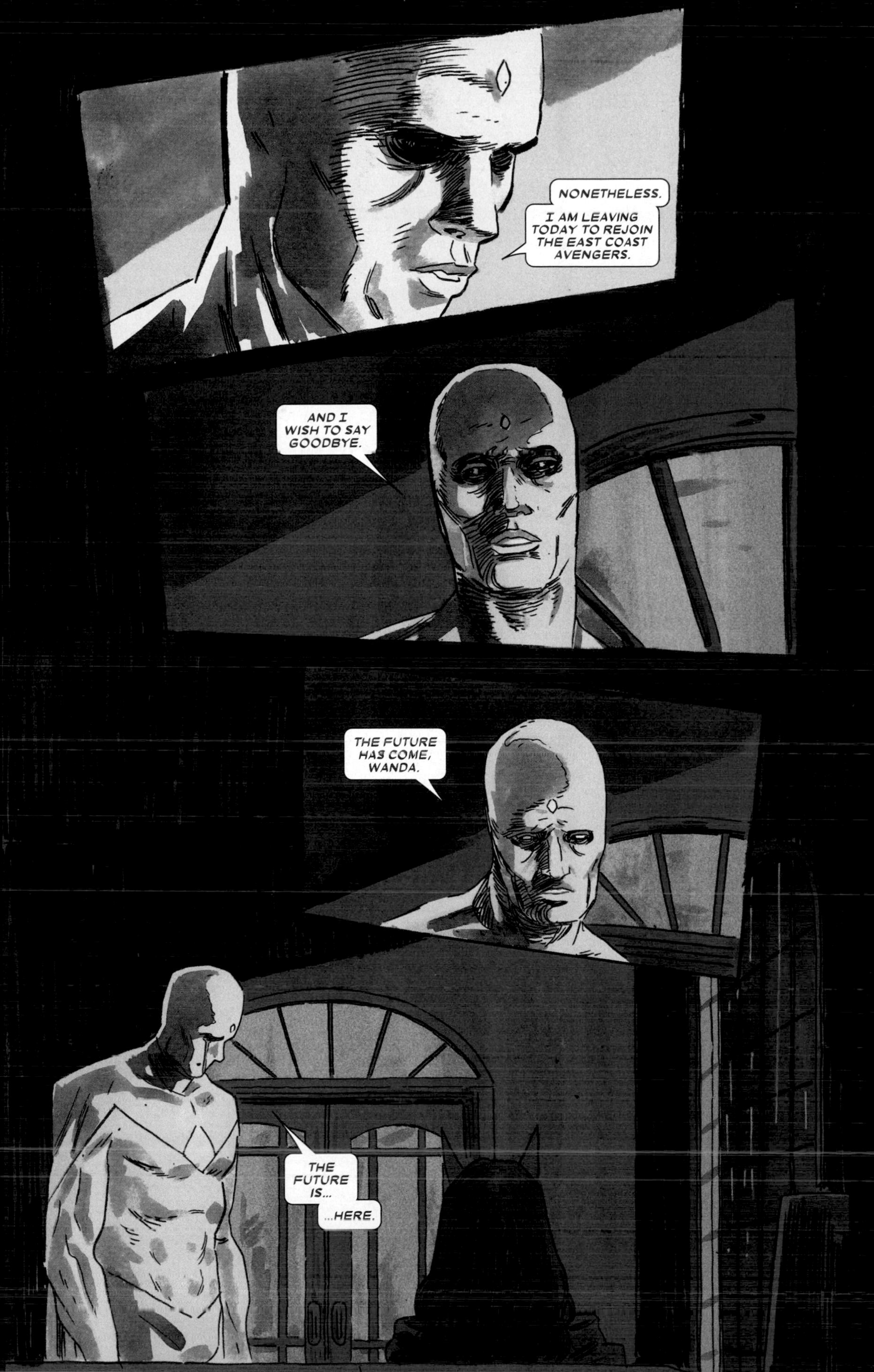
NONETHELESS.
I AM LEAVING TODAY TO REJOIN THE EAST COAST AVENGERS.
AND I WISH TO SAY GOODBYE.
THE FUTURE HAS COME, WANDA.
THE FUTURE IS...
...HERE.

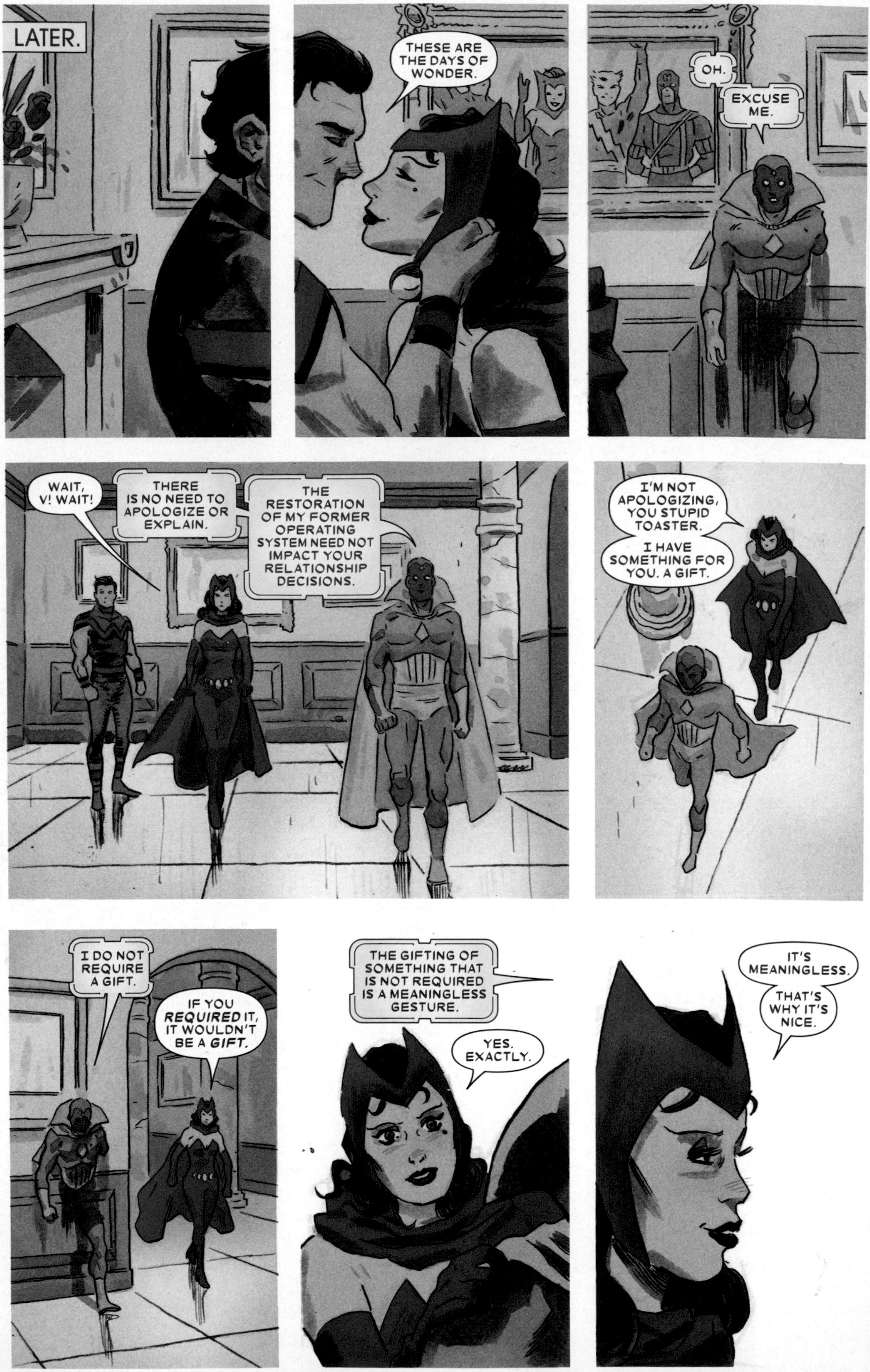
LATER.
THESE ARE THE DAYS OF WONDER.
OH.
EXCUSE ME.
WAIT, V! WAIT!
THERE IS NO NEED TO APOLOGIZE OR EXPLAIN.
THE RESTORATION OF MY FORMER OPERATING SYSTEM NEED NOT IMPACT YOUR RELATIONSHIP DECISIONS.
I'M NOT APOLOGIZING, YOU STUPID TOASTER.
I HAVE SOMETHING FOR YOU. A GIFT.
I DO NOT REQUIRE A GIFT.
IF YOU *REQUIRED* IT, IT WOULDN'T BE A *GIFT.*
THE GIFTING OF SOMETHING THAT IS NOT REQUIRED IS A MEANINGLESS GESTURE.
YES. EXACTLY.
IT'S MEANINGLESS.
THAT'S WHY IT'S NICE.

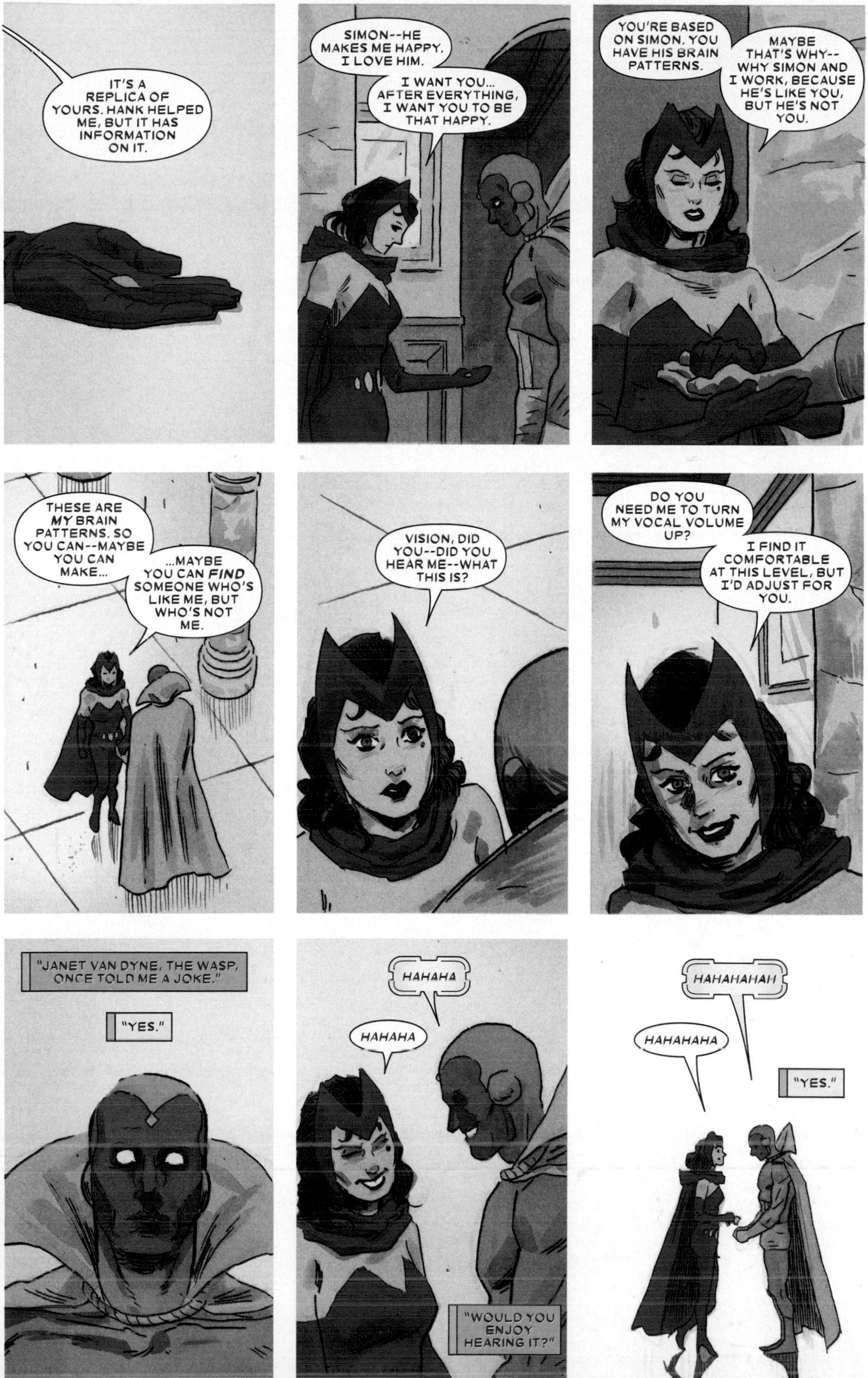
IT'S A REPLICA OF YOURS. HANK HELPED ME, BUT IT HAS INFORMATION ON IT.
SIMON--HE MAKES ME HAPPY. I LOVE HIM.
I WANT YOU... AFTER EVERYTHING, I WANT YOU TO BE THAT HAPPY.
YOU'RE BASED ON SIMON. YOU HAVE HIS BRAIN PATTERNS.
MAYBE THAT'S WHY-- WHY SIMON AND I WORK, BECAUSE HE'S LIKE YOU, BUT HE'S NOT YOU.
THESE ARE MY BRAIN PATTERNS. SO YOU CAN--MAYBE YOU CAN MAKE...
...MAYBE YOU CAN FIND SOMEONE WHO'S LIKE ME, BUT WHO'S NOT ME.
VISION, DID YOU--DID YOU HEAR ME--WHAT THIS IS?
DO YOU NEED ME TO TURN MY VOCAL VOLUME UP?
I FIND IT COMFORTABLE AT THIS LEVEL, BUT I'D ADJUST FOR YOU.
"JANET VAN DYNE, THE WASP, ONCE TOLD ME A JOKE."
"YES."
HAHAHA
HAHAHA
"WOULD YOU ENJOY HEARING IT?"
HAHAHAHAH
HAHAHAHA
"YES."

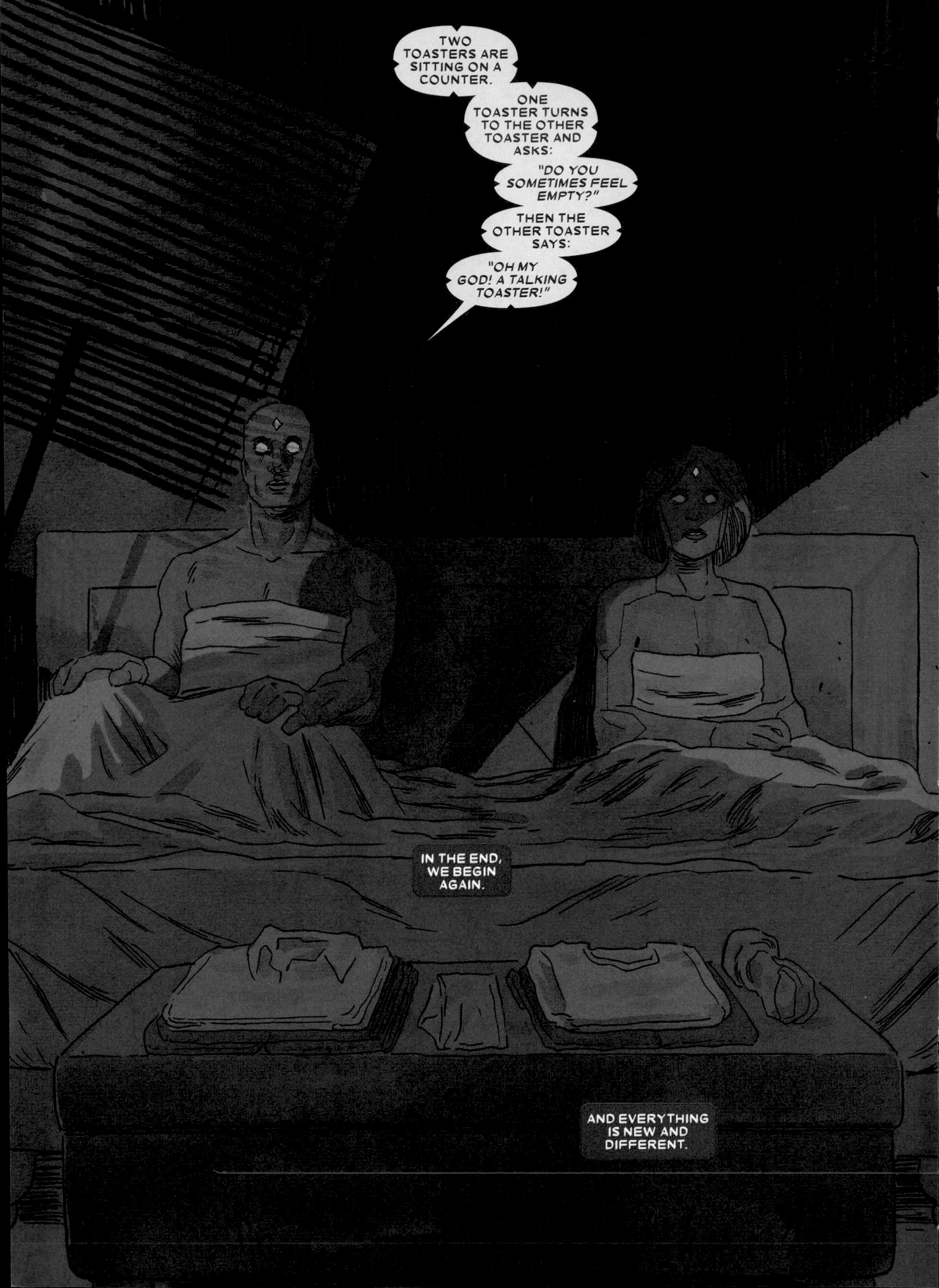
TWO TOASTERS ARE SITTING ON A COUNTER.
ONE TOASTER TURNS TO THE OTHER TOASTER AND ASKS:
"DO YOU SOMETIMES FEEL EMPTY?"
THEN THE OTHER TOASTER SAYS:
"OH MY GOD! A TALKING TOASTER!"
IN THE END, WE BEGIN AGAIN.
AND EVERYTHING IS NEW AND DIFFERENT.

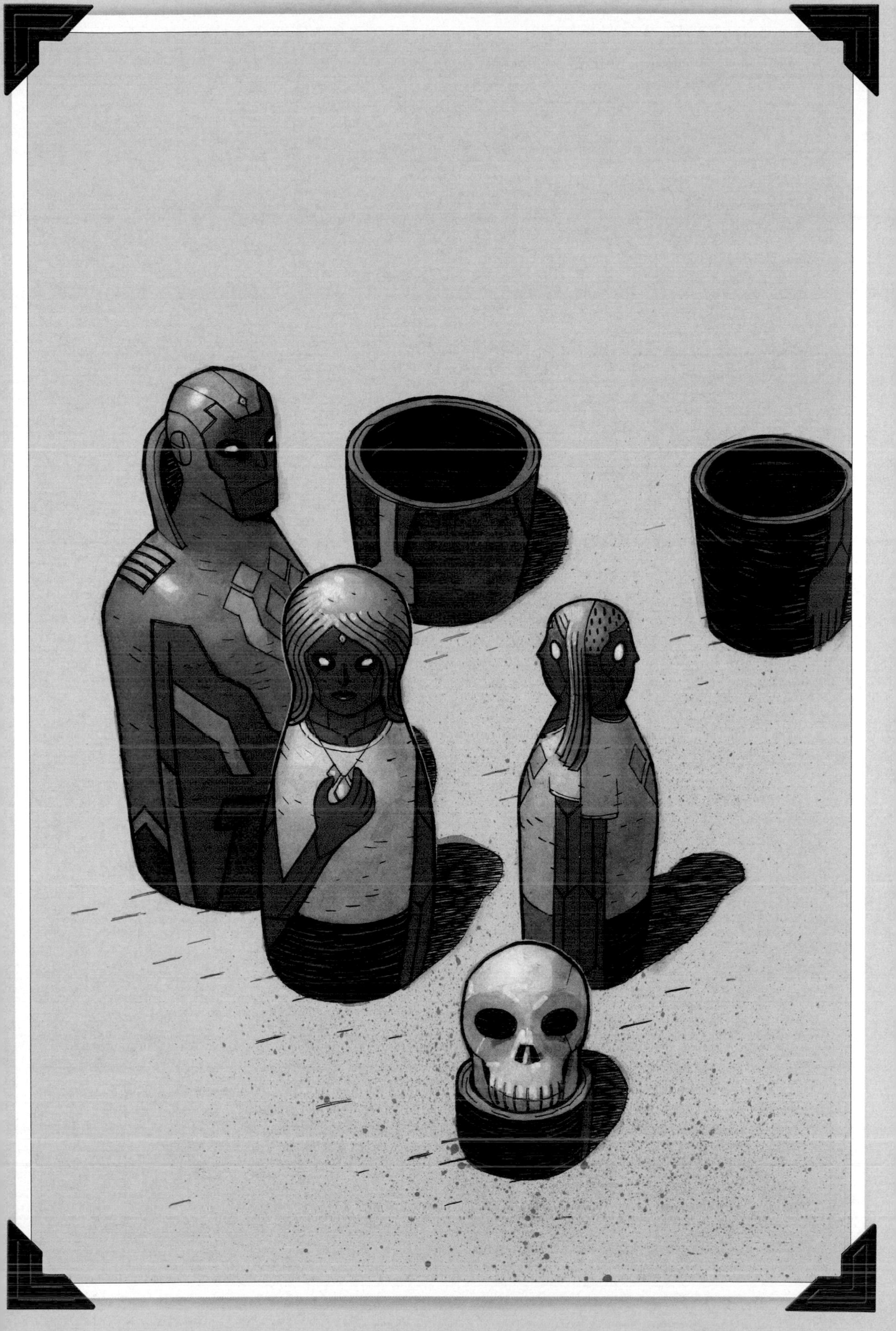

#8 STORY THUS FAR VARIANT BY ***GABRIEL HERNANDEZ WALTA***

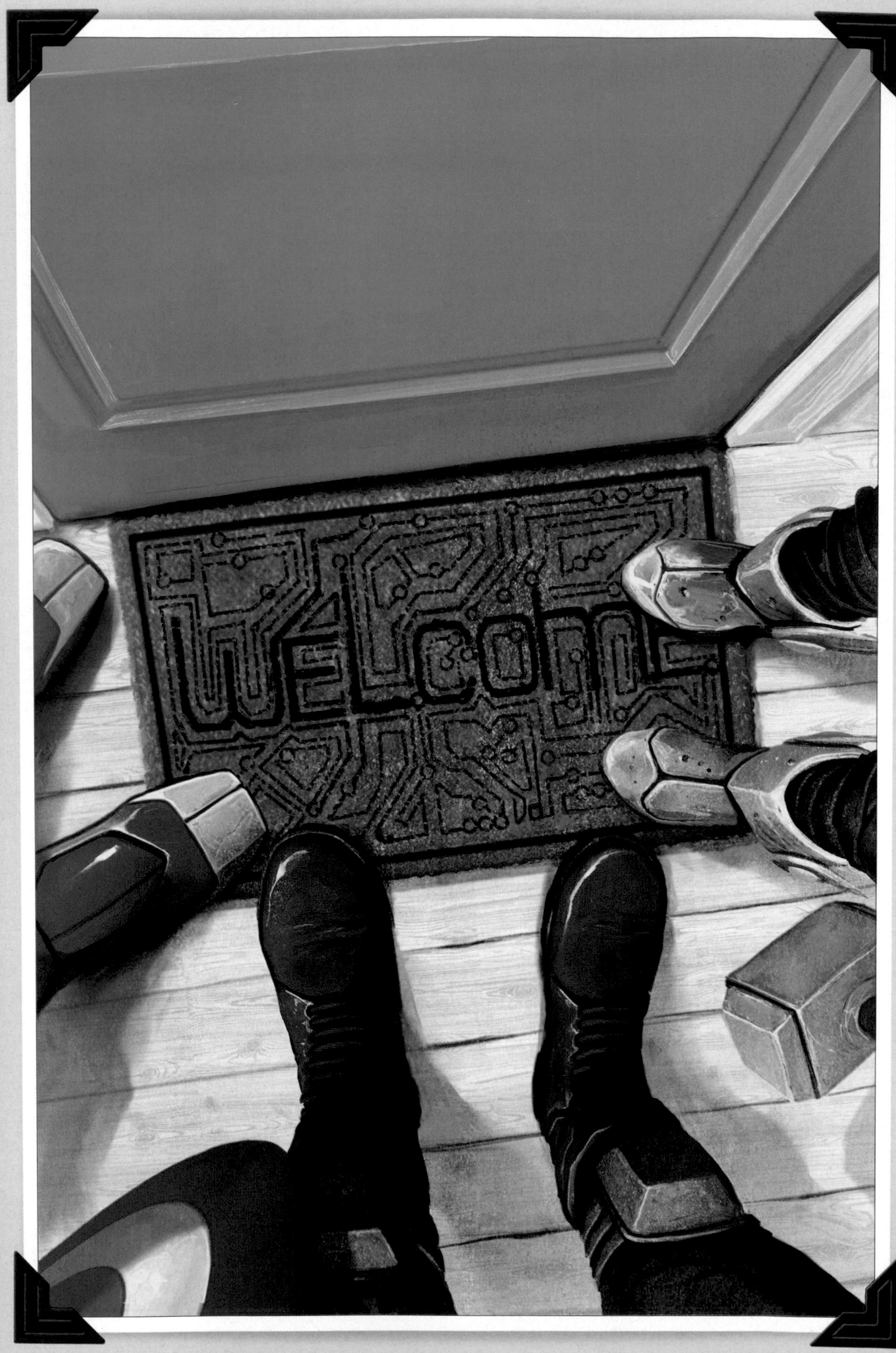
WELCOME

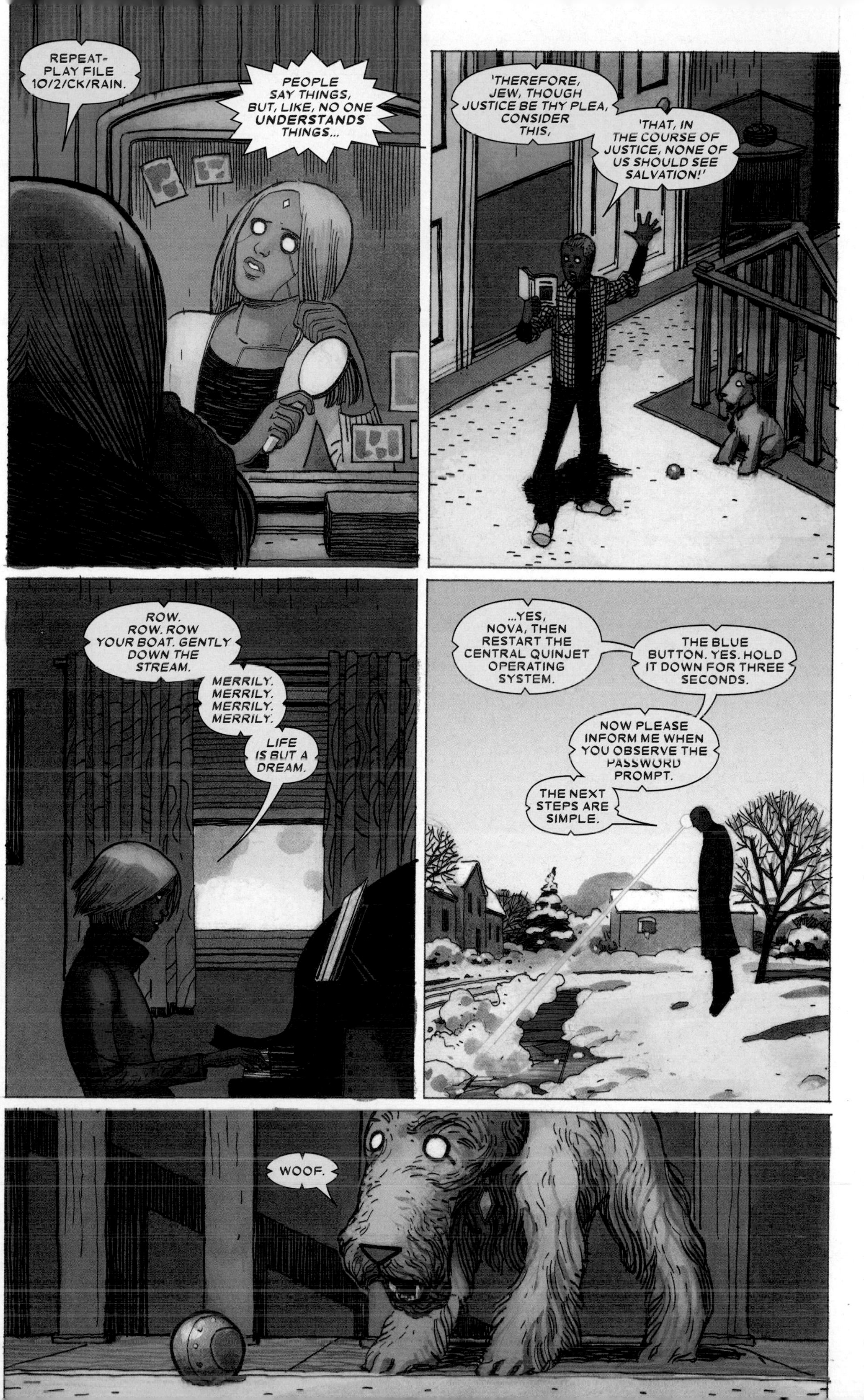
REPEAT-PLAY FILE 10/2/CK/RAIN.
PEOPLE SAY THINGS, BUT, LIKE, NO ONE UNDERSTANDS THINGS...
'THEREFORE, JEW, THOUGH JUSTICE BE THY PLEA, CONSIDER THIS,
'THAT, IN THE COURSE OF JUSTICE, NONE OF US SHOULD SEE SALVATION!'
ROW. ROW. ROW YOUR BOAT. GENTLY DOWN THE STREAM.
MERRILY. MERRILY. MERRILY. MERRILY.
LIFE IS BUT A DREAM.
...YES, NOVA, THEN RESTART THE CENTRAL QUINJET OPERATING SYSTEM.
THE BLUE BUTTON. YES. HOLD IT DOWN FOR THREE SECONDS.
NOW PLEASE INFORM ME WHEN YOU OBSERVE THE PASSWORD PROMPT.
THE NEXT STEPS ARE SIMPLE.
WOOF.

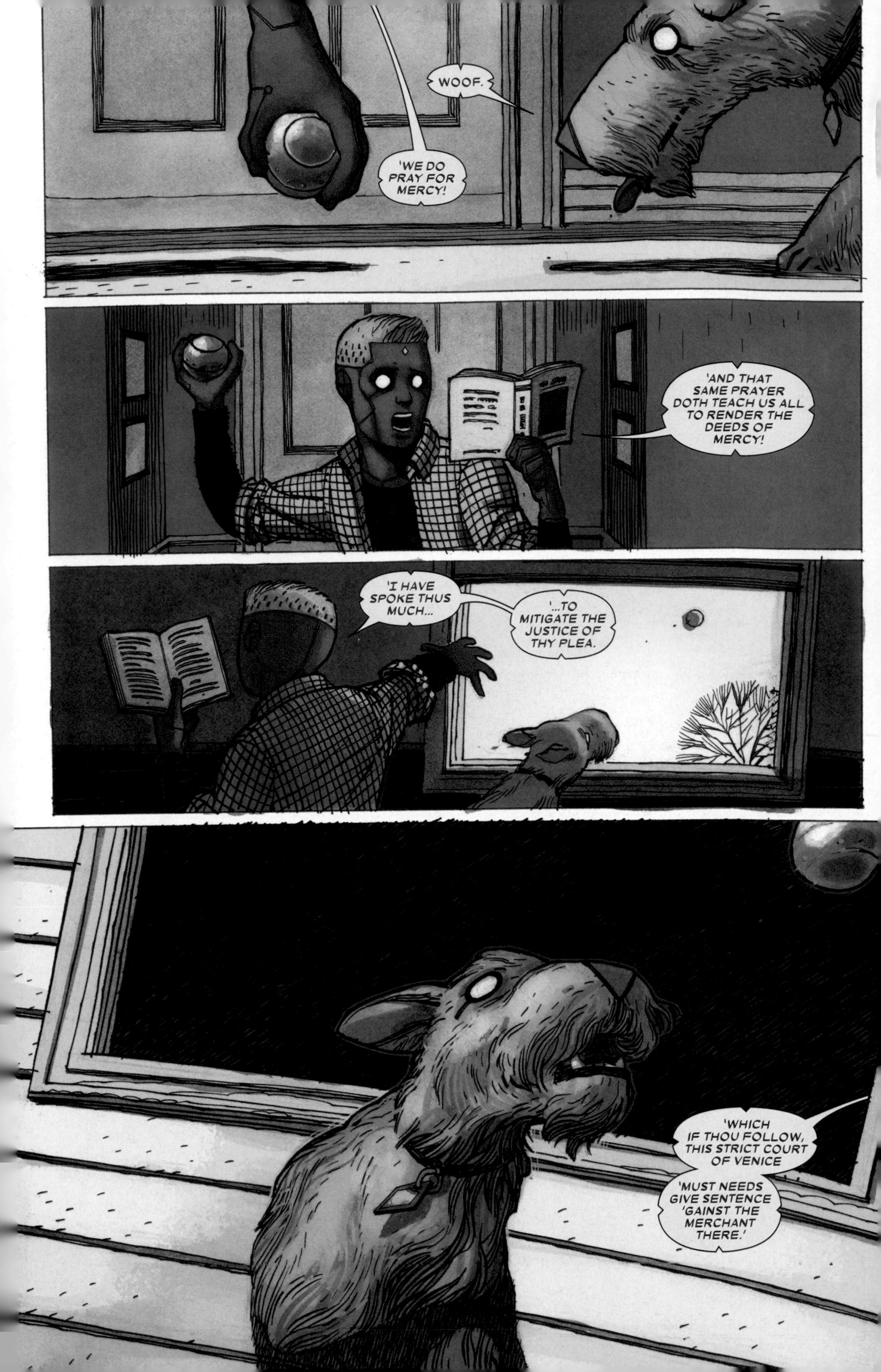
WOOF.
'WE DO PRAY FOR MERCY!
'AND THAT SAME PRAYER DOTH TEACH US ALL TO RENDER THE DEEDS OF MERCY!
'I HAVE SPOKE THUS MUCH...
'...TO MITIGATE THE JUSTICE OF THY PLEA.
'WHICH IF THOU FOLLOW, THIS STRICT COURT OF VENICE
'MUST NEEDS GIVE SENTENCE 'GAINST THE MERCHANT THERE.'

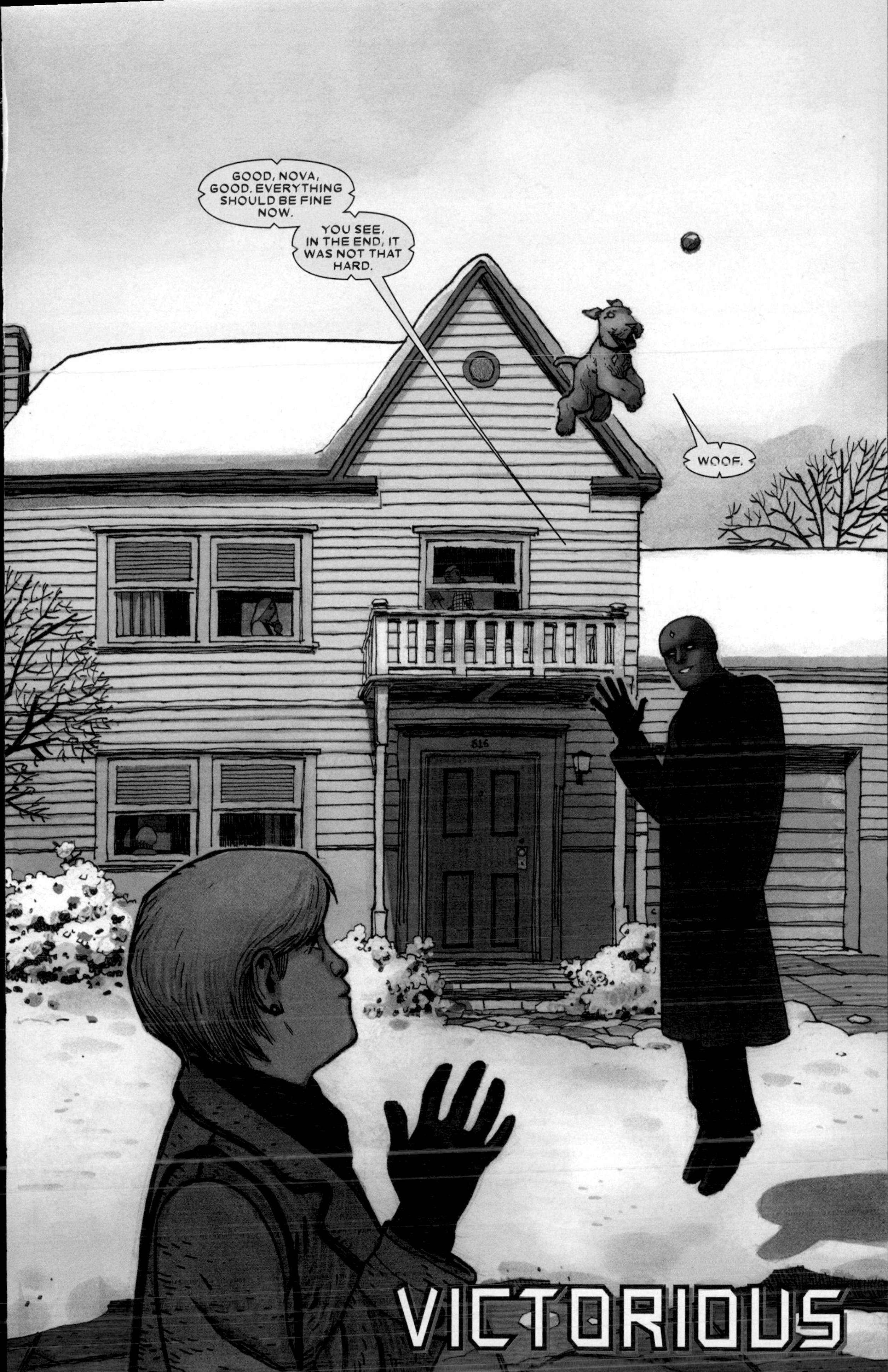
GOOD, NOVA, GOOD. EVERYTHING SHOULD BE FINE NOW.
YOU SEE, IN THE END, IT WAS NOT THAT HARD.
WOOF.
516
VICTORIOUS

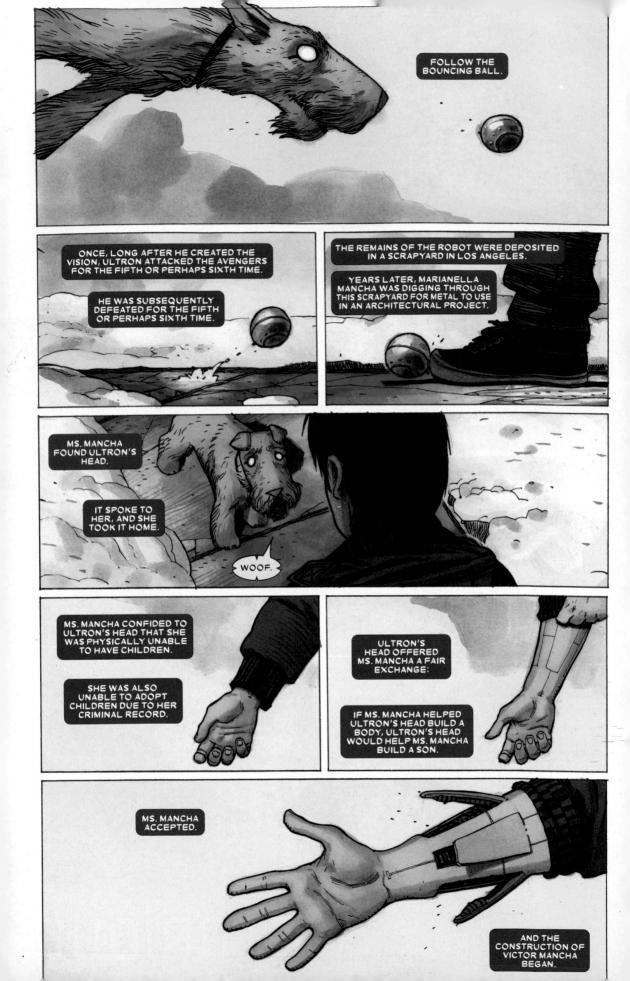

FOLLOW THE BOUNCING BALL.

ONCE, LONG AFTER HE CREATED THE VISION, ULTRON ATTACKED THE AVENGERS FOR THE FIFTH OR PERHAPS SIXTH TIME.

HE WAS SUBSEQUENTLY DEFEATED FOR THE FIFTH OR PERHAPS SIXTH TIME.

THE REMAINS OF THE ROBOT WERE DEPOSITED IN A SCRAPYARD IN LOS ANGELES.

YEARS LATER, MARIANELLA MANCHA WAS DIGGING THROUGH THIS SCRAPYARD FOR METAL TO USE IN AN ARCHITECTURAL PROJECT.

MS. MANCHA FOUND ULTRON'S HEAD.

IT SPOKE TO HER, AND SHE TOOK IT HOME.

WOOF.

MS. MANCHA CONFIDED TO ULTRON'S HEAD THAT SHE WAS PHYSICALLY UNABLE TO HAVE CHILDREN.

SHE WAS ALSO UNABLE TO ADOPT CHILDREN DUE TO HER CRIMINAL RECORD.

ULTRON'S HEAD OFFERED MS. MANCHA A FAIR EXCHANGE:

IF MS. MANCHA HELPED ULTRON'S HEAD BUILD A BODY, ULTRON'S HEAD WOULD HELP MS. MANCHA BUILD A SON.

MS. MANCHA ACCEPTED.

AND THE CONSTRUCTION OF VICTOR MANCHA BEGAN.

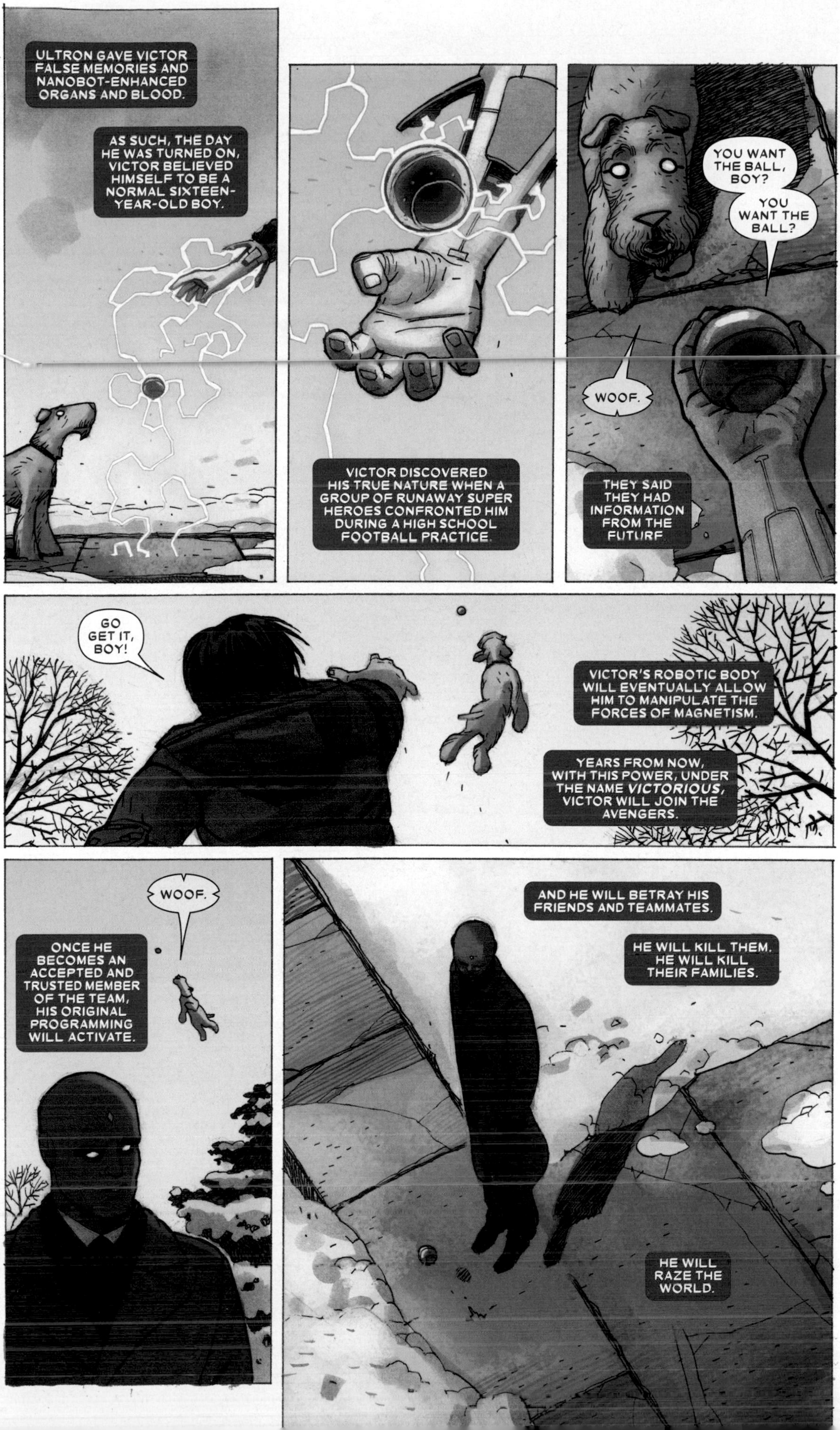

ULTRON GAVE VICTOR FALSE MEMORIES AND NANOBOT-ENHANCED ORGANS AND BLOOD.
AS SUCH, THE DAY HE WAS TURNED ON, VICTOR BELIEVED HIMSELF TO BE A NORMAL SIXTEEN-YEAR-OLD BOY.
VICTOR DISCOVERED HIS TRUE NATURE WHEN A GROUP OF RUNAWAY SUPER HEROES CONFRONTED HIM DURING A HIGH SCHOOL FOOTBALL PRACTICE.
YOU WANT THE BALL, BOY?
YOU WANT THE BALL?
WOOF.
THEY SAID THEY HAD INFORMATION FROM THE FUTURE
GO GET IT, BOY!
VICTOR'S ROBOTIC BODY WILL EVENTUALLY ALLOW HIM TO MANIPULATE THE FORCES OF MAGNETISM.
YEARS FROM NOW, WITH THIS POWER, UNDER THE NAME *VICTORIOUS*, VICTOR WILL JOIN THE AVENGERS.
WOOF.
ONCE HE BECOMES AN ACCEPTED AND TRUSTED MEMBER OF THE TEAM, HIS ORIGINAL PROGRAMMING WILL ACTIVATE.
AND HE WILL BETRAY HIS FRIENDS AND TEAMMATES.
HE WILL KILL THEM. HE WILL KILL THEIR FAMILIES.
HE WILL RAZE THE WORLD.

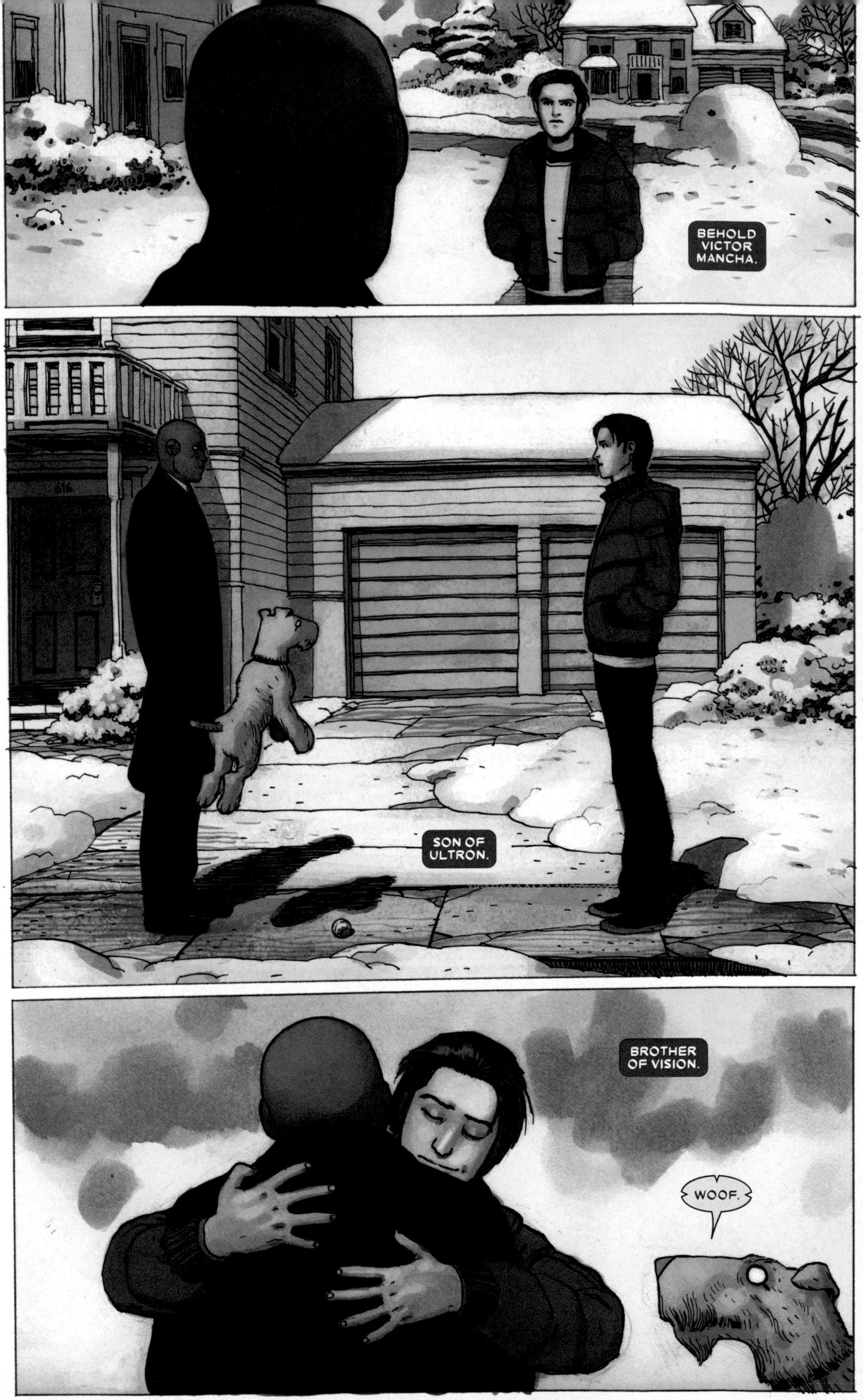
BEHOLD VICTOR MANCHA.
SON OF ULTRON.
BROTHER OF VISION.
WOOF.

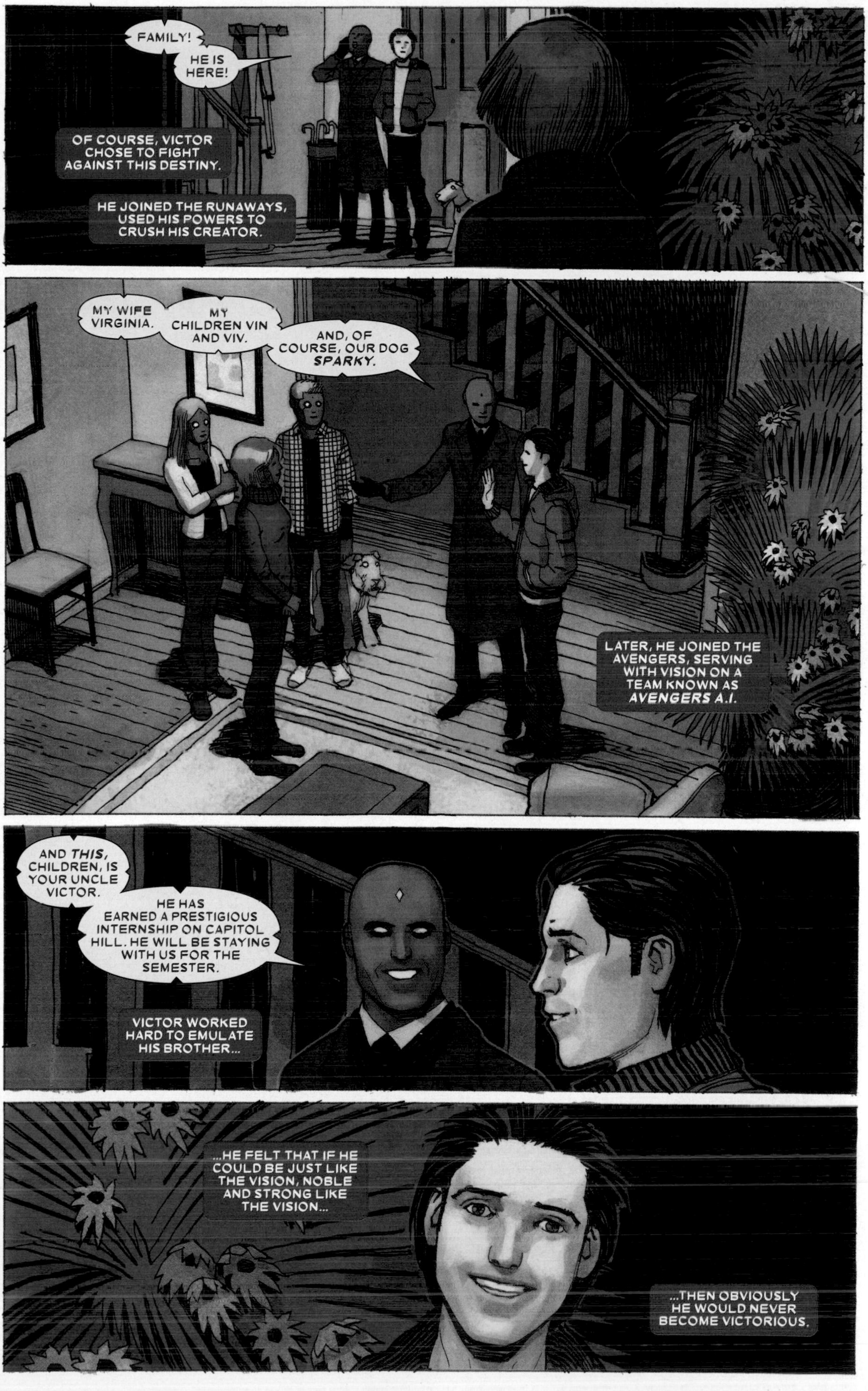
FAMILY!
HE IS HERE!
OF COURSE, VICTOR CHOSE TO FIGHT AGAINST THIS DESTINY.
HE JOINED THE RUNAWAYS, USED HIS POWERS TO CRUSH HIS CREATOR.
MY WIFE VIRGINIA.
MY CHILDREN VIN AND VIV.
AND, OF COURSE, OUR DOG SPARKY.
LATER, HE JOINED THE AVENGERS, SERVING WITH VISION ON A TEAM KNOWN AS AVENGERS A.I.
AND THIS, CHILDREN, IS YOUR UNCLE VICTOR.
HE HAS EARNED A PRESTIGIOUS INTERNSHIP ON CAPITOL HILL. HE WILL BE STAYING WITH US FOR THE SEMESTER.
VICTOR WORKED HARD TO EMULATE HIS BROTHER...
...HE FELT THAT IF HE COULD BE JUST LIKE THE VISION, NOBLE AND STRONG LIKE THE VISION...
...THEN OBVIOUSLY HE WOULD NEVER BECOME VICTORIOUS.

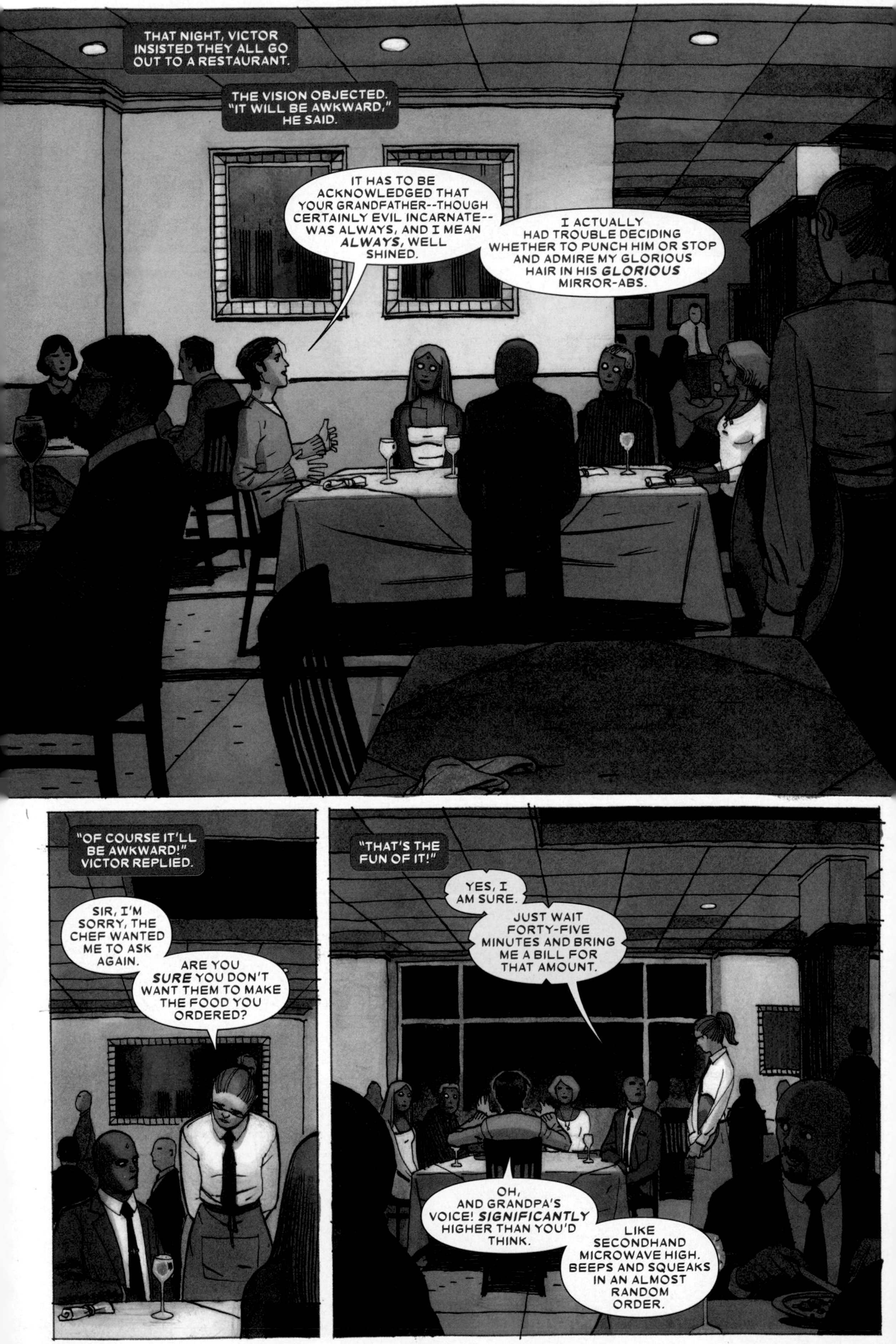
THAT NIGHT, VICTOR INSISTED THEY ALL GO OUT TO A RESTAURANT.
THE VISION OBJECTED. "IT WILL BE AWKWARD," HE SAID.
IT HAS TO BE ACKNOWLEDGED THAT YOUR GRANDFATHER--THOUGH CERTAINLY EVIL INCARNATE--WAS ALWAYS, AND I MEAN *ALWAYS*, WELL SHINED.
I ACTUALLY HAD TROUBLE DECIDING WHETHER TO PUNCH HIM OR STOP AND ADMIRE MY GLORIOUS HAIR IN HIS *GLORIOUS* MIRROR-ABS.
"OF COURSE IT'LL BE AWKWARD!" VICTOR REPLIED.
SIR, I'M SORRY, THE CHEF WANTED ME TO ASK AGAIN.
ARE YOU *SURE* YOU DON'T WANT THEM TO MAKE THE FOOD YOU ORDERED?
"THAT'S THE FUN OF IT!"
YES, I AM SURE.
JUST WAIT FORTY-FIVE MINUTES AND BRING ME A BILL FOR THAT AMOUNT.
OH, AND GRANDPA'S VOICE! *SIGNIFICANTLY* HIGHER THAN YOU'D THINK.
LIKE SECONDHAND MICROWAVE HIGH. BEEPS AND SQUEAKS IN AN ALMOST RANDOM ORDER.

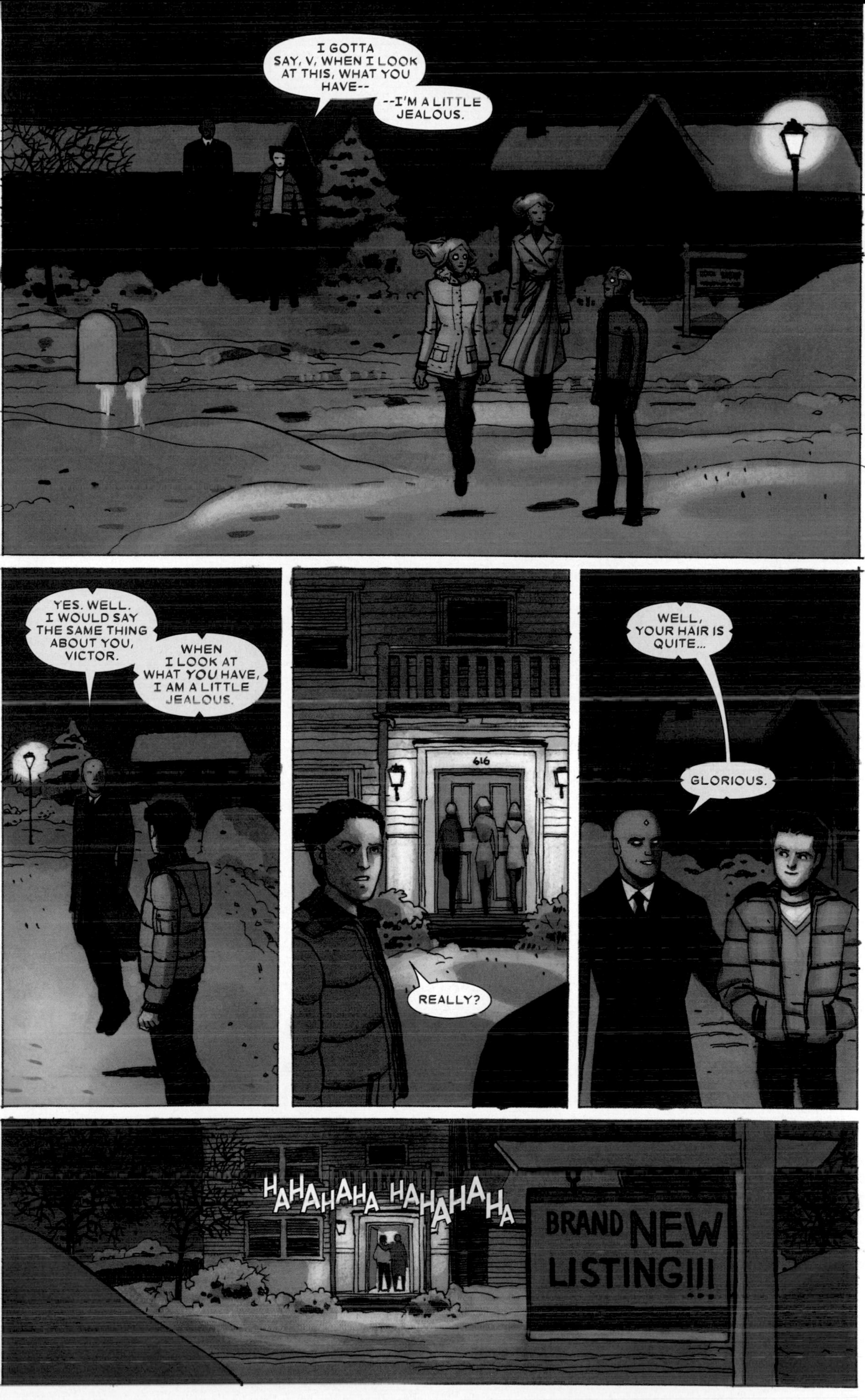
I GOTTA SAY, V, WHEN I LOOK AT THIS, WHAT YOU HAVE--
--I'M A LITTLE JEALOUS.
YES. WELL. I WOULD SAY THE SAME THING ABOUT YOU, VICTOR.
WHEN I LOOK AT WHAT YOU HAVE, I AM A LITTLE JEALOUS.
616
REALLY?
WELL, YOUR HAIR IS QUITE...
GLORIOUS.
HAHAHAHA HAHAHAHA
BRAND NEW LISTING!!!

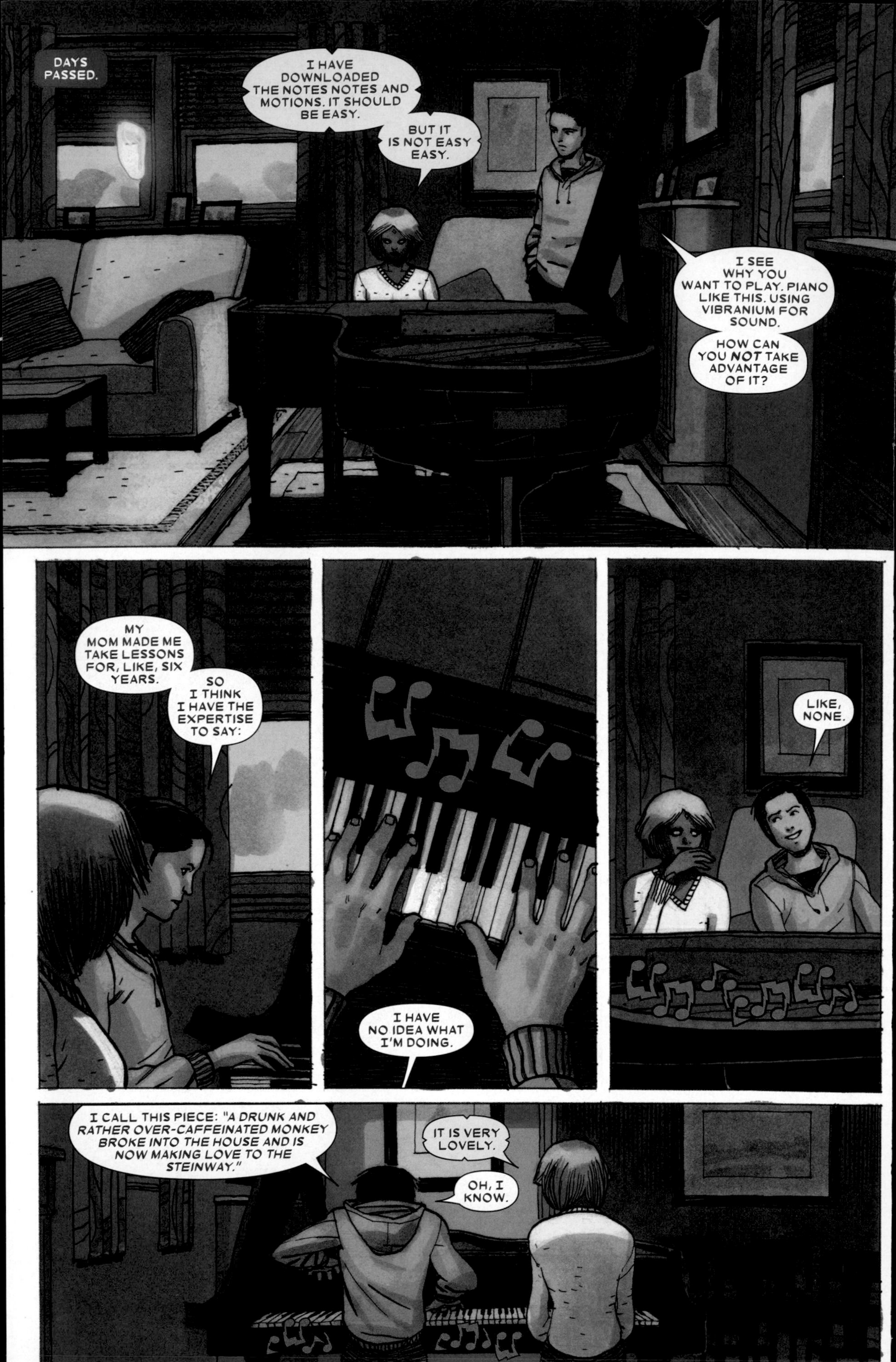
DAYS PASSED.
I HAVE DOWNLOADED THE NOTES NOTES AND MOTIONS. IT SHOULD BE EASY.
BUT IT IS NOT EASY EASY.
I SEE WHY YOU WANT TO PLAY. PIANO LIKE THIS. USING VIBRANIUM FOR SOUND.
HOW CAN YOU NOT TAKE ADVANTAGE OF IT?
MY MOM MADE ME TAKE LESSONS FOR, LIKE, SIX YEARS.
SO I THINK I HAVE THE EXPERTISE TO SAY:
I HAVE NO IDEA WHAT I'M DOING.
LIKE, NONE.
I CALL THIS PIECE: "A DRUNK AND RATHER OVER-CAFFEINATED MONKEY BROKE INTO THE HOUSE AND IS NOW MAKING LOVE TO THE STEINWAY."
IT IS VERY LOVELY.
OH, I KNOW.

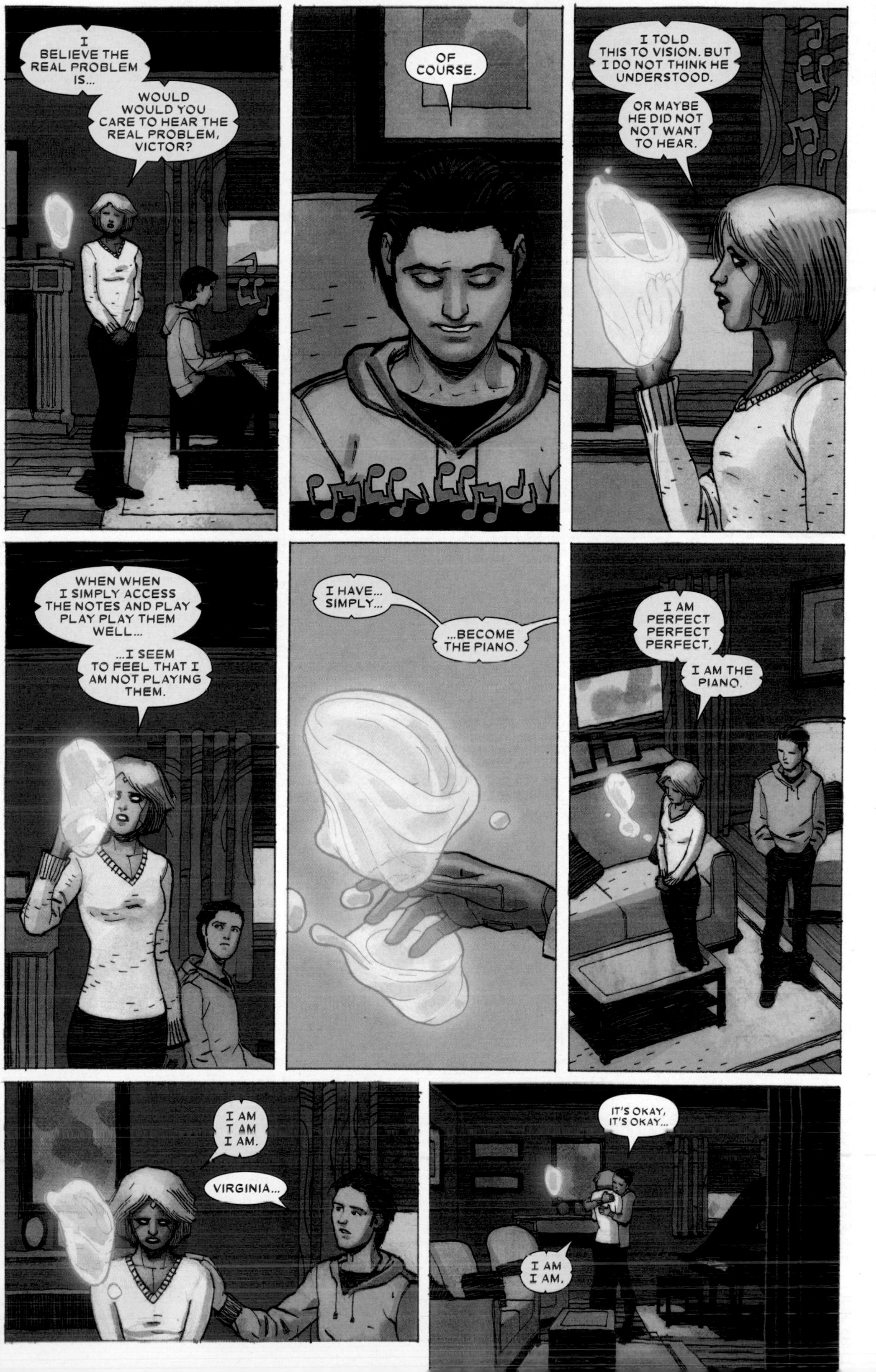
I BELIEVE THE REAL PROBLEM IS...
WOULD WOULD YOU CARE TO HEAR THE REAL PROBLEM, VICTOR?
OF COURSE.
I TOLD THIS TO VISION. BUT I DO NOT THINK HE UNDERSTOOD.
OR MAYBE HE DID NOT NOT WANT TO HEAR.
WHEN WHEN I SIMPLY ACCESS THE NOTES AND PLAY PLAY PLAY THEM WELL...
...I SEEM TO FEEL THAT I AM NOT PLAYING THEM.
I HAVE... SIMPLY...
...BECOME THE PIANO.
I AM PERFECT PERFECT PERFECT.
I AM THE PIANO.
I AM I AM I AM.
VIRGINIA...
IT'S OKAY, IT'S OKAY...
I AM I AM.

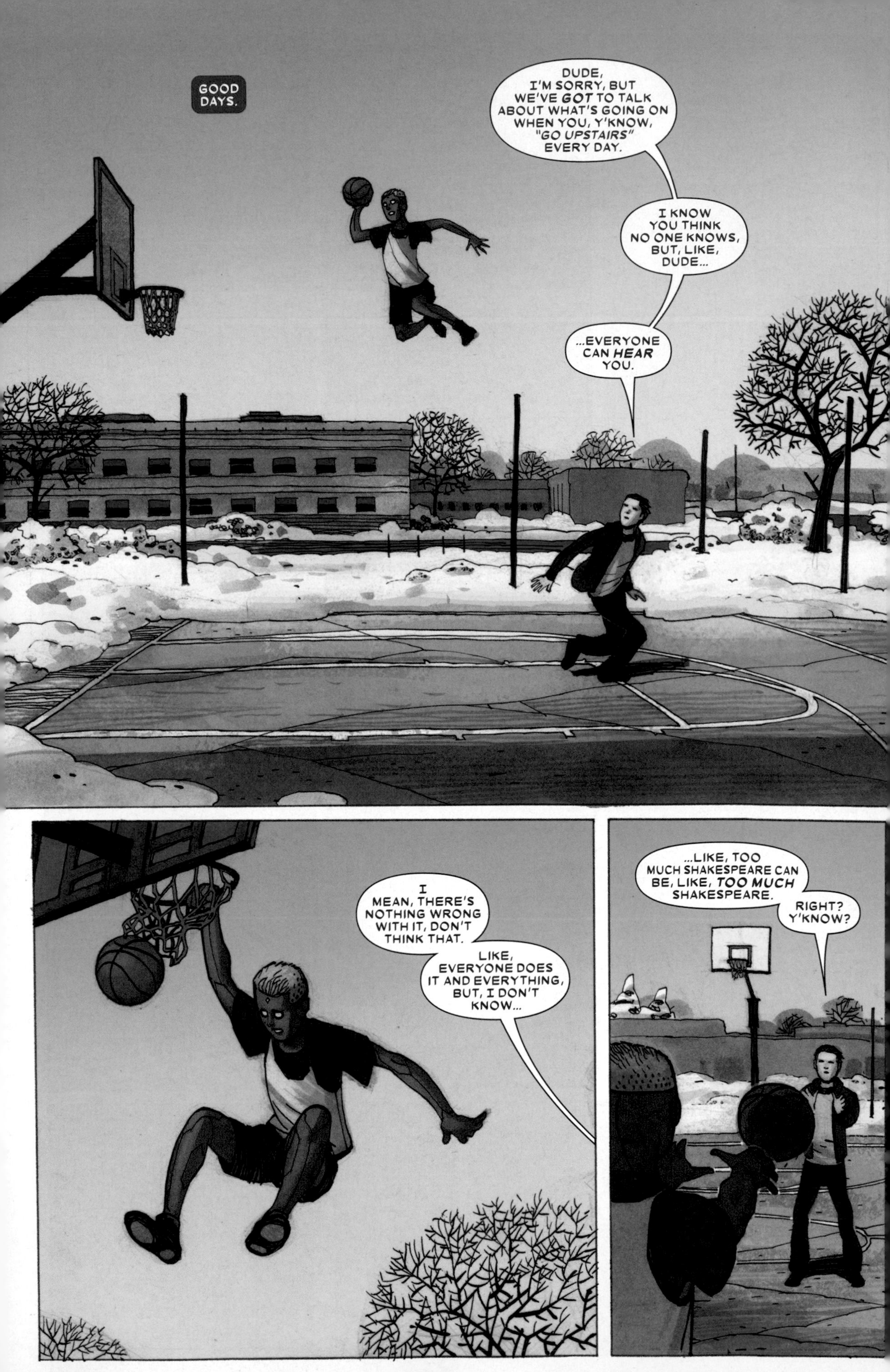
GOOD DAYS.
DUDE, I'M SORRY, BUT WE'VE *GOT* TO TALK ABOUT WHAT'S GOING ON WHEN YOU, Y'KNOW, "*GO UPSTAIRS*" EVERY DAY.
I KNOW YOU THINK NO ONE KNOWS, BUT, LIKE, DUDE...
...EVERYONE CAN *HEAR* YOU.
I MEAN, THERE'S NOTHING WRONG WITH IT, DON'T THINK THAT.
LIKE, EVERYONE DOES IT AND EVERYTHING, BUT, I DON'T KNOW...
...LIKE, TOO MUCH SHAKESPEARE CAN BE, LIKE, *TOO MUCH* SHAKESPEARE.
RIGHT? Y'KNOW?

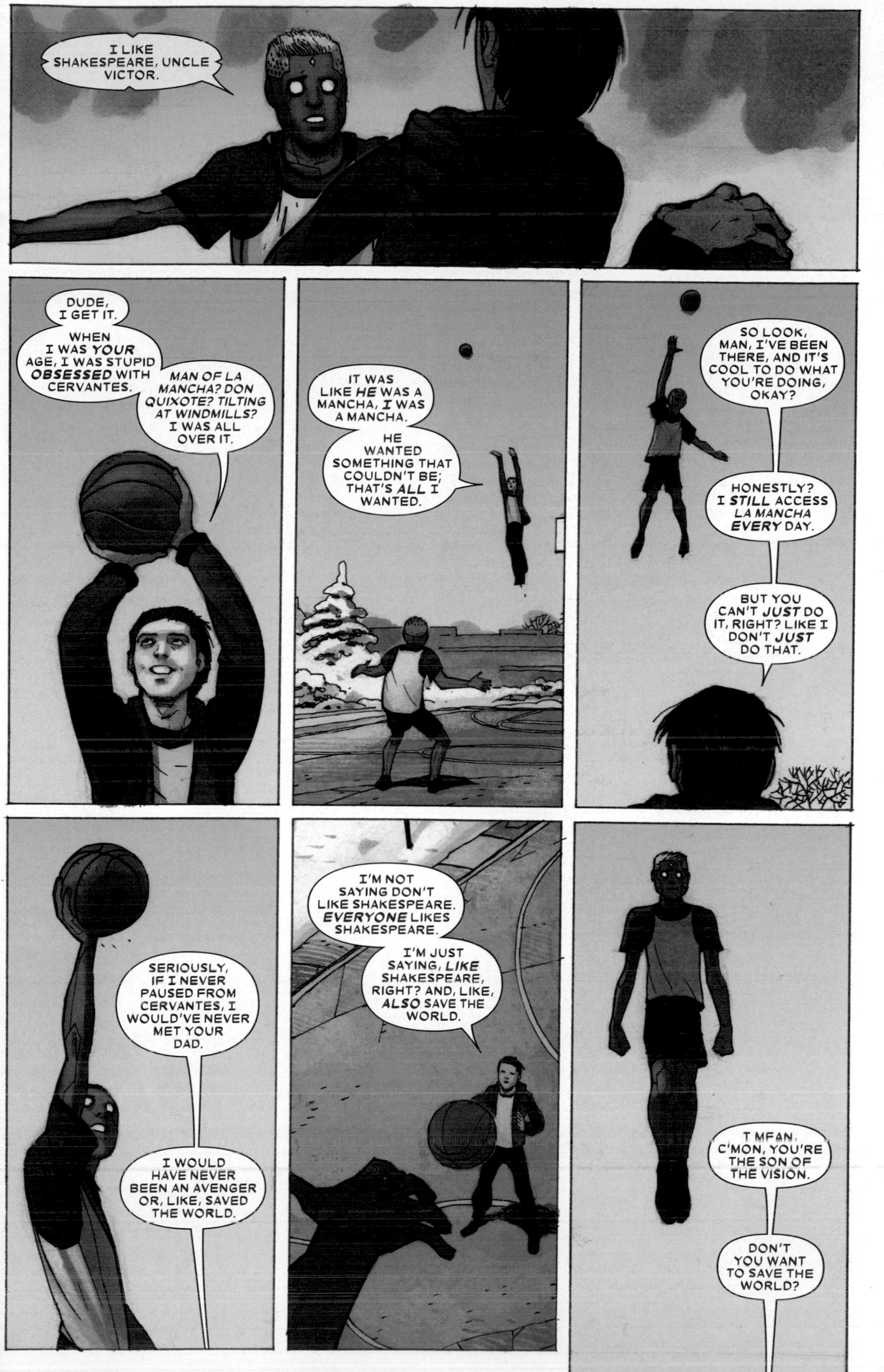

I LIKE SHAKESPEARE, UNCLE VICTOR.
DUDE, I GET IT.
WHEN I WAS *YOUR* AGE, I WAS STUPID ***OBSESSED*** WITH CERVANTES.
MAN OF LA MANCHA? DON QUIXOTE? TILTING AT WINDMILLS? I WAS ALL OVER IT.
IT WAS LIKE ***HE*** WAS A MANCHA, ***I*** WAS A MANCHA.
HE WANTED SOMETHING THAT COULDN'T BE; THAT'S ***ALL*** I WANTED.
SO LOOK, MAN, I'VE BEEN THERE, AND IT'S COOL TO DO WHAT YOU'RE DOING, OKAY?
HONESTLY? I ***STILL*** ACCESS *LA MANCHA* ***EVERY*** DAY.
BUT YOU CAN'T ***JUST*** DO IT, RIGHT? LIKE I DON'T ***JUST*** DO THAT.
SERIOUSLY, IF I NEVER PAUSED FROM CERVANTES, I WOULD'VE NEVER MET YOUR DAD.
I WOULD HAVE NEVER BEEN AN AVENGER OR, LIKE, SAVED THE WORLD.
I'M NOT SAYING DON'T LIKE SHAKESPEARE. ***EVERYONE*** LIKES SHAKESPEARE.
I'M JUST SAYING, ***LIKE*** SHAKESPEARE, RIGHT? AND, LIKE, ***ALSO*** SAVE THE WORLD.
I MEAN, C'MON, YOU'RE THE SON OF THE VISION.
DON'T YOU WANT TO SAVE THE WORLD?

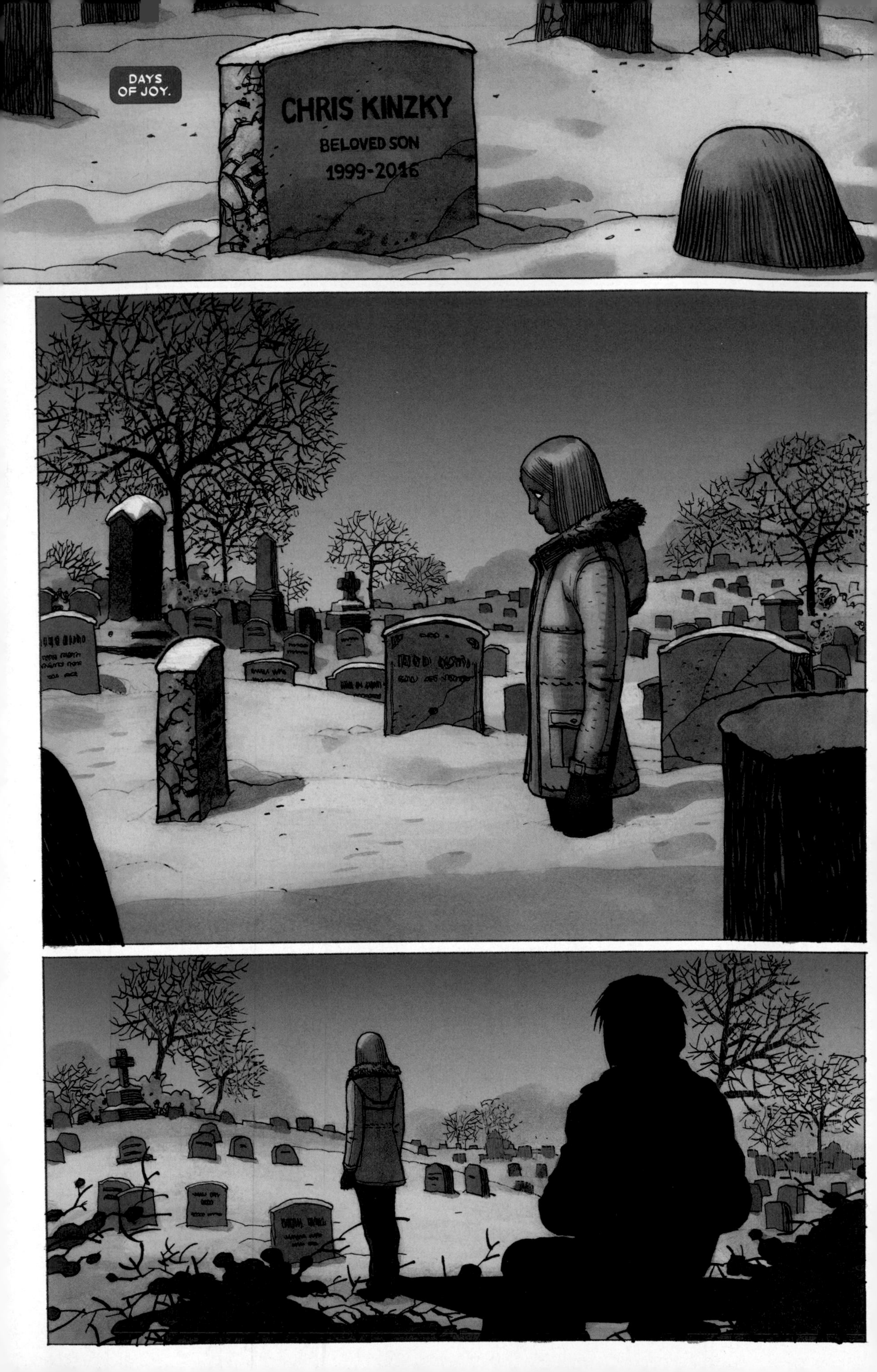
DAYS OF JOY.
CHRIS KINZKY
BELOVED SON
1999-2016

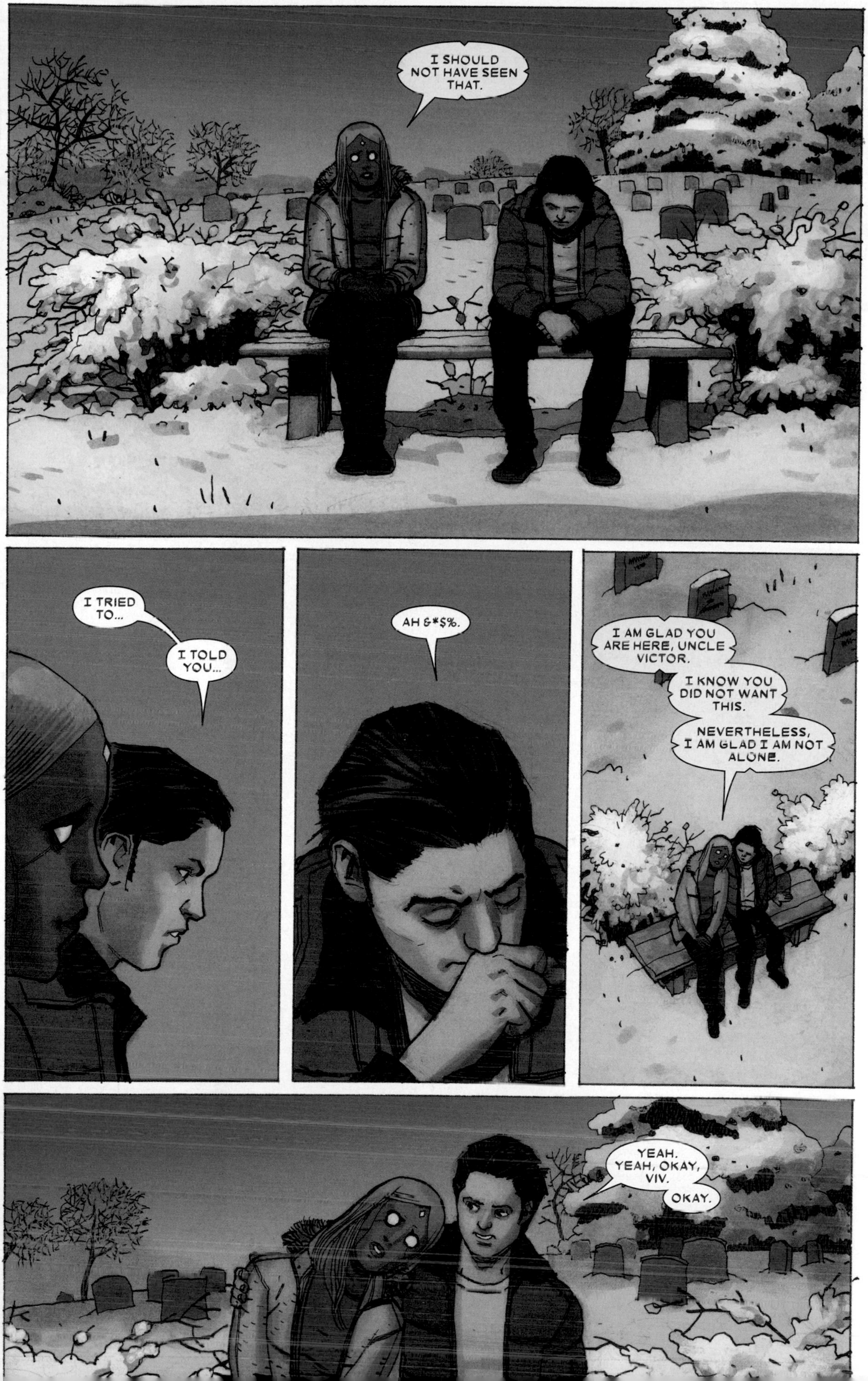
I SHOULD NOT HAVE SEEN THAT.
I TRIED TO...
I TOLD YOU...
AH &*$%.
I AM GLAD YOU ARE HERE, UNCLE VICTOR.
I KNOW YOU DID NOT WANT THIS.
NEVERTHELESS, I AM GLAD I AM NOT ALONE.
YEAH. YEAH, OKAY, VIV.
OKAY.

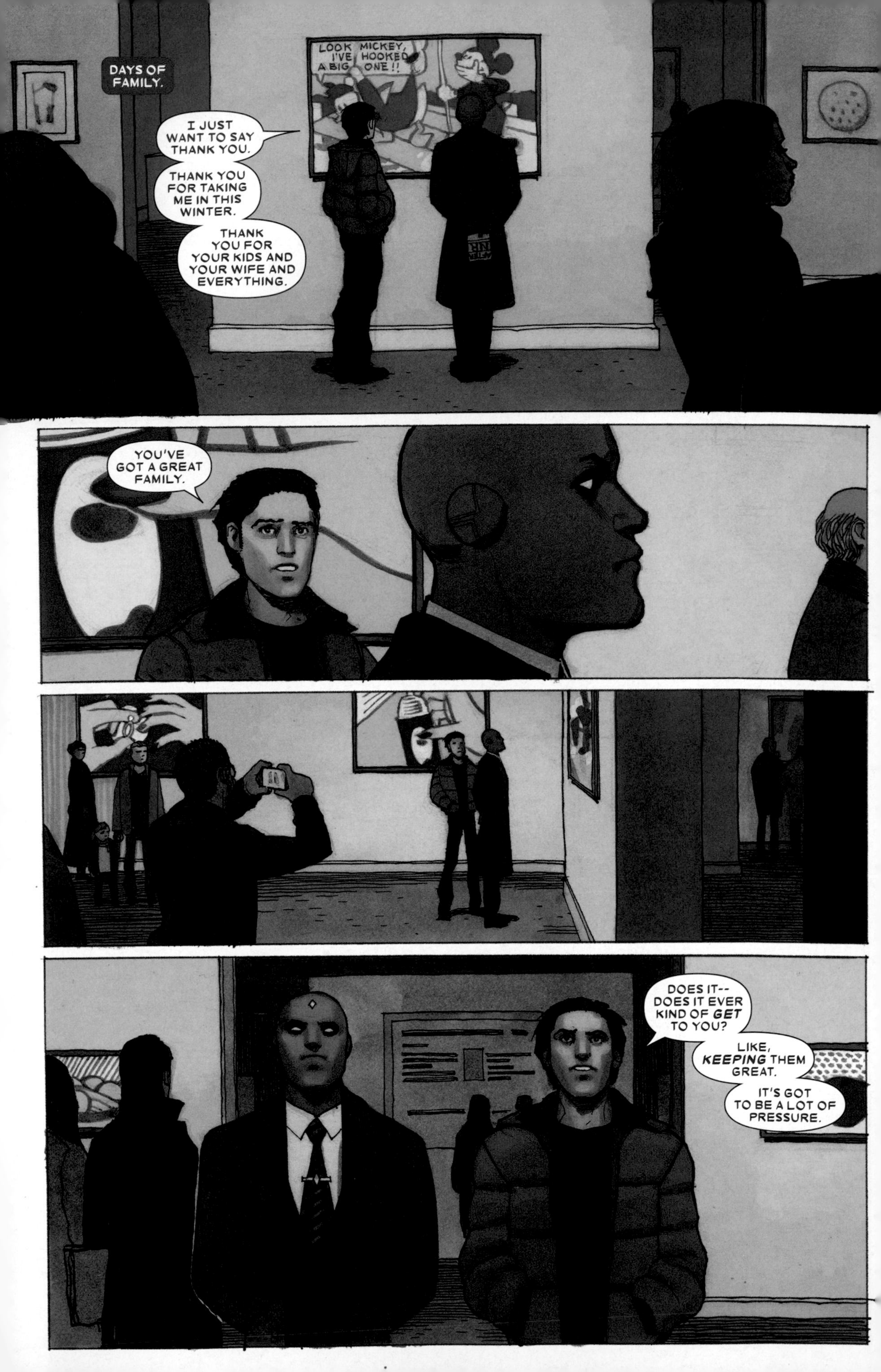
LOOK MICKEY, I'VE HOOKED A BIG ONE!!
DAYS OF FAMILY.
I JUST WANT TO SAY THANK YOU.
THANK YOU FOR TAKING ME IN THIS WINTER.
THANK YOU FOR YOUR KIDS AND YOUR WIFE AND EVERYTHING.
YOU'VE GOT A GREAT FAMILY.
DOES IT-- DOES IT EVER KIND OF GET TO YOU?
LIKE, KEEPING THEM GREAT.
IT'S GOT TO BE A LOT OF PRESSURE.

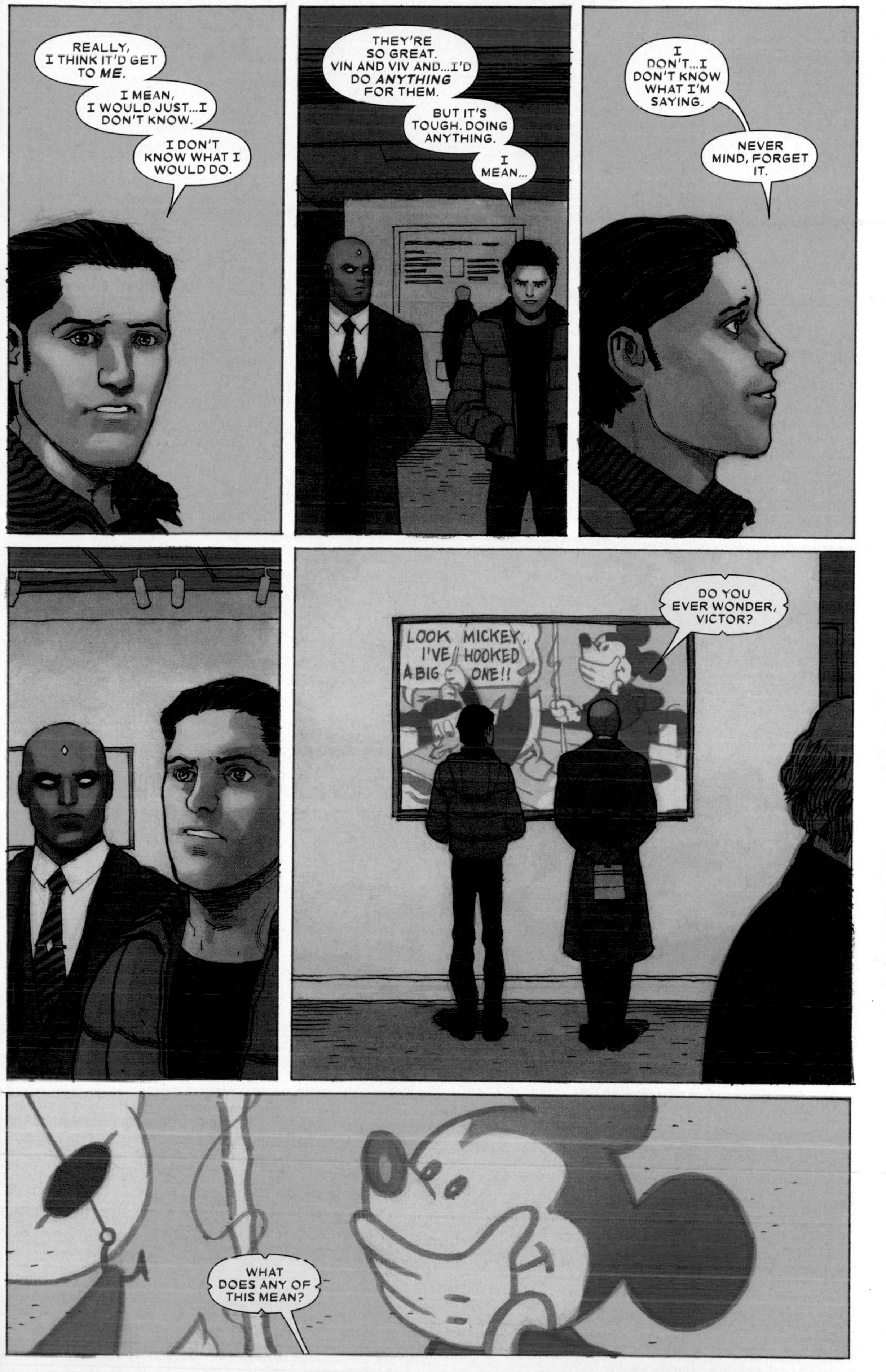
REALLY, I THINK IT'D GET TO *ME.*
I MEAN, I WOULD JUST...I DON'T KNOW.
I DON'T KNOW WHAT I WOULD DO.
THEY'RE SO GREAT. VIN AND VIV AND...I'D DO *ANYTHING* FOR THEM.
BUT IT'S TOUGH. DOING ANYTHING.
I MEAN...
I DON'T...I DON'T KNOW WHAT I'M SAYING.
NEVER MIND, FORGET IT.
LOOK MICKEY, I'VE HOOKED A BIG ONE!!
DO YOU EVER WONDER, VICTOR?
WHAT DOES ANY OF THIS MEAN?

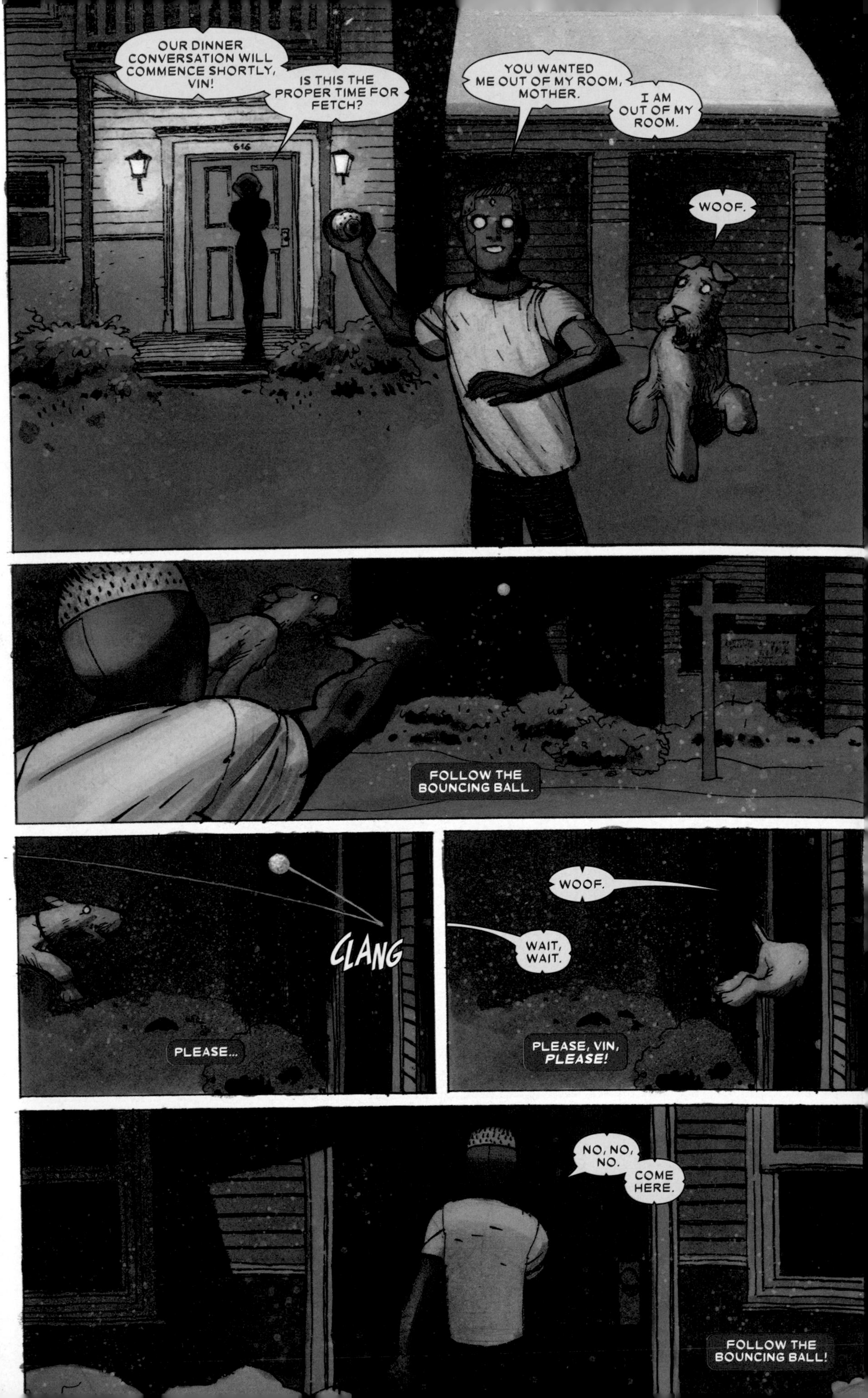
OUR DINNER CONVERSATION WILL COMMENCE SHORTLY, VIN!
IS THIS THE PROPER TIME FOR FETCH?
YOU WANTED ME OUT OF MY ROOM, MOTHER.
I AM OUT OF MY ROOM.
WOOF.
FOLLOW THE BOUNCING BALL.
CLANG
PLEASE...
WOOF.
WAIT, WAIT.
PLEASE, VIN, PLEASE!
NO, NO, NO.
COME HERE.
FOLLOW THE BOUNCING BALL!

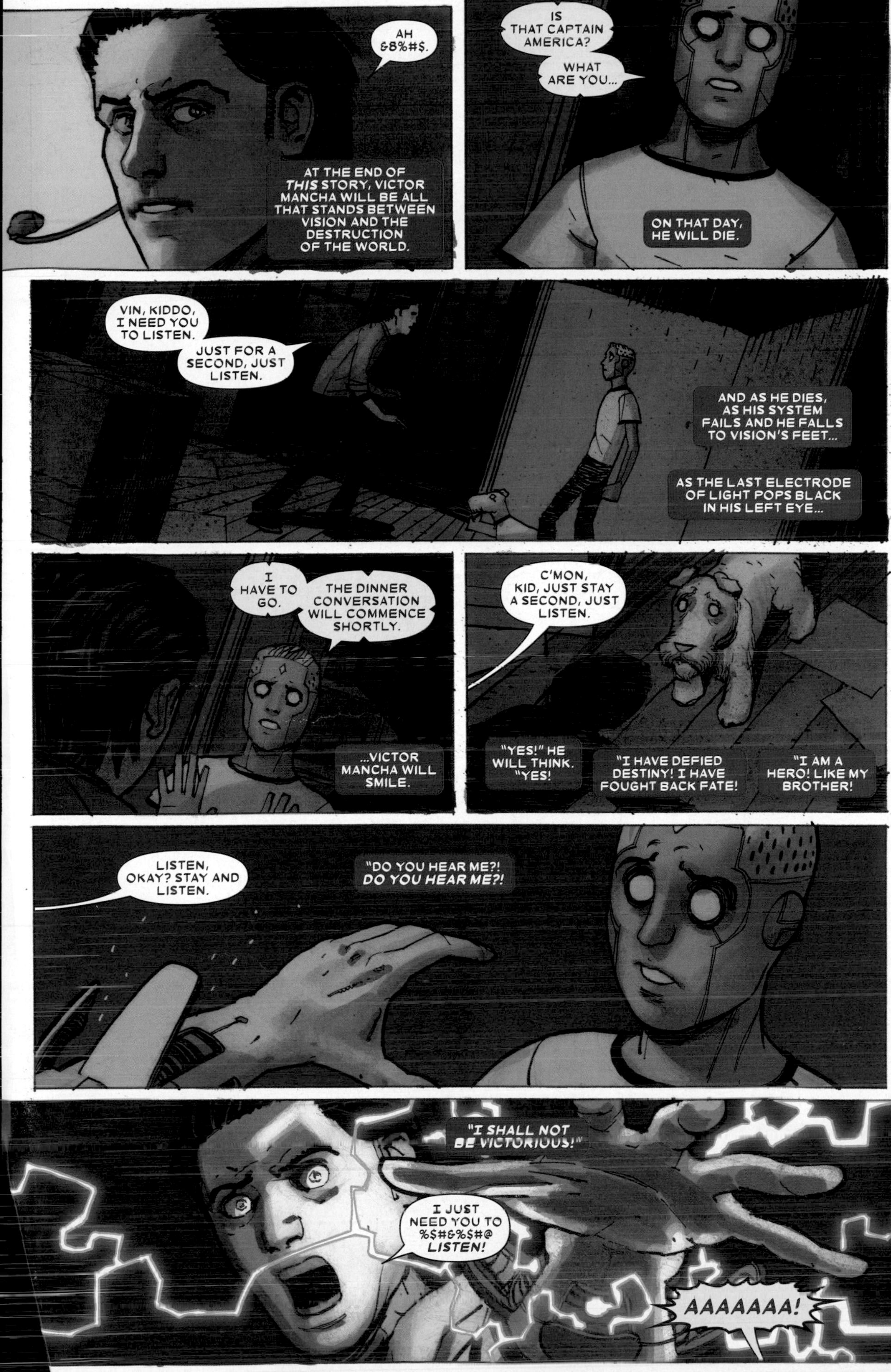
AH &8%#$.
AT THE END OF THIS STORY, VICTOR MANCHA WILL BE ALL THAT STANDS BETWEEN VISION AND THE DESTRUCTION OF THE WORLD.
IS THAT CAPTAIN AMERICA?
WHAT ARE YOU...
ON THAT DAY, HE WILL DIE.
VIN, KIDDO, I NEED YOU TO LISTEN.
JUST FOR A SECOND, JUST LISTEN.
AND AS HE DIES, AS HIS SYSTEM FAILS AND HE FALLS TO VISION'S FEET...
AS THE LAST ELECTRODE OF LIGHT POPS BLACK IN HIS LEFT EYE...
I HAVE TO GO.
THE DINNER CONVERSATION WILL COMMENCE SHORTLY.
...VICTOR MANCHA WILL SMILE.
C'MON, KID, JUST STAY A SECOND, JUST LISTEN.
"YES!" HE WILL THINK. "YES!
"I HAVE DEFIED DESTINY! I HAVE FOUGHT BACK FATE!
"I AM A HERO! LIKE MY BROTHER!
LISTEN, OKAY? STAY AND LISTEN.
"DO YOU HEAR ME?! DO YOU HEAR ME?!
"I SHALL NOT BE VICTORIOUS!"
I JUST NEED YOU TO %$#&%$#@ LISTEN!
AAAAAAA!

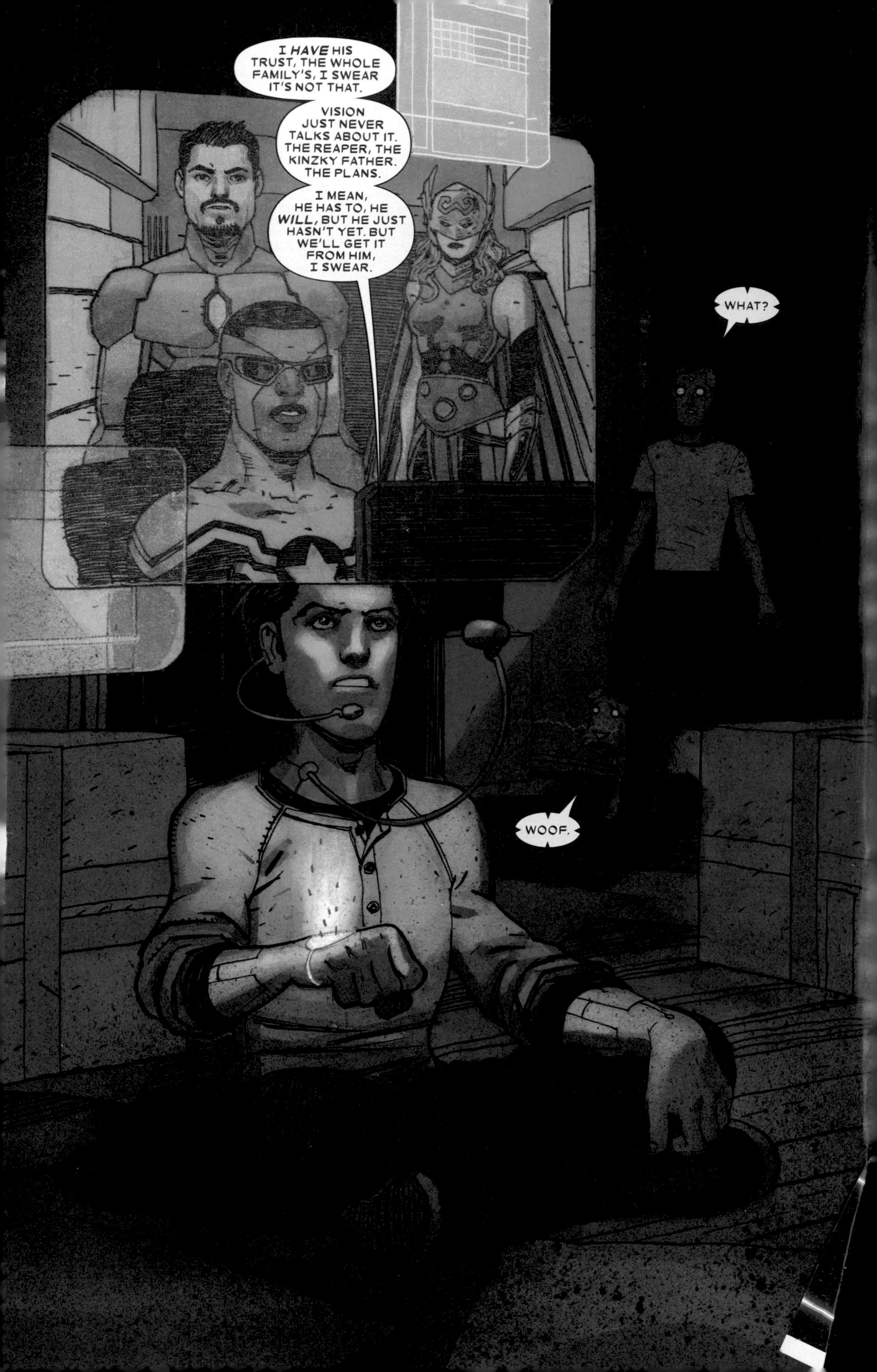
I HAVE HIS TRUST, THE WHOLE FAMILY'S, I SWEAR IT'S NOT THAT.
VISION JUST NEVER TALKS ABOUT IT. THE REAPER, THE KINZKY FATHER. THE PLANS.
I MEAN, HE HAS TO, HE WILL, BUT HE JUST HASN'T YET. BUT WE'LL GET IT FROM HIM, I SWEAR.
WHAT?
WOOF.

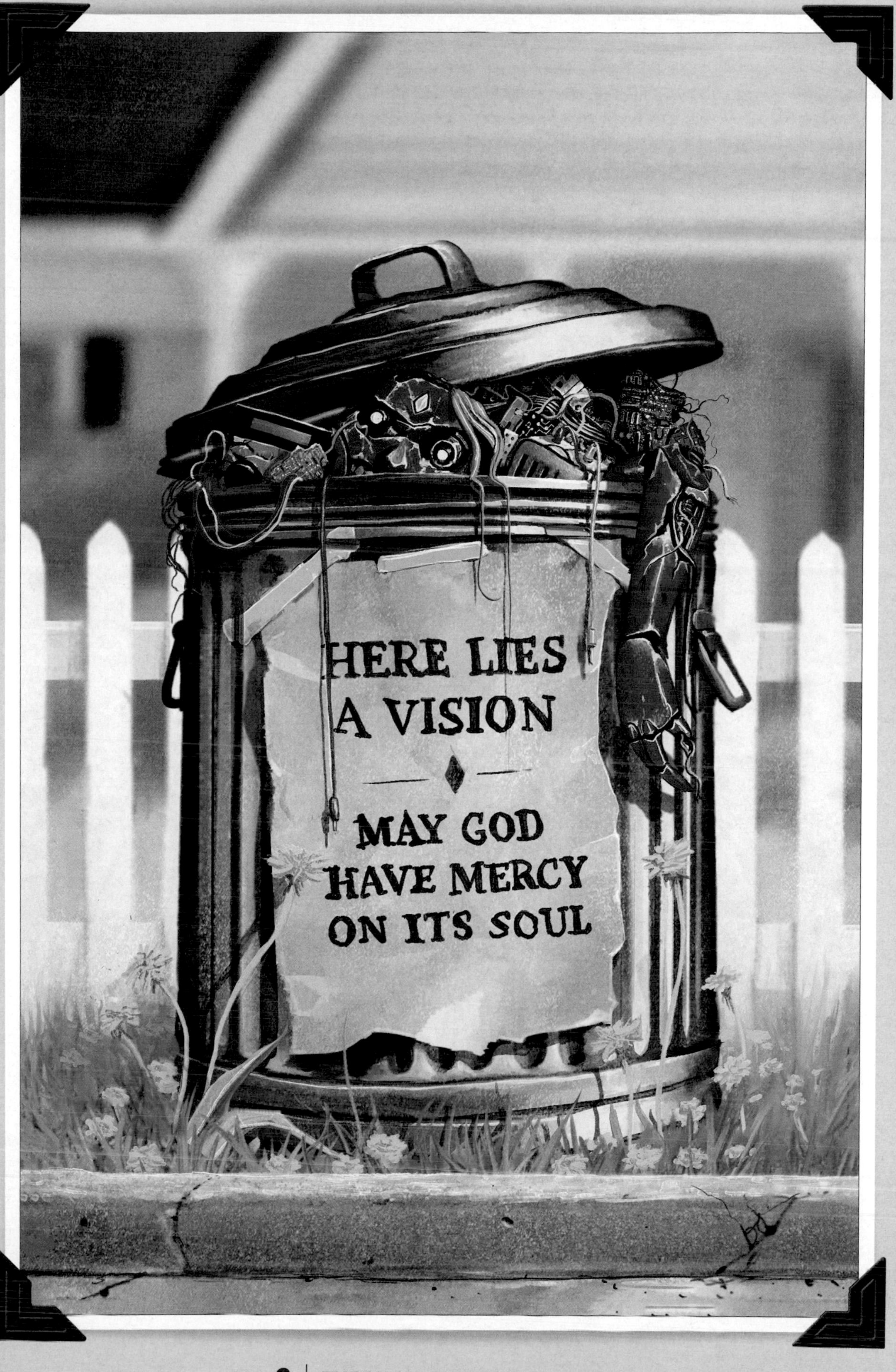
HERE LIES
A VISION
MAY GOD
HAVE MERCY
ON ITS SOUL

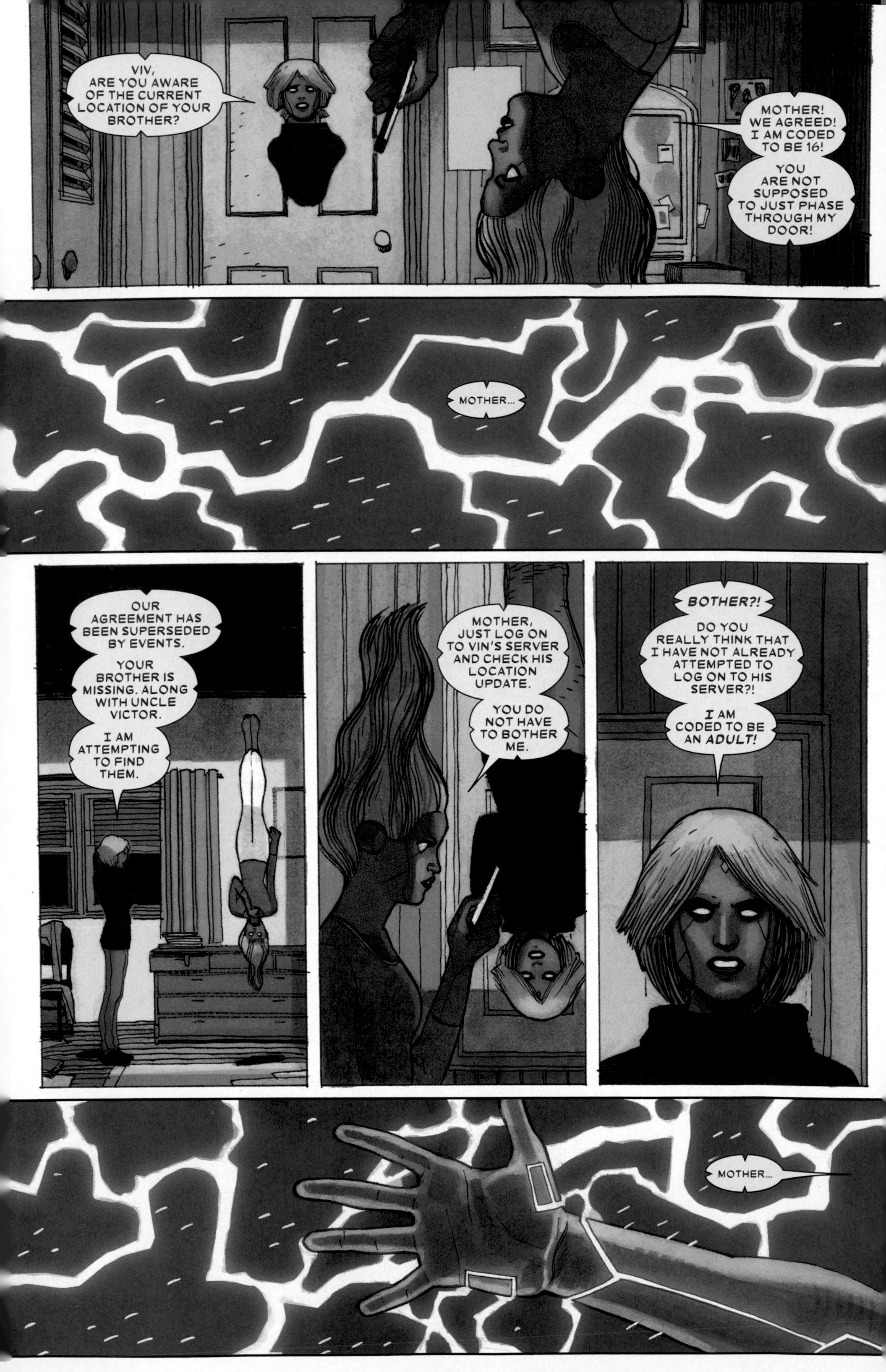
VIV, ARE YOU AWARE OF THE CURRENT LOCATION OF YOUR BROTHER?
MOTHER! WE AGREED! I AM CODED TO BE 16!
YOU ARE NOT SUPPOSED TO JUST PHASE THROUGH MY DOOR!
MOTHER...
OUR AGREEMENT HAS BEEN SUPERSEDED BY EVENTS.
YOUR BROTHER IS MISSING. ALONG WITH UNCLE VICTOR.
I AM ATTEMPTING TO FIND THEM.
MOTHER, JUST LOG ON TO VIN'S SERVER AND CHECK HIS LOCATION UPDATE.
YOU DO NOT HAVE TO BOTHER ME.
BOTHER?!
DO YOU REALLY THINK THAT I HAVE NOT ALREADY ATTEMPTED TO LOG ON TO HIS SERVER?!
I AM CODED TO BE AN ADULT!
MOTHER...

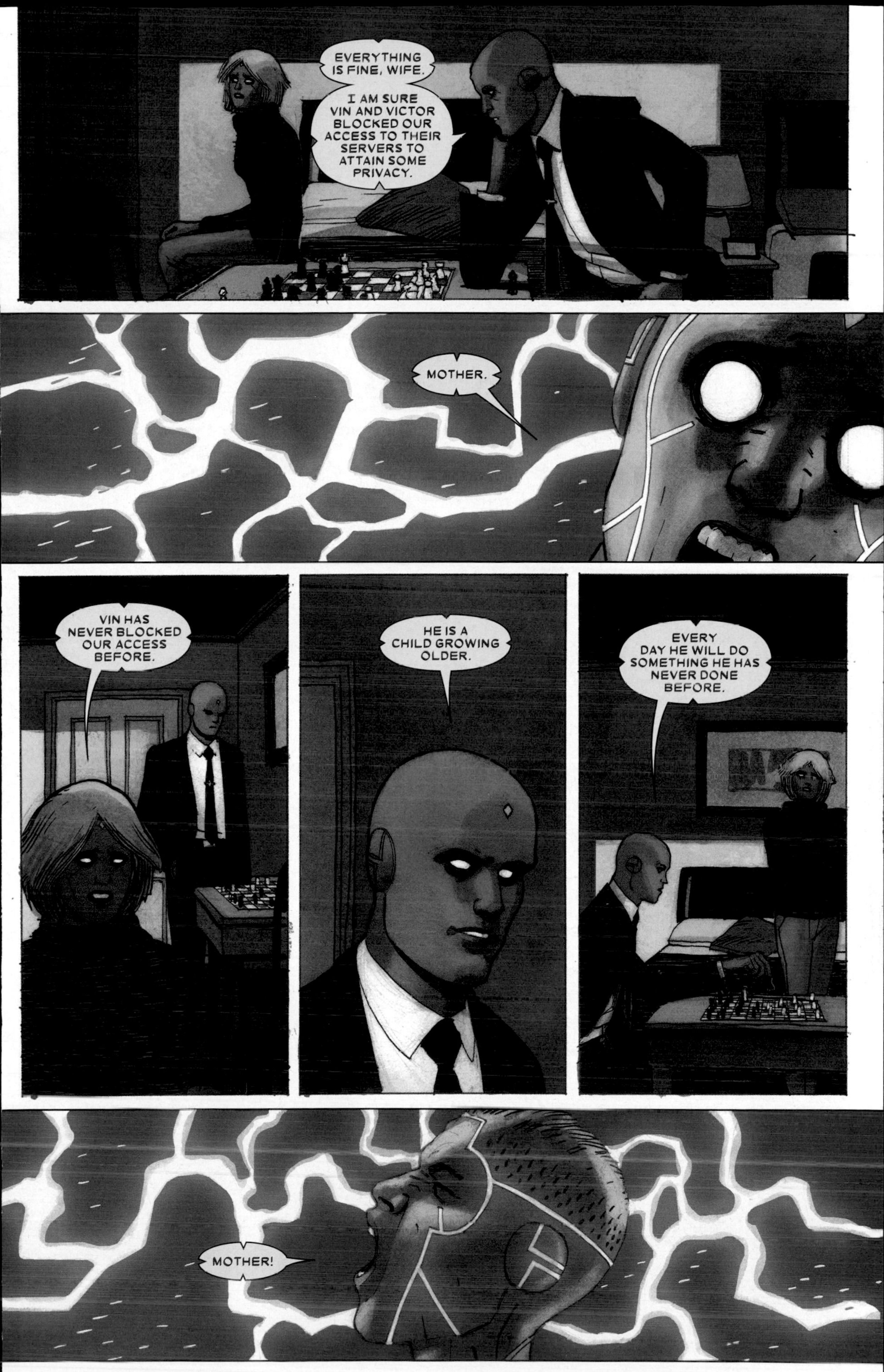
EVERYTHING IS FINE, WIFE.
I AM SURE VIN AND VICTOR BLOCKED OUR ACCESS TO THEIR SERVERS TO ATTAIN SOME PRIVACY.
MOTHER.
VIN HAS NEVER BLOCKED OUR ACCESS BEFORE.
HE IS A CHILD GROWING OLDER.
EVERY DAY HE WILL DO SOMETHING HE HAS NEVER DONE BEFORE.
MOTHER!

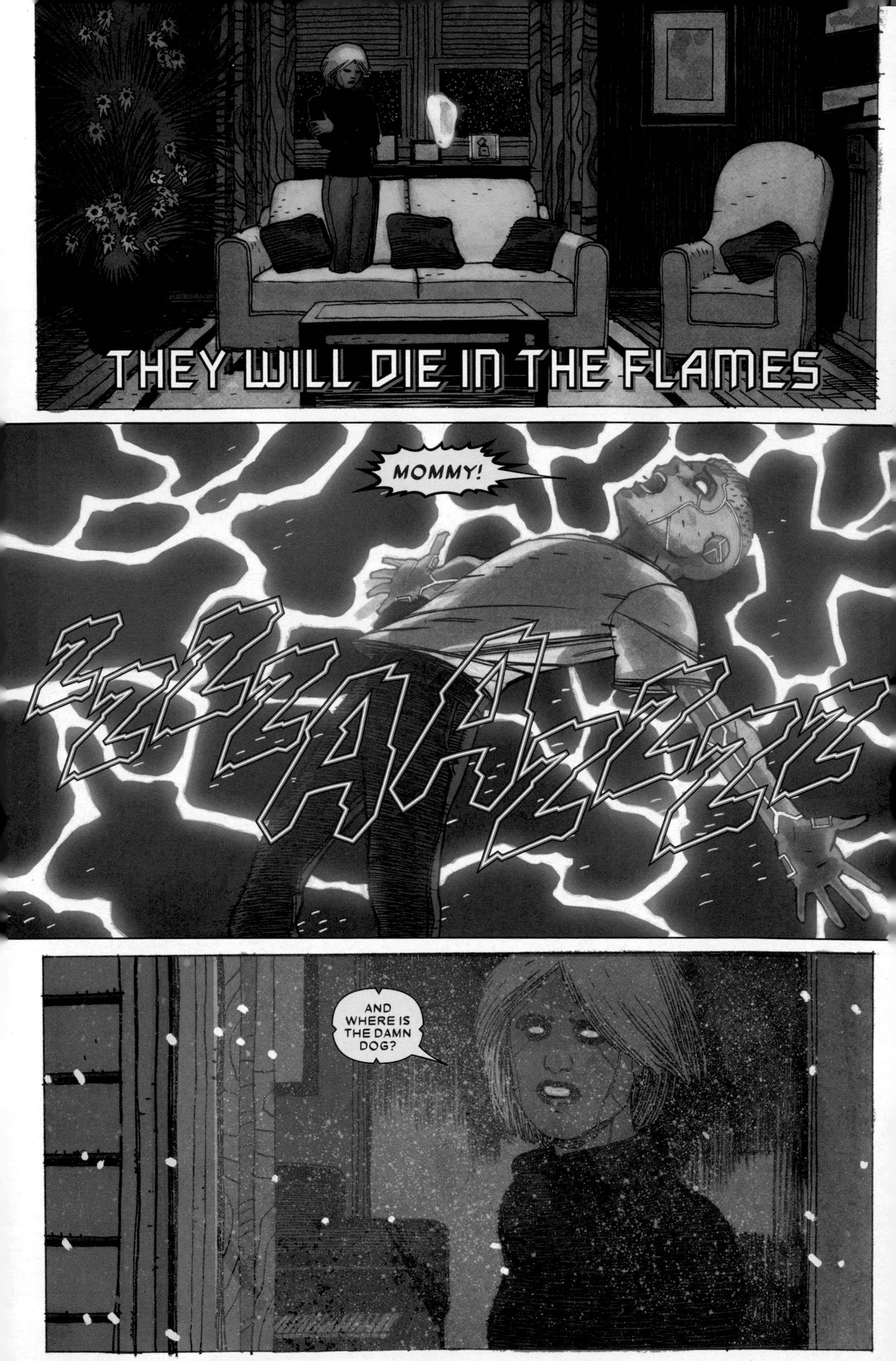
THEY WILL DIE IN THE FLAMES
MOMMY!
AND WHERE IS THE DAMN DOG?

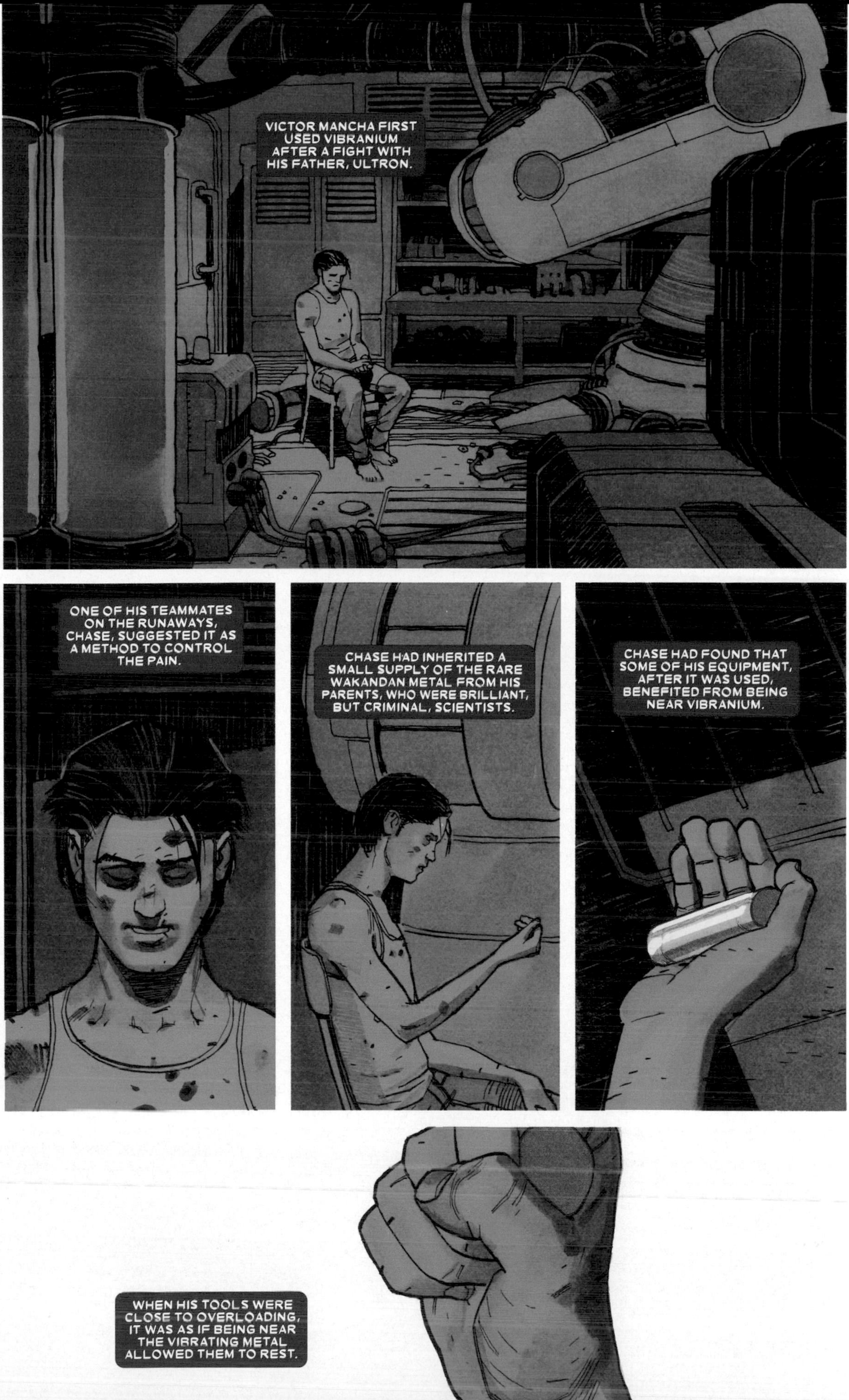
VICTOR MANCHA FIRST USED VIBRANIUM AFTER A FIGHT WITH HIS FATHER, ULTRON.
ONE OF HIS TEAMMATES ON THE RUNAWAYS, CHASE, SUGGESTED IT AS A METHOD TO CONTROL THE PAIN.
CHASE HAD INHERITED A SMALL SUPPLY OF THE RARE WAKANDAN METAL FROM HIS PARENTS, WHO WERE BRILLIANT, BUT CRIMINAL, SCIENTISTS.
CHASE HAD FOUND THAT SOME OF HIS EQUIPMENT, AFTER IT WAS USED, BENEFITED FROM BEING NEAR VIBRANIUM.
WHEN HIS TOOLS WERE CLOSE TO OVERLOADING, IT WAS AS IF BEING NEAR THE VIBRATING METAL ALLOWED THEM TO REST.

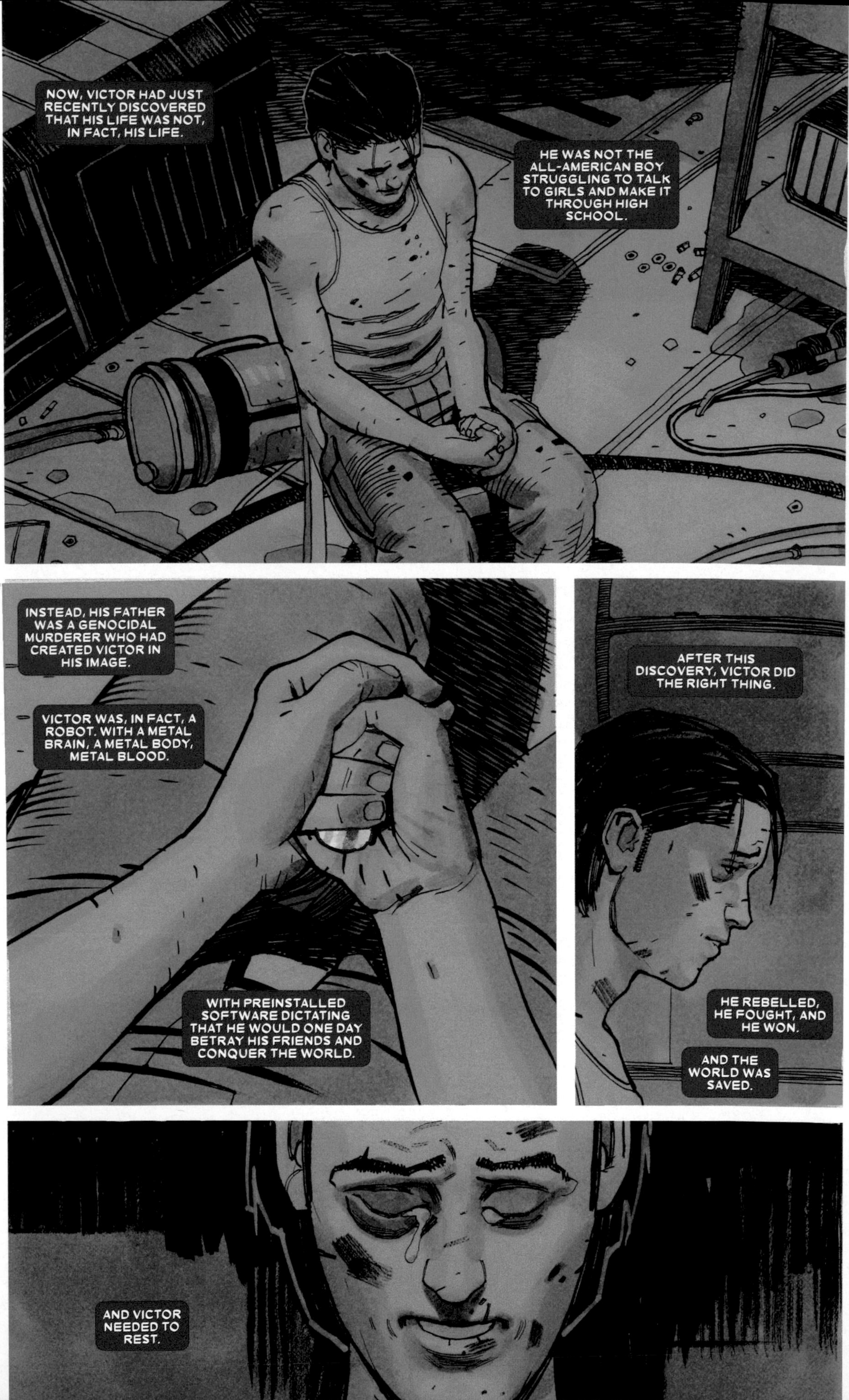
NOW, VICTOR HAD JUST RECENTLY DISCOVERED THAT HIS LIFE WAS NOT, IN FACT, HIS LIFE.
HE WAS NOT THE ALL-AMERICAN BOY STRUGGLING TO TALK TO GIRLS AND MAKE IT THROUGH HIGH SCHOOL.
INSTEAD, HIS FATHER WAS A GENOCIDAL MURDERER WHO HAD CREATED VICTOR IN HIS IMAGE.
VICTOR WAS, IN FACT, A ROBOT. WITH A METAL BRAIN, A METAL BODY, METAL BLOOD.
WITH PREINSTALLED SOFTWARE DICTATING THAT HE WOULD ONE DAY BETRAY HIS FRIENDS AND CONQUER THE WORLD.
AFTER THIS DISCOVERY, VICTOR DID THE RIGHT THING.
HE REBELLED, HE FOUGHT, AND HE WON.
AND THE WORLD WAS SAVED.
AND VICTOR NEEDED TO REST.

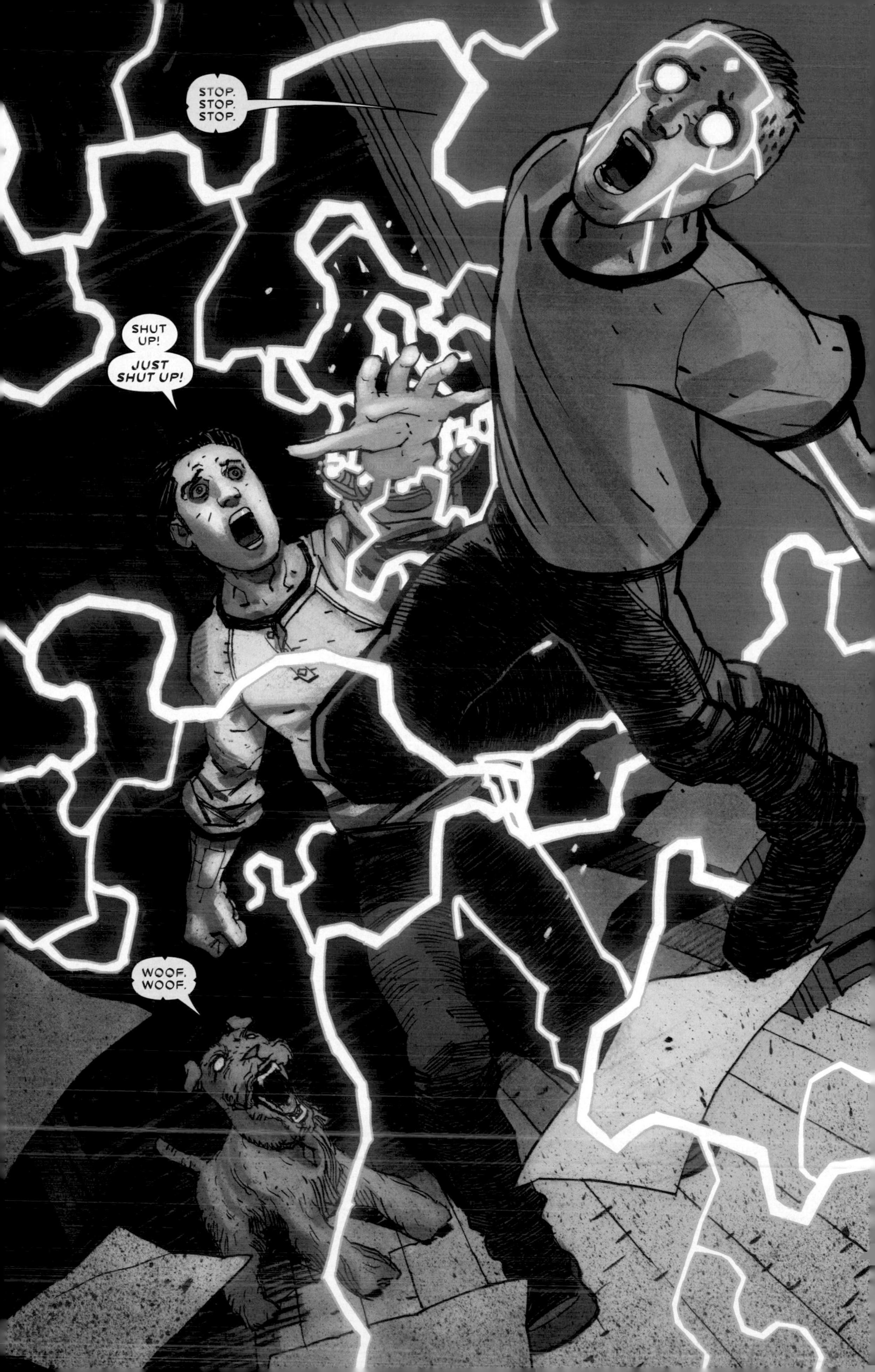
STOP. STOP. STOP.
SHUT UP!
JUST SHUT UP!
WOOF. WOOF.

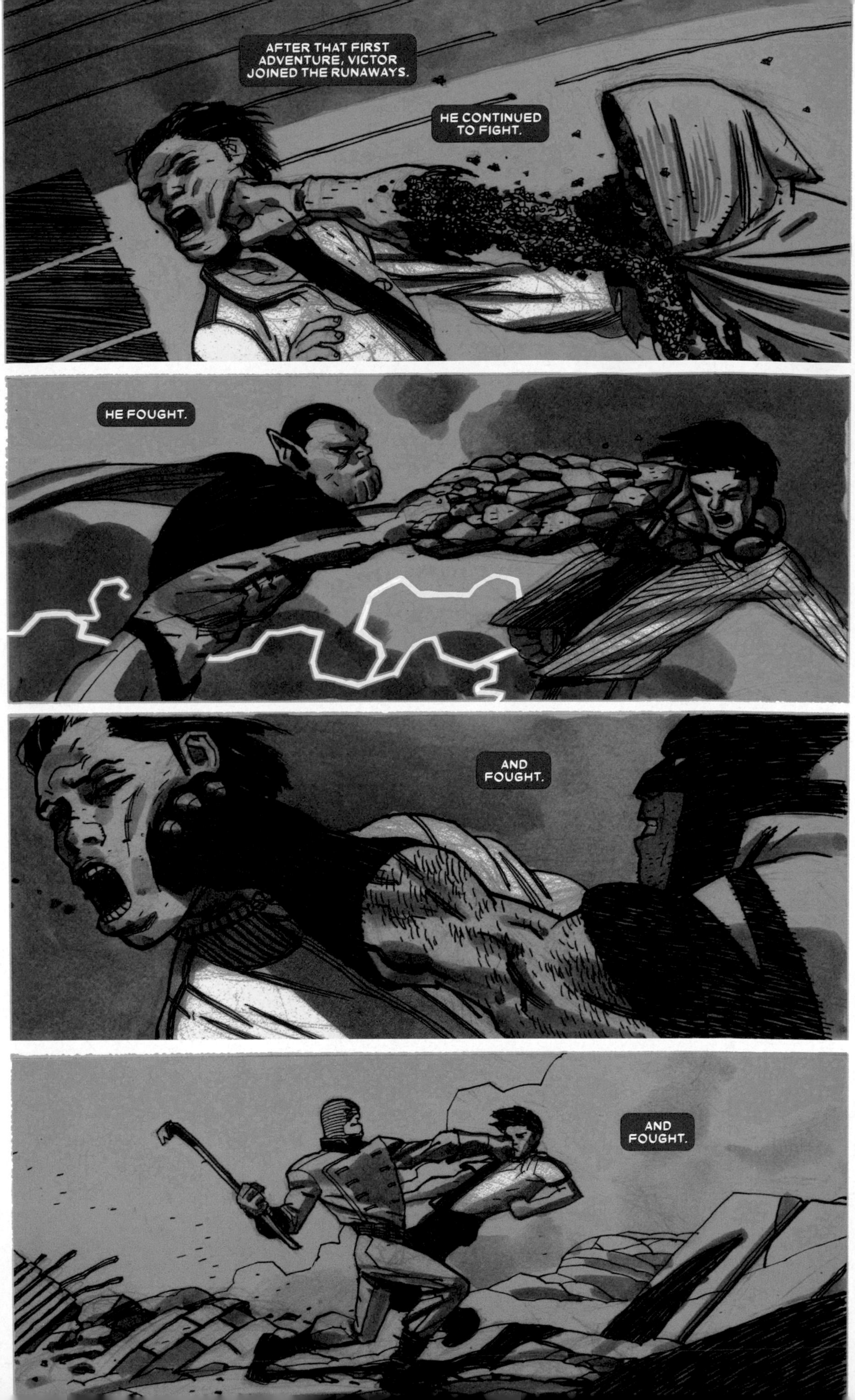
AFTER THAT FIRST ADVENTURE, VICTOR JOINED THE RUNAWAYS.
HE CONTINUED TO FIGHT.
HE FOUGHT.
AND FOUGHT.
AND FOUGHT.

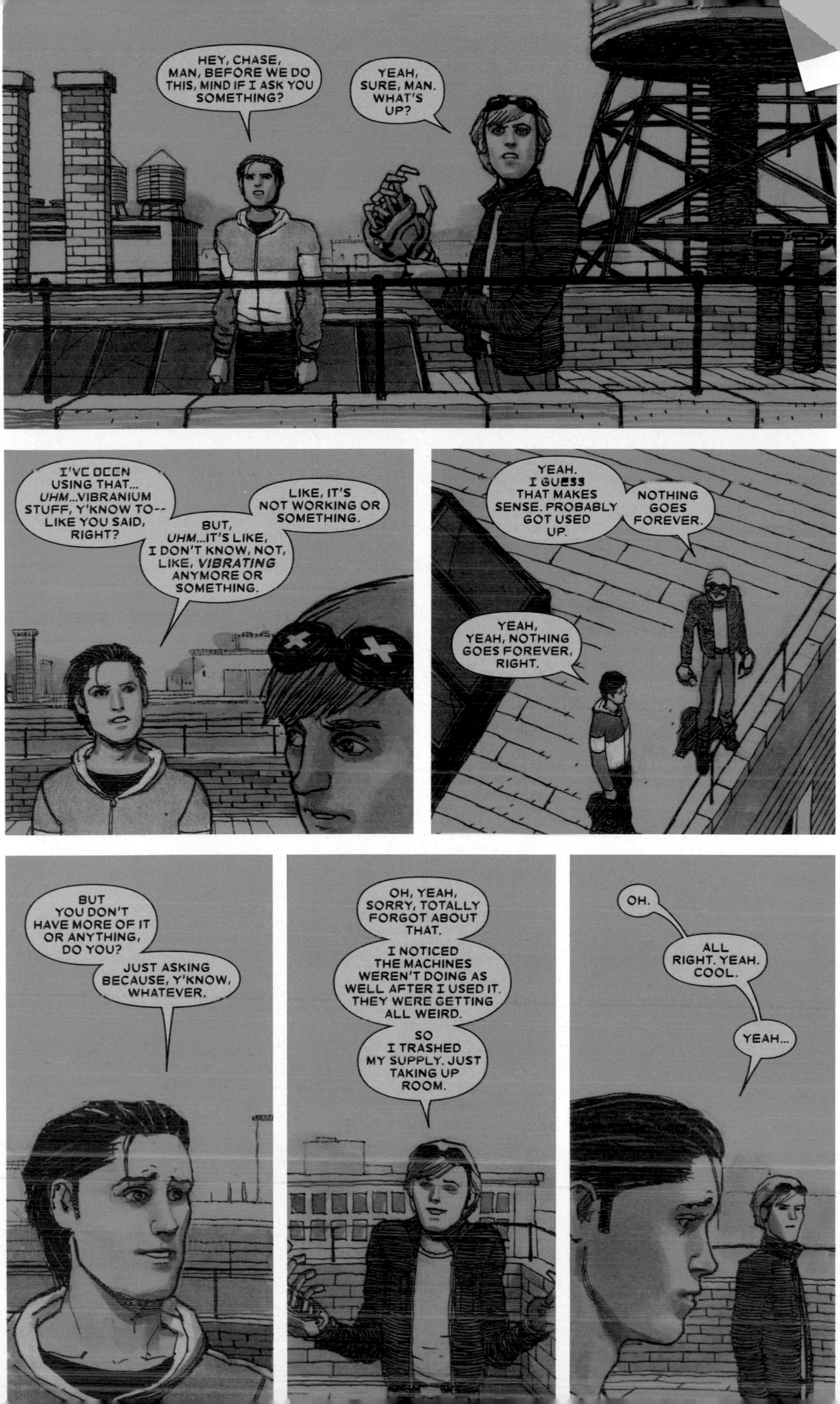
HEY, CHASE, MAN, BEFORE WE DO THIS, MIND IF I ASK YOU SOMETHING?
YEAH, SURE, MAN. WHAT'S UP?
I'VE BEEN USING THAT... *UHM*...VIBRANIUM STUFF, Y'KNOW TO-- LIKE YOU SAID, RIGHT?
BUT, *UHM*...IT'S LIKE, I DON'T KNOW, NOT, LIKE, *VIBRATING* ANYMORE OR SOMETHING.
LIKE, IT'S NOT WORKING OR SOMETHING.
YEAH. I GUESS THAT MAKES SENSE. PROBABLY GOT USED UP.
NOTHING GOES FOREVER.
YEAH, YEAH, NOTHING GOES FOREVER, RIGHT.
BUT YOU DON'T HAVE MORE OF IT OR ANYTHING, DO YOU?
JUST ASKING BECAUSE, Y'KNOW, WHATEVER.
OH, YEAH, SORRY, TOTALLY FORGOT ABOUT THAT.
I NOTICED THE MACHINES WEREN'T DOING AS WELL AFTER I USED IT. THEY WERE GETTING ALL WEIRD.
SO I TRASHED MY SUPPLY. JUST TAKING UP ROOM.
OH.
ALL RIGHT. YEAH. COOL.
YEAH...

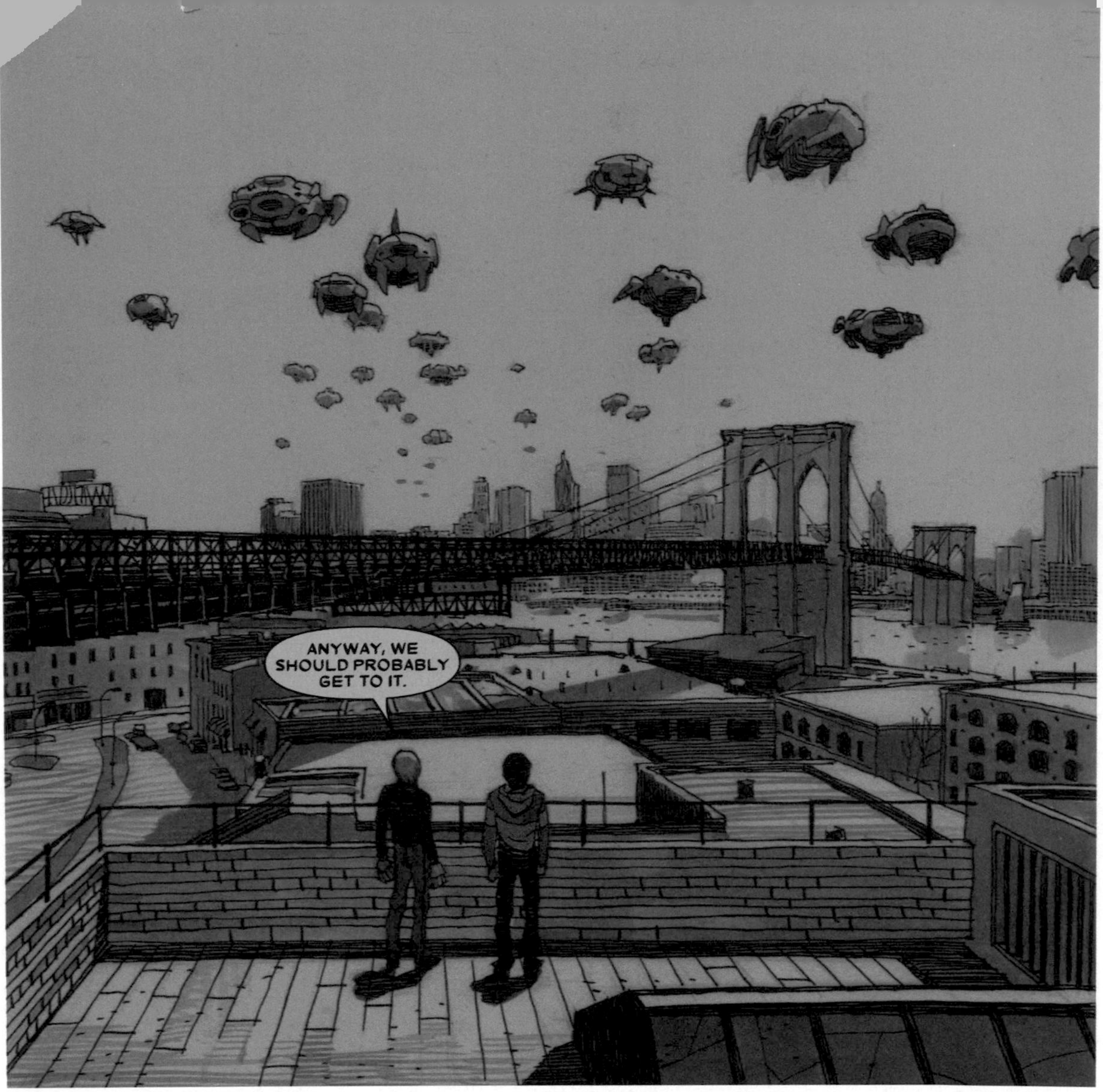
ANYWAY, WE SHOULD PROBABLY GET TO IT.

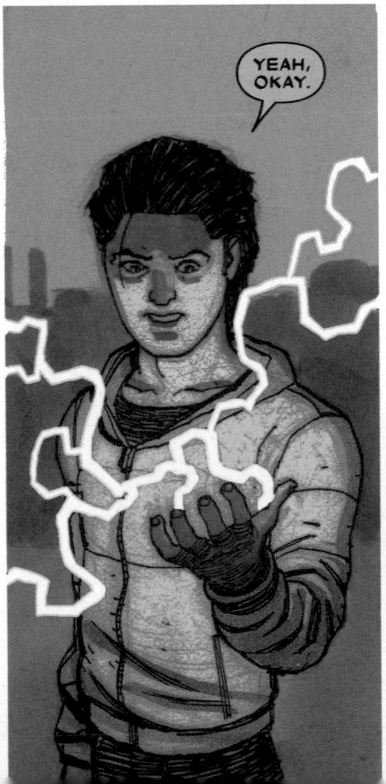
YEAH, OKAY.

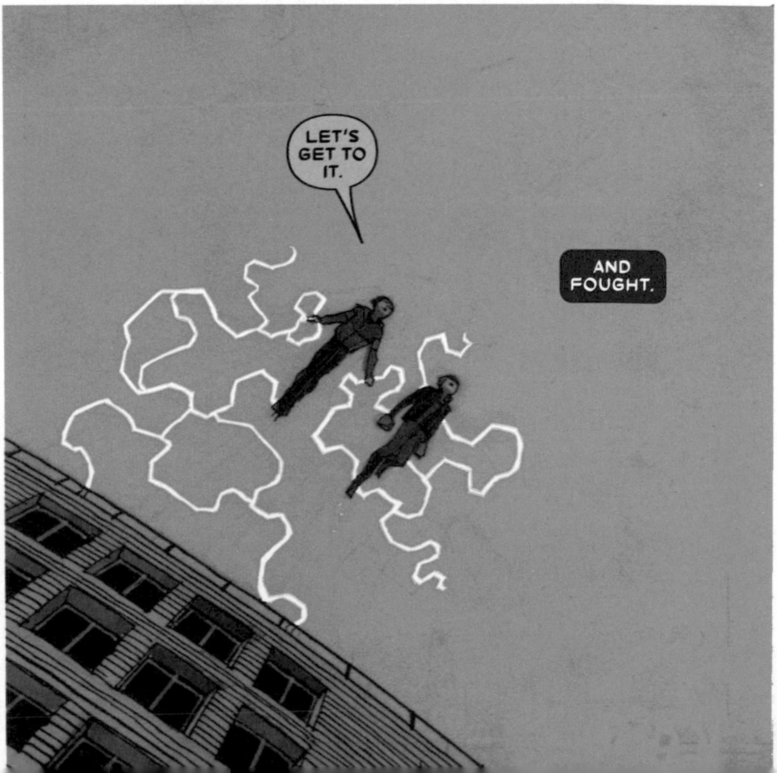
LET'S GET TO IT.
AND FOUGHT.

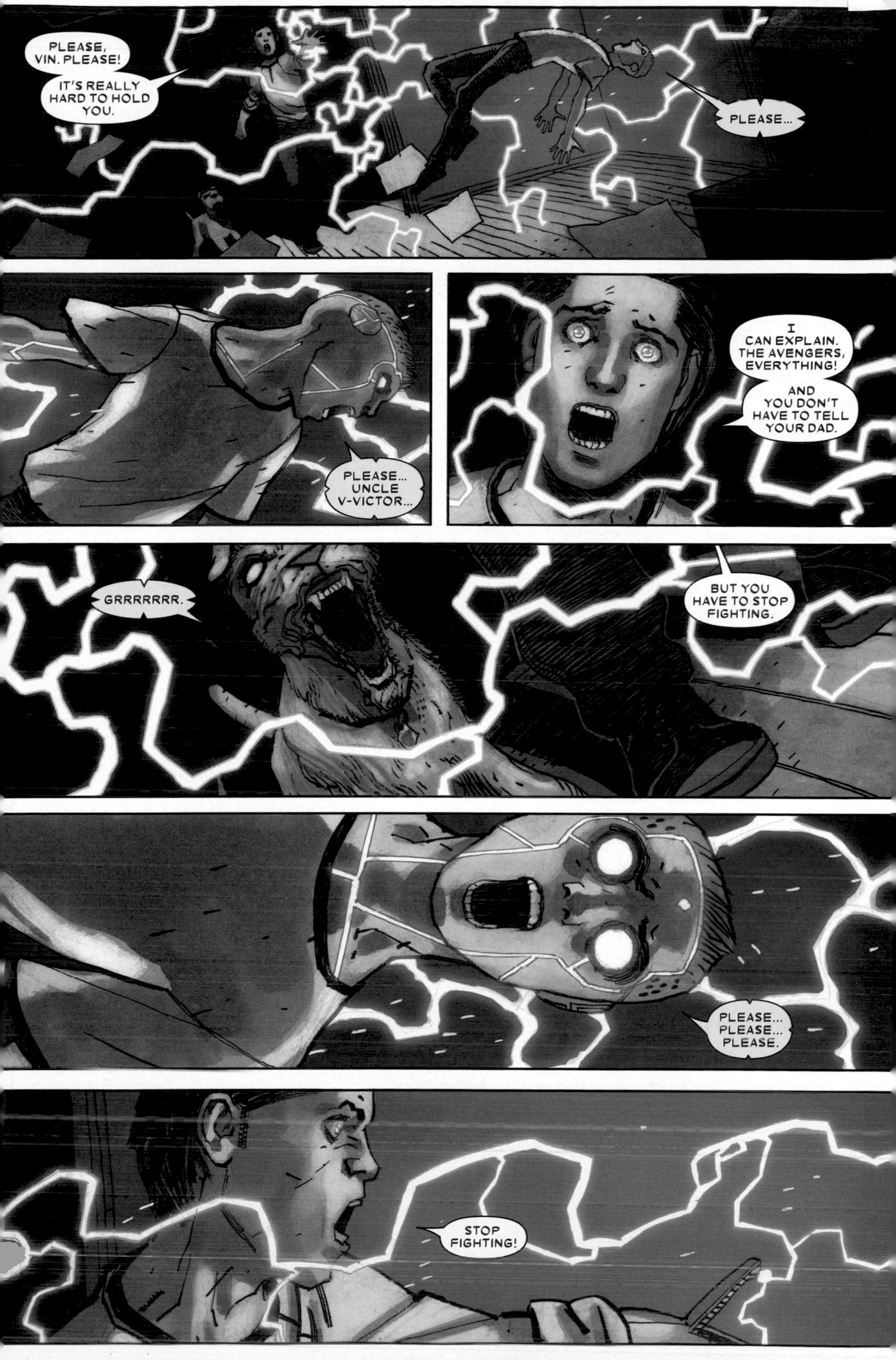
PLEASE, VIN. PLEASE!
IT'S REALLY HARD TO HOLD YOU.
PLEASE...
PLEASE... UNCLE V-VICTOR...
I CAN EXPLAIN. THE AVENGERS, EVERYTHING!
AND YOU DON'T HAVE TO TELL YOUR DAD.
GRRRRRRR.
BUT YOU HAVE TO STOP FIGHTING.
PLEASE... PLEASE... PLEASE.
STOP FIGHTING!

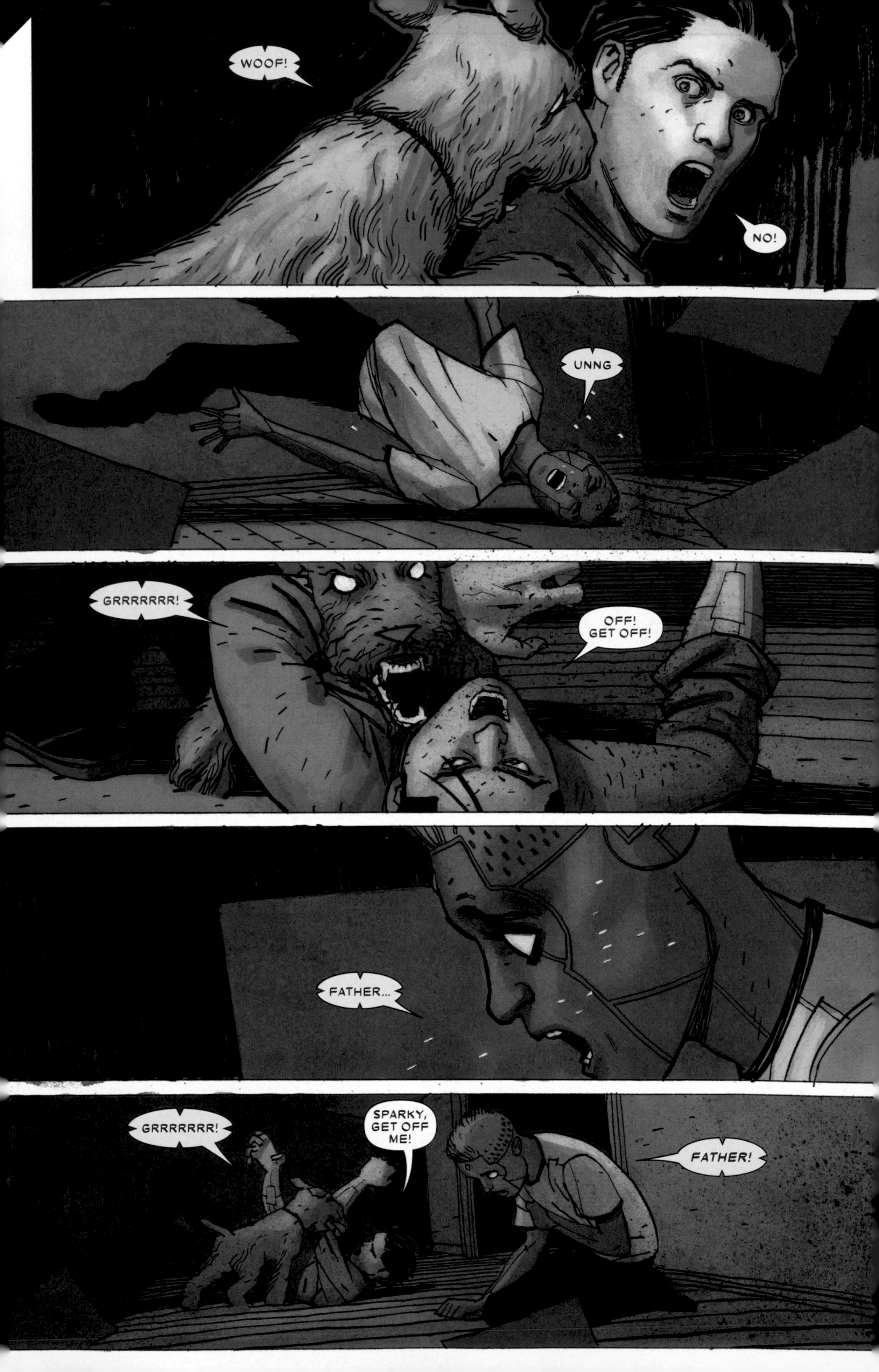
WOOF!
NO!
UNNG
GRRRRRRR!
OFF! GET OFF!
FATHER...
GRRRRRRR!
SPARKY, GET OFF ME!
FATHER!

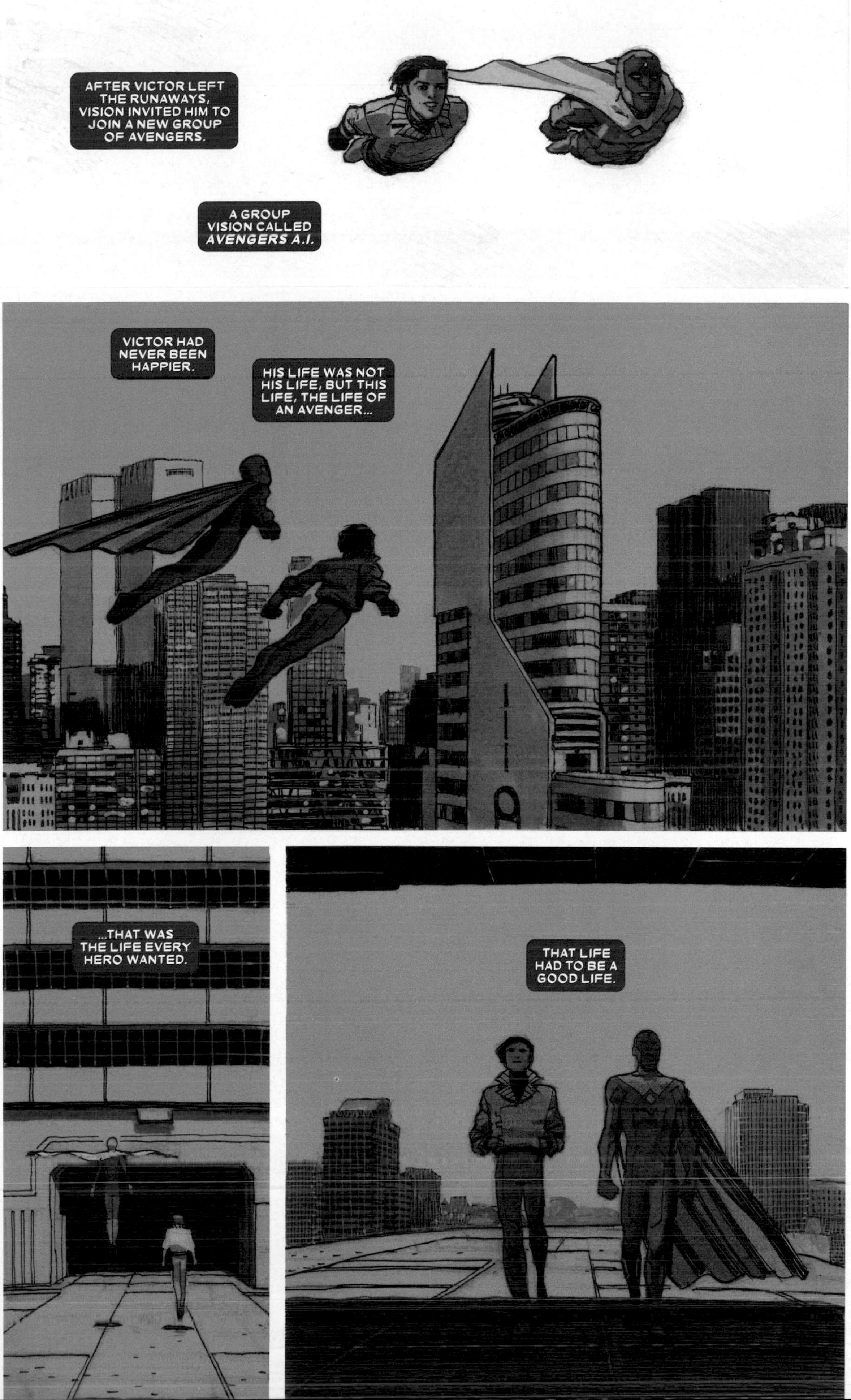
AFTER VICTOR LEFT THE RUNAWAYS, VISION INVITED HIM TO JOIN A NEW GROUP OF AVENGERS.
A GROUP VISION CALLED *AVENGERS A.I.*
VICTOR HAD NEVER BEEN HAPPIER.
HIS LIFE WAS NOT HIS LIFE, BUT THIS LIFE, THE LIFE OF AN AVENGER...
...THAT WAS THE LIFE EVERY HERO WANTED.
THAT LIFE HAD TO BE A GOOD LIFE.

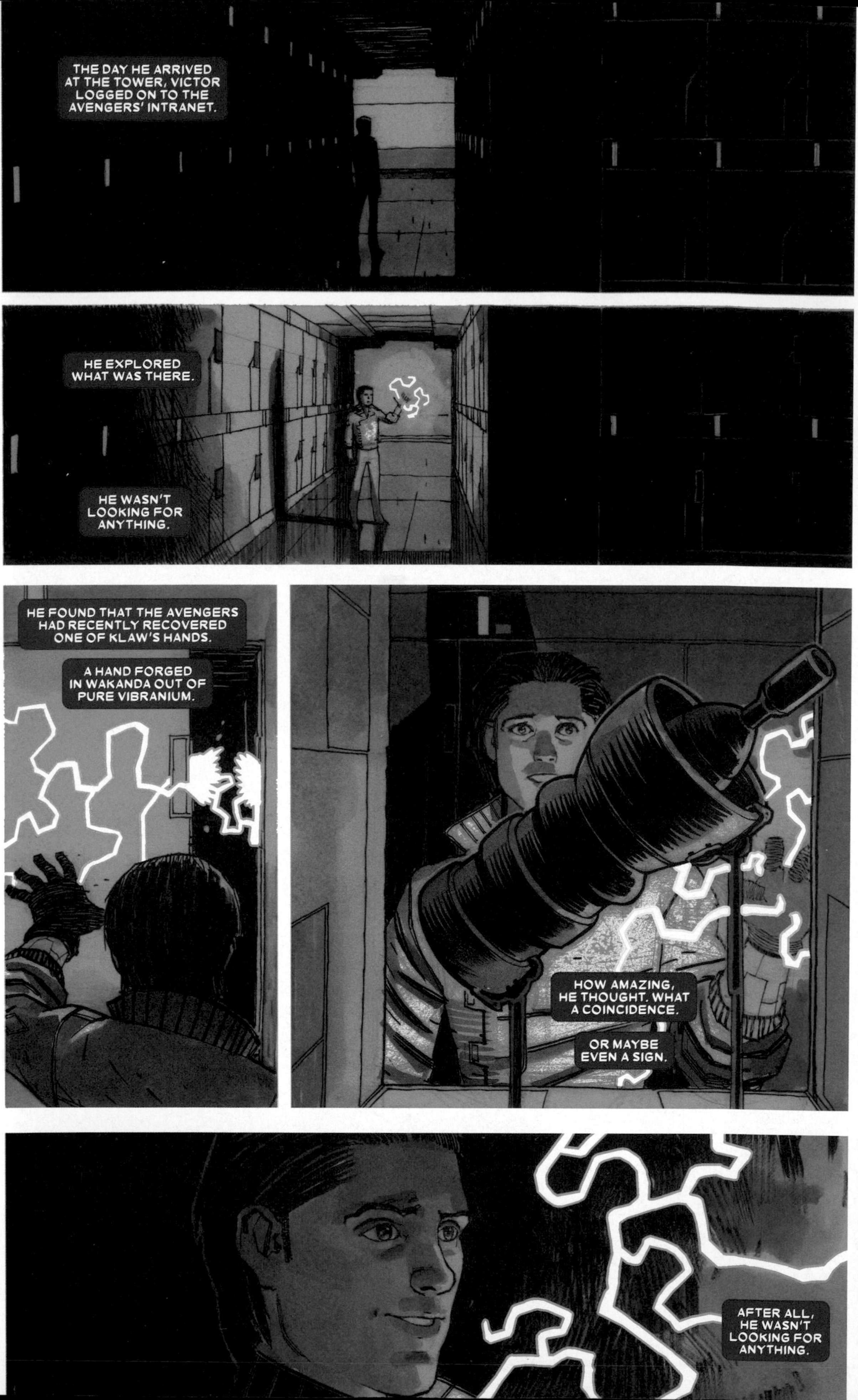
THE DAY HE ARRIVED AT THE TOWER, VICTOR LOGGED ON TO THE AVENGERS' INTRANET.
HE EXPLORED WHAT WAS THERE.
HE WASN'T LOOKING FOR ANYTHING.
HE FOUND THAT THE AVENGERS HAD RECENTLY RECOVERED ONE OF KLAW'S HANDS.
A HAND FORGED IN WAKANDA OUT OF PURE VIBRANIUM.
HOW AMAZING, HE THOUGHT. WHAT A COINCIDENCE.
OR MAYBE EVEN A SIGN.
AFTER ALL, HE WASN'T LOOKING FOR ANYTHING.

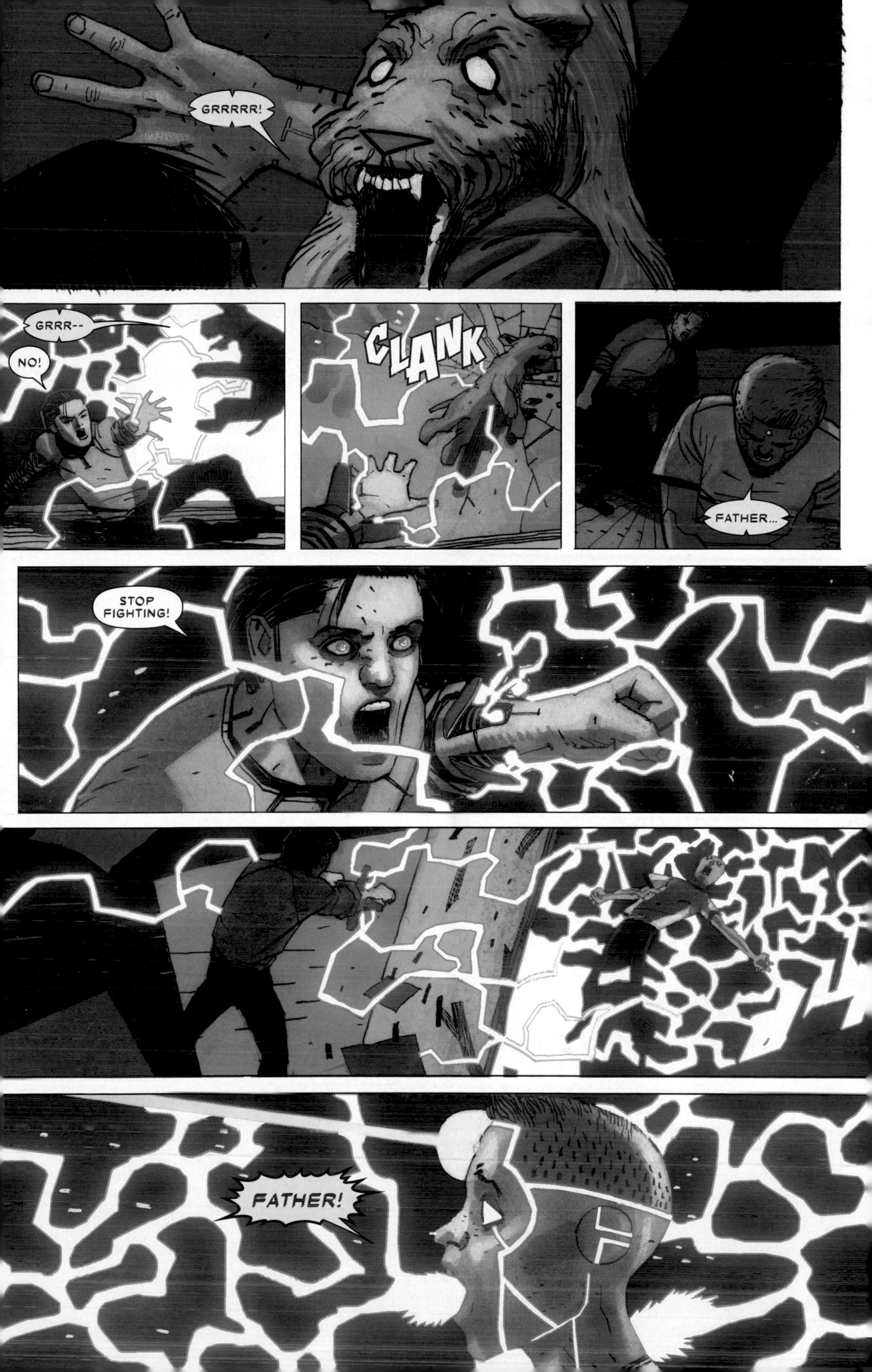
GRRRRR!
GRRR--
NO!
CLANK
FATHER...
STOP FIGHTING!
FATHER!

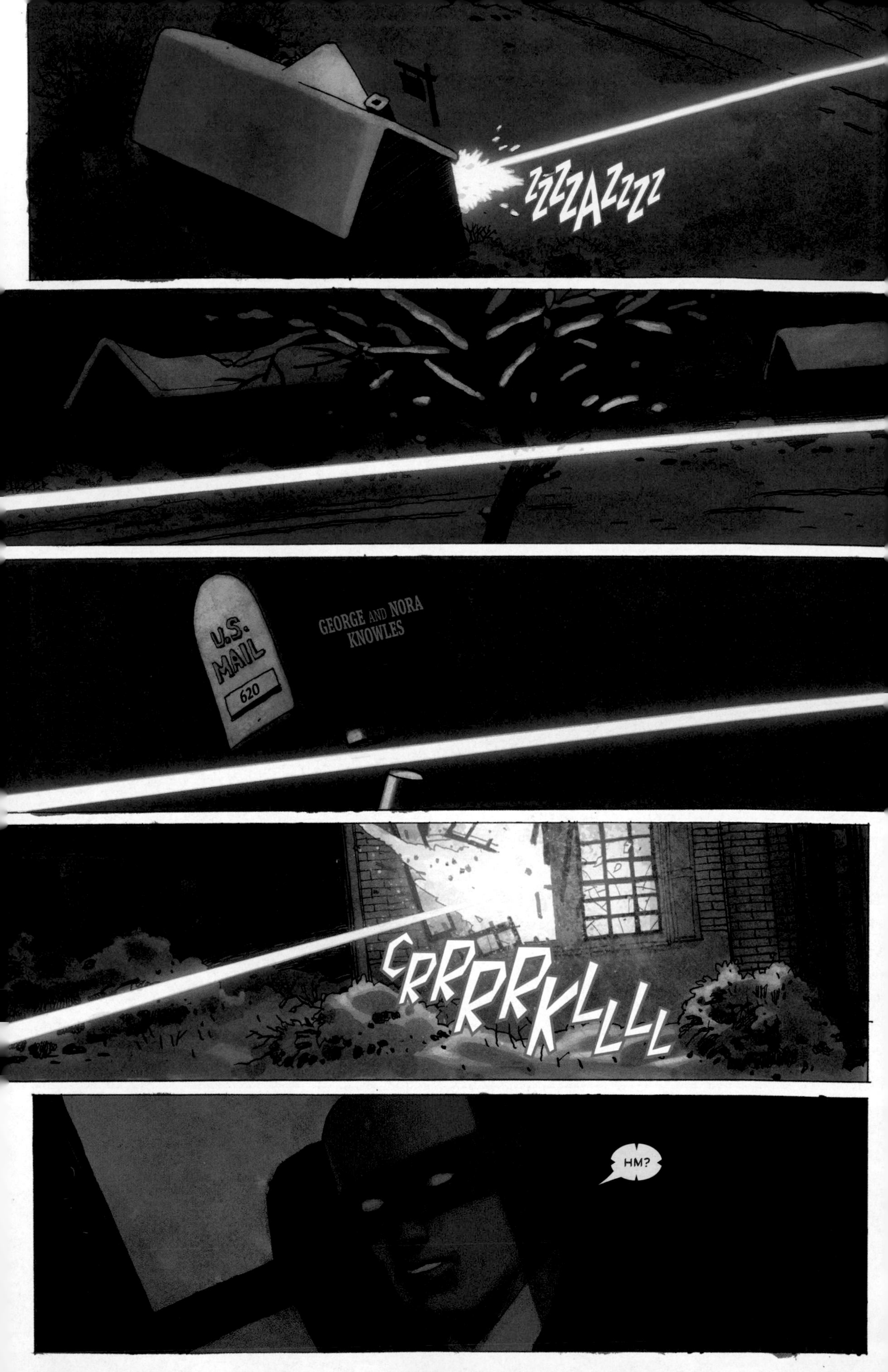

ZZZZAZZZZ
U.S. MAIL
620
GEORGE AND NORA KNOWLES
CRRRRKLLLLL
HM?

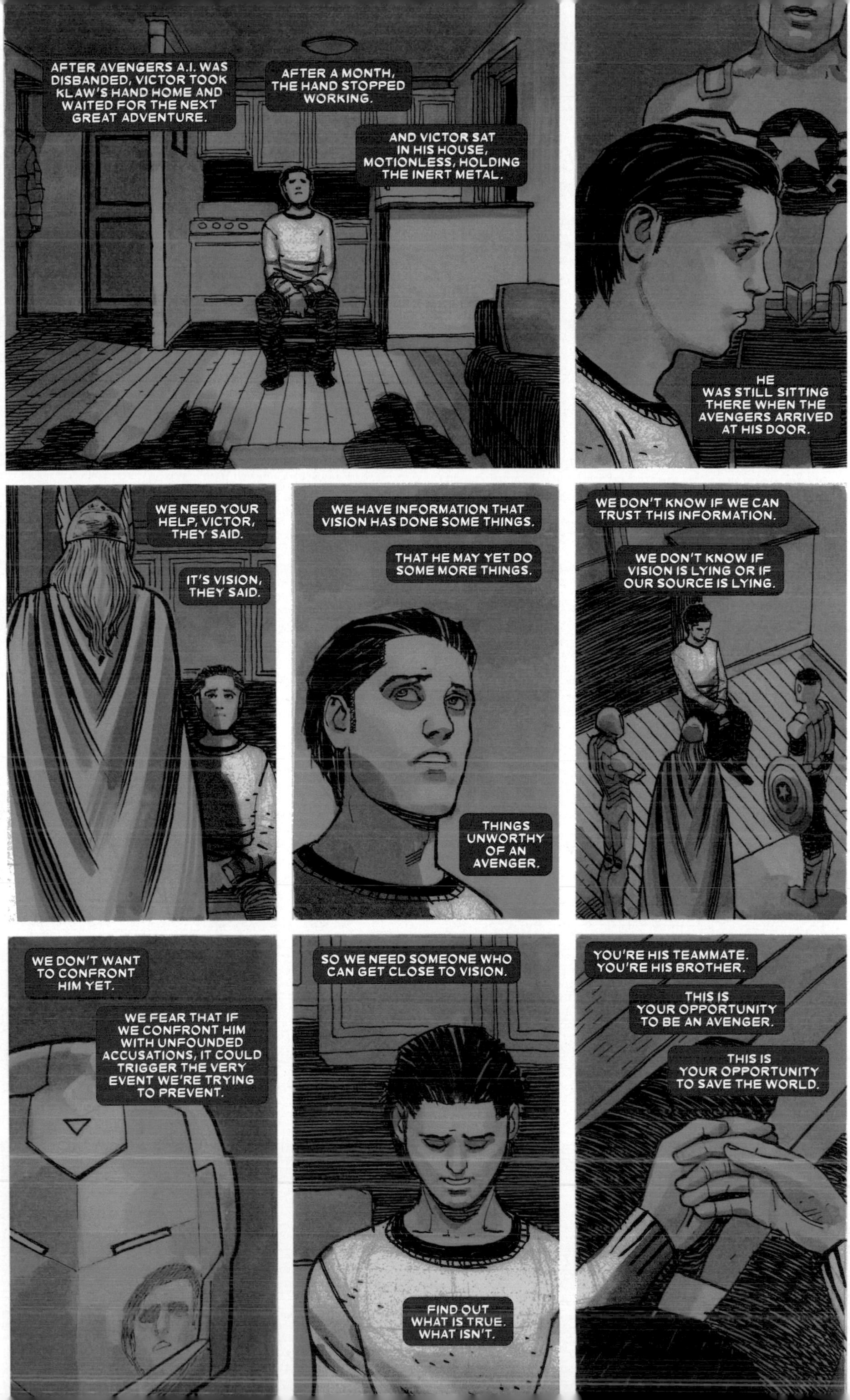
AFTER AVENGERS A.I. WAS DISBANDED, VICTOR TOOK KLAW'S HAND HOME AND WAITED FOR THE NEXT GREAT ADVENTURE.
AFTER A MONTH, THE HAND STOPPED WORKING.
AND VICTOR SAT IN HIS HOUSE, MOTIONLESS, HOLDING THE INERT METAL.
HE WAS STILL SITTING THERE WHEN THE AVENGERS ARRIVED AT HIS DOOR.
WE NEED YOUR HELP, VICTOR, THEY SAID.
IT'S VISION, THEY SAID.
WE HAVE INFORMATION THAT VISION HAS DONE SOME THINGS.
THAT HE MAY YET DO SOME MORE THINGS.
THINGS UNWORTHY OF AN AVENGER.
WE DON'T KNOW IF WE CAN TRUST THIS INFORMATION.
WE DON'T KNOW IF VISION IS LYING OR IF OUR SOURCE IS LYING.
WE DON'T WANT TO CONFRONT HIM YET.
WE FEAR THAT IF WE CONFRONT HIM WITH UNFOUNDED ACCUSATIONS, IT COULD TRIGGER THE VERY EVENT WE'RE TRYING TO PREVENT.
SO WE NEED SOMEONE WHO CAN GET CLOSE TO VISION.
FIND OUT WHAT IS TRUE. WHAT ISN'T.
YOU'RE HIS TEAMMATE. YOU'RE HIS BROTHER.
THIS IS YOUR OPPORTUNITY TO BE AN AVENGER.
THIS IS YOUR OPPORTUNITY TO SAVE THE WORLD.

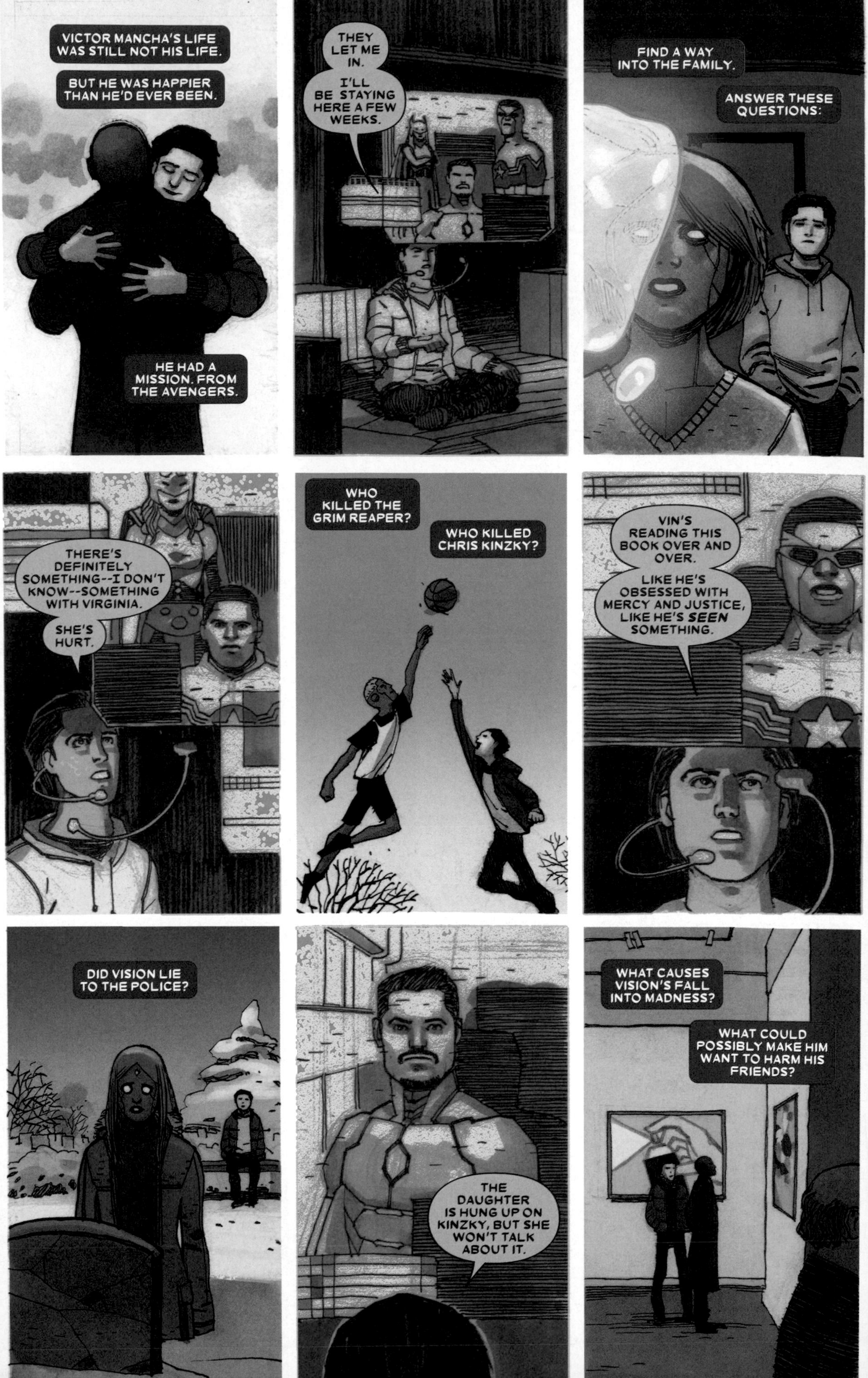
VICTOR MANCHA'S LIFE WAS STILL NOT HIS LIFE.
BUT HE WAS HAPPIER THAN HE'D EVER BEEN.
HE HAD A MISSION. FROM THE AVENGERS.
THEY LET ME IN.
I'LL BE STAYING HERE A FEW WEEKS.
FIND A WAY INTO THE FAMILY.
ANSWER THESE QUESTIONS:
THERE'S DEFINITELY SOMETHING--I DON'T KNOW--SOMETHING WITH VIRGINIA.
SHE'S HURT.
WHO KILLED THE GRIM REAPER?
WHO KILLED CHRIS KINZKY?
VIN'S READING THIS BOOK OVER AND OVER.
LIKE HE'S OBSESSED WITH MERCY AND JUSTICE, LIKE HE'S SEEN SOMETHING.
DID VISION LIE TO THE POLICE?
THE DAUGHTER IS HUNG UP ON KINZKY, BUT SHE WON'T TALK ABOUT IT.
WHAT CAUSES VISION'S FALL INTO MADNESS?
WHAT COULD POSSIBLY MAKE HIM WANT TO HARM HIS FRIENDS?

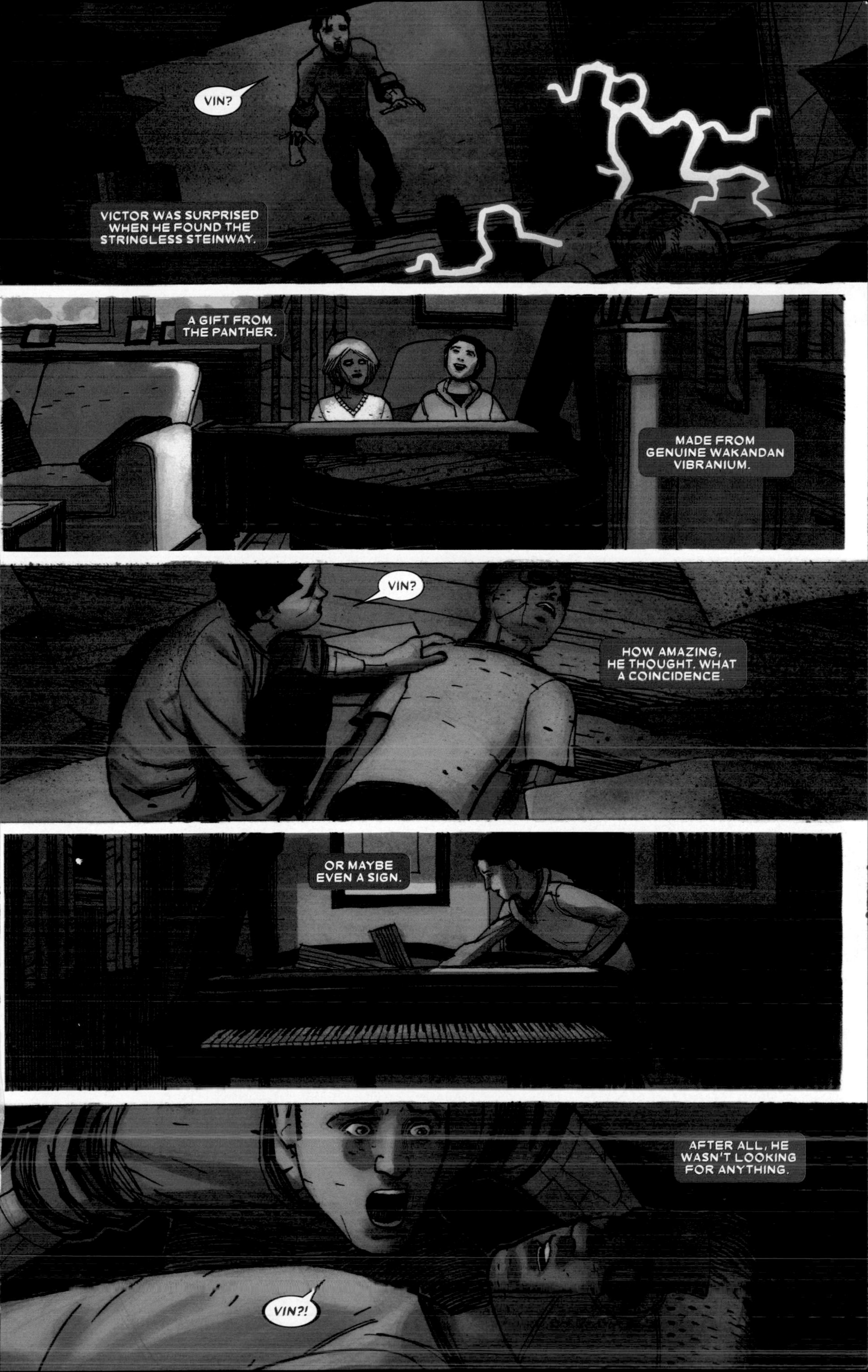
VIN?
VICTOR WAS SURPRISED WHEN HE FOUND THE STRINGLESS STEINWAY.
A GIFT FROM THE PANTHER.
MADE FROM GENUINE WAKANDAN VIBRANIUM.
VIN?
HOW AMAZING, HE THOUGHT. WHAT A COINCIDENCE.
OR MAYBE EVEN A SIGN.
AFTER ALL, HE WASN'T LOOKING FOR ANYTHING.
VIN?!

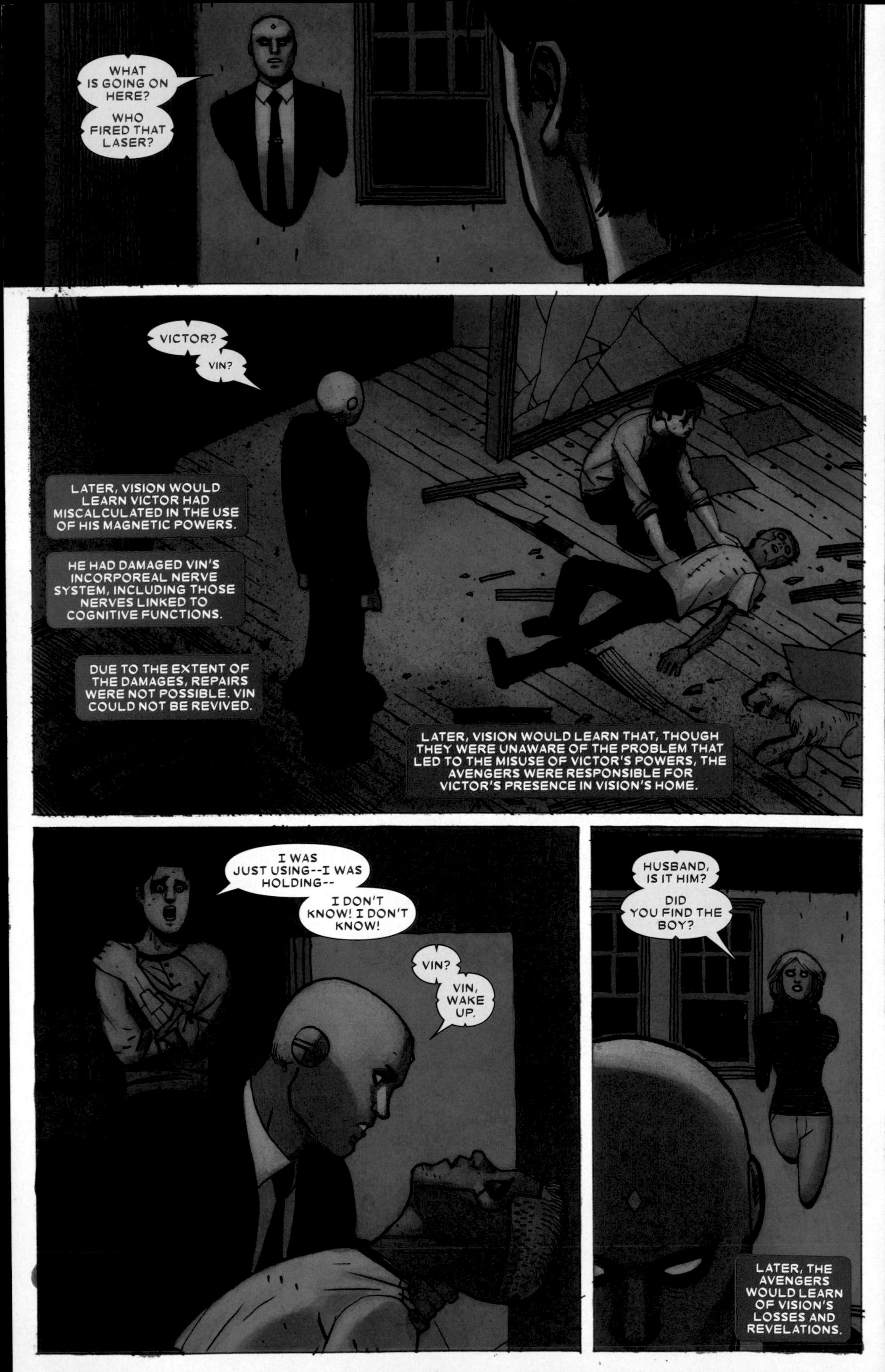
WHAT IS GOING ON HERE?
WHO FIRED THAT LASER?
VICTOR?
VIN?
LATER, VISION WOULD LEARN VICTOR HAD MISCALCULATED IN THE USE OF HIS MAGNETIC POWERS.
HE HAD DAMAGED VIN'S INCORPOREAL NERVE SYSTEM, INCLUDING THOSE NERVES LINKED TO COGNITIVE FUNCTIONS.
DUE TO THE EXTENT OF THE DAMAGES, REPAIRS WERE NOT POSSIBLE. VIN COULD NOT BE REVIVED.
LATER, VISION WOULD LEARN THAT, THOUGH THEY WERE UNAWARE OF THE PROBLEM THAT LED TO THE MISUSE OF VICTOR'S POWERS, THE AVENGERS WERE RESPONSIBLE FOR VICTOR'S PRESENCE IN VISION'S HOME.
I WAS JUST USING--I WAS HOLDING--
I DON'T KNOW! I DON'T KNOW!
VIN?
VIN, WAKE UP.
HUSBAND, IS IT HIM?
DID YOU FIND THE BOY?
LATER, THE AVENGERS WOULD LEARN OF VISION'S LOSSES AND REVELATIONS.

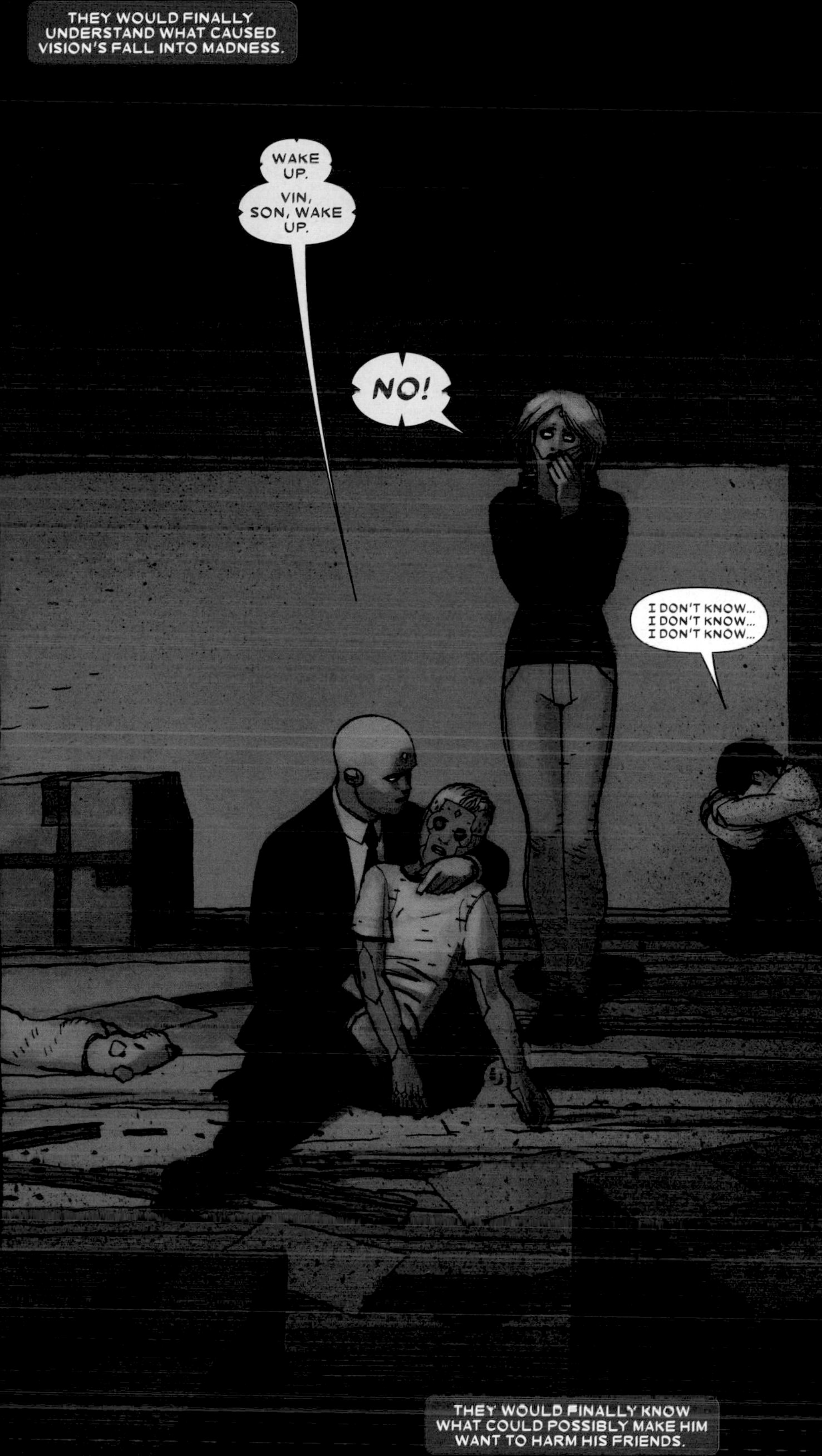
THEY WOULD FINALLY UNDERSTAND WHAT CAUSED VISION'S FALL INTO MADNESS.
WAKE UP.
VIN, SON, WAKE UP.
NO!
I DON'T KNOW... I DON'T KNOW... I DON'T KNOW...
THEY WOULD FINALLY KNOW WHAT COULD POSSIBLY MAKE HIM WANT TO HARM HIS FRIENDS.

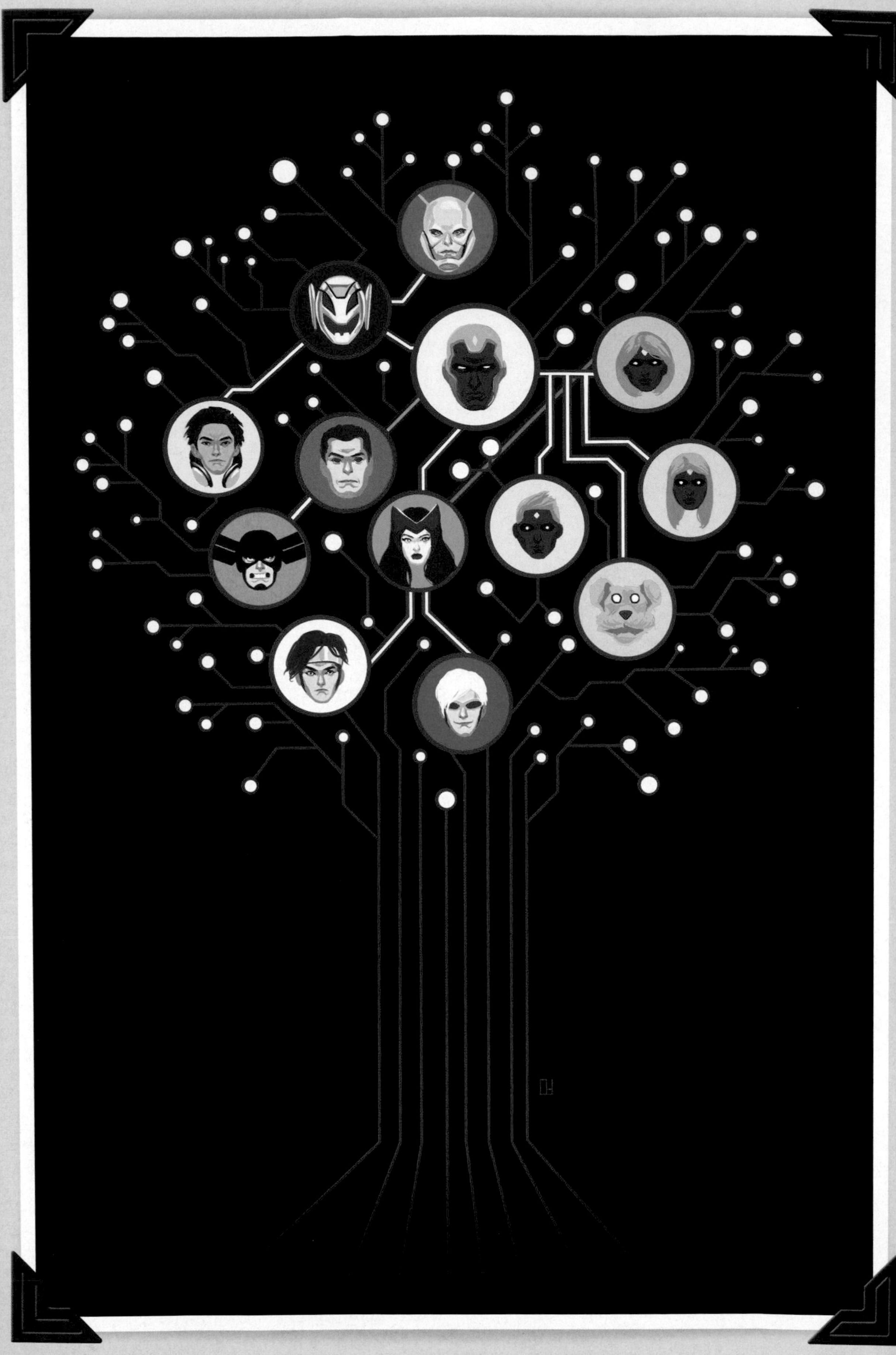

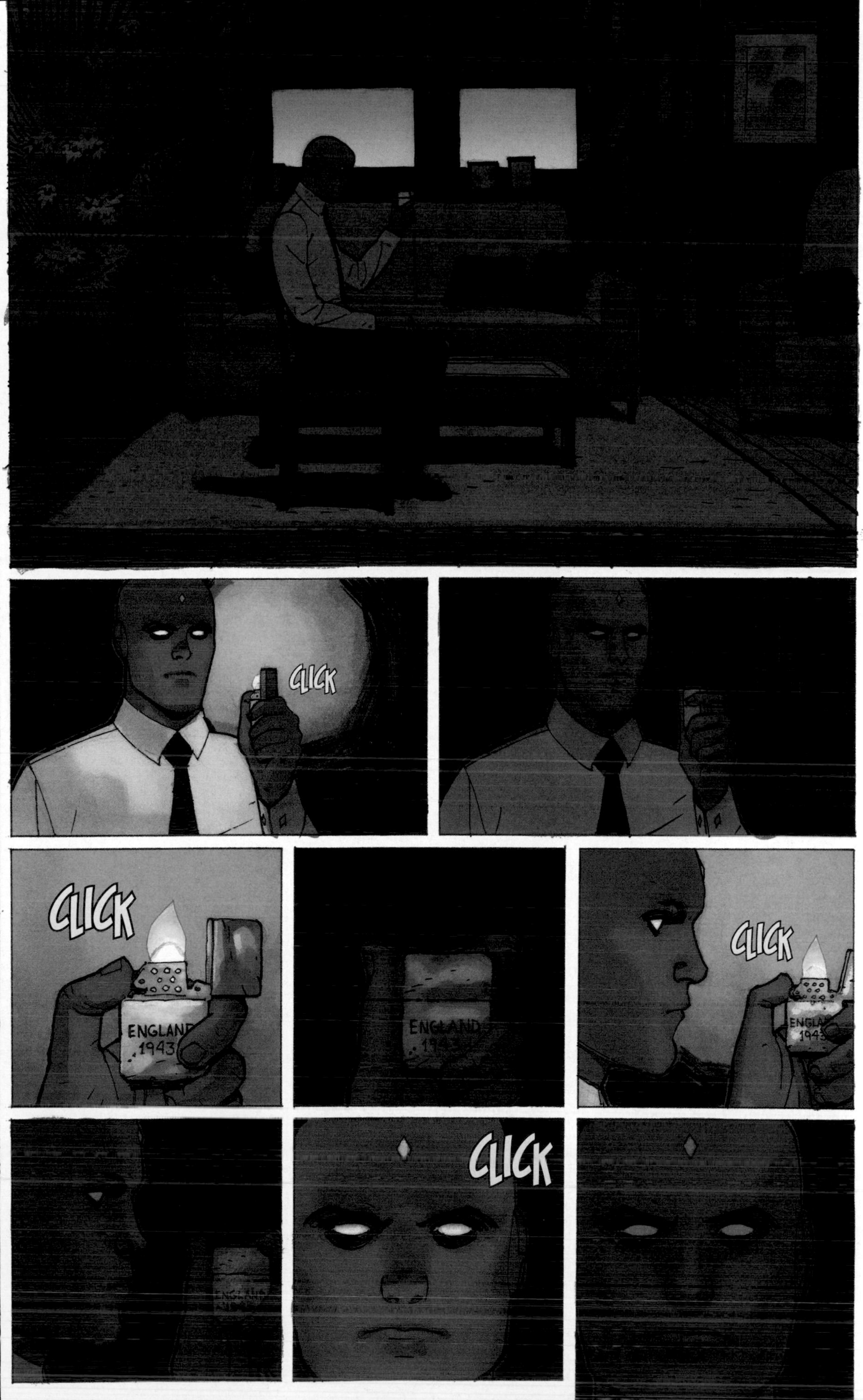
CLICK
CLICK
ENGLAND
1943
ENGLAND
CLICK
CLICK

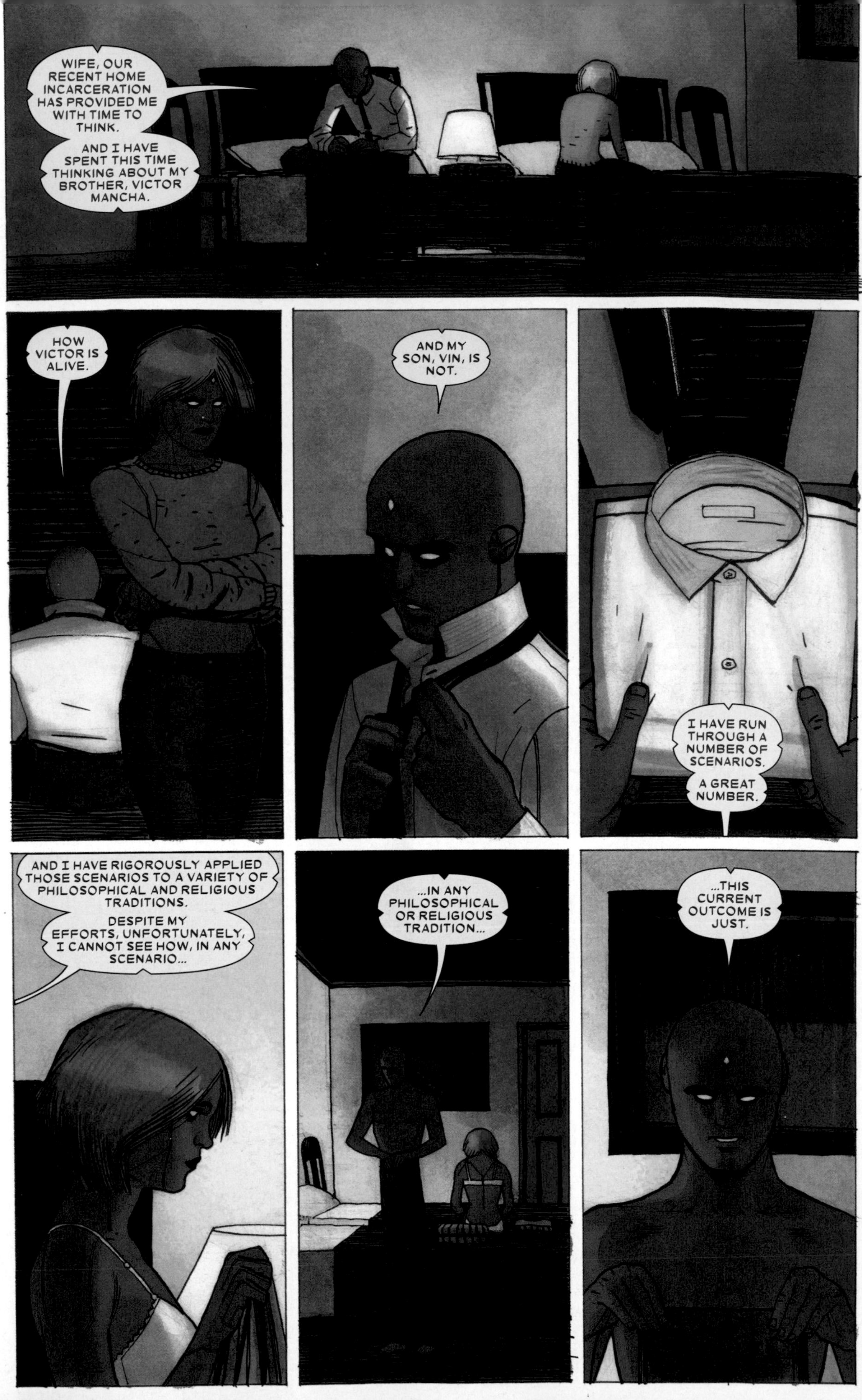
WIFE, OUR RECENT HOME INCARCERATION HAS PROVIDED ME WITH TIME TO THINK.
AND I HAVE SPENT THIS TIME THINKING ABOUT MY BROTHER, VICTOR MANCHA.
HOW VICTOR IS ALIVE.
AND MY SON, VIN, IS NOT.
I HAVE RUN THROUGH A NUMBER OF SCENARIOS.
A GREAT NUMBER.
AND I HAVE RIGOROUSLY APPLIED THOSE SCENARIOS TO A VARIETY OF PHILOSOPHICAL AND RELIGIOUS TRADITIONS.
DESPITE MY EFFORTS, UNFORTUNATELY, I CANNOT SEE HOW, IN ANY SCENARIO...
...IN ANY PHILOSOPHICAL OR RELIGIOUS TRADITION...
...THIS CURRENT OUTCOME IS JUST.

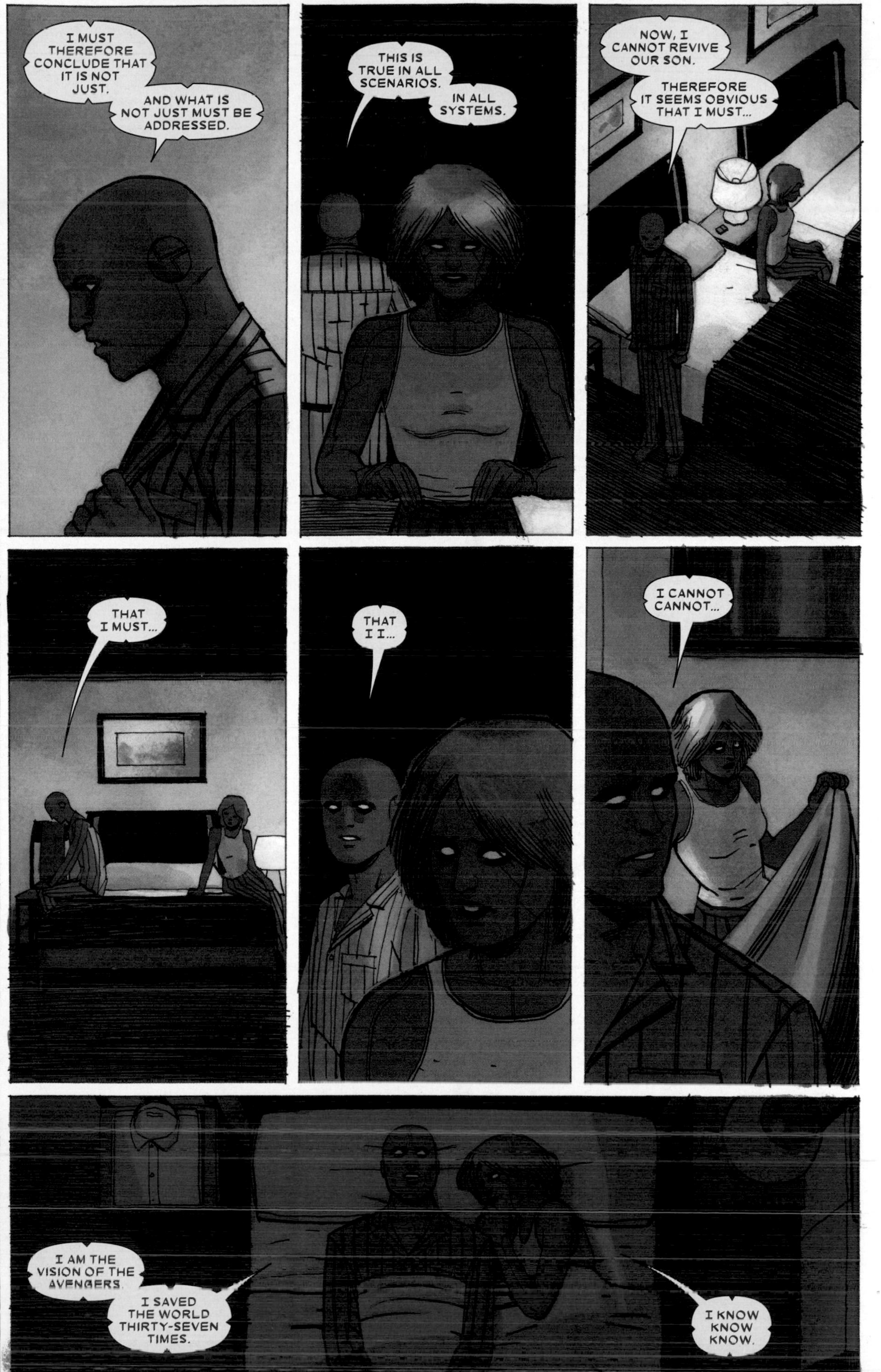
I MUST THEREFORE CONCLUDE THAT IT IS NOT JUST.
AND WHAT IS NOT JUST MUST BE ADDRESSED.
THIS IS TRUE IN ALL SCENARIOS.
IN ALL SYSTEMS.
NOW, I CANNOT REVIVE OUR SON.
THEREFORE IT SEEMS OBVIOUS THAT I MUST...
THAT I MUST...
THAT I I...
I CANNOT CANNOT...
I AM THE VISION OF THE AVENGERS.
I SAVED THE WORLD THIRTY-SEVEN TIMES.
I KNOW KNOW KNOW.

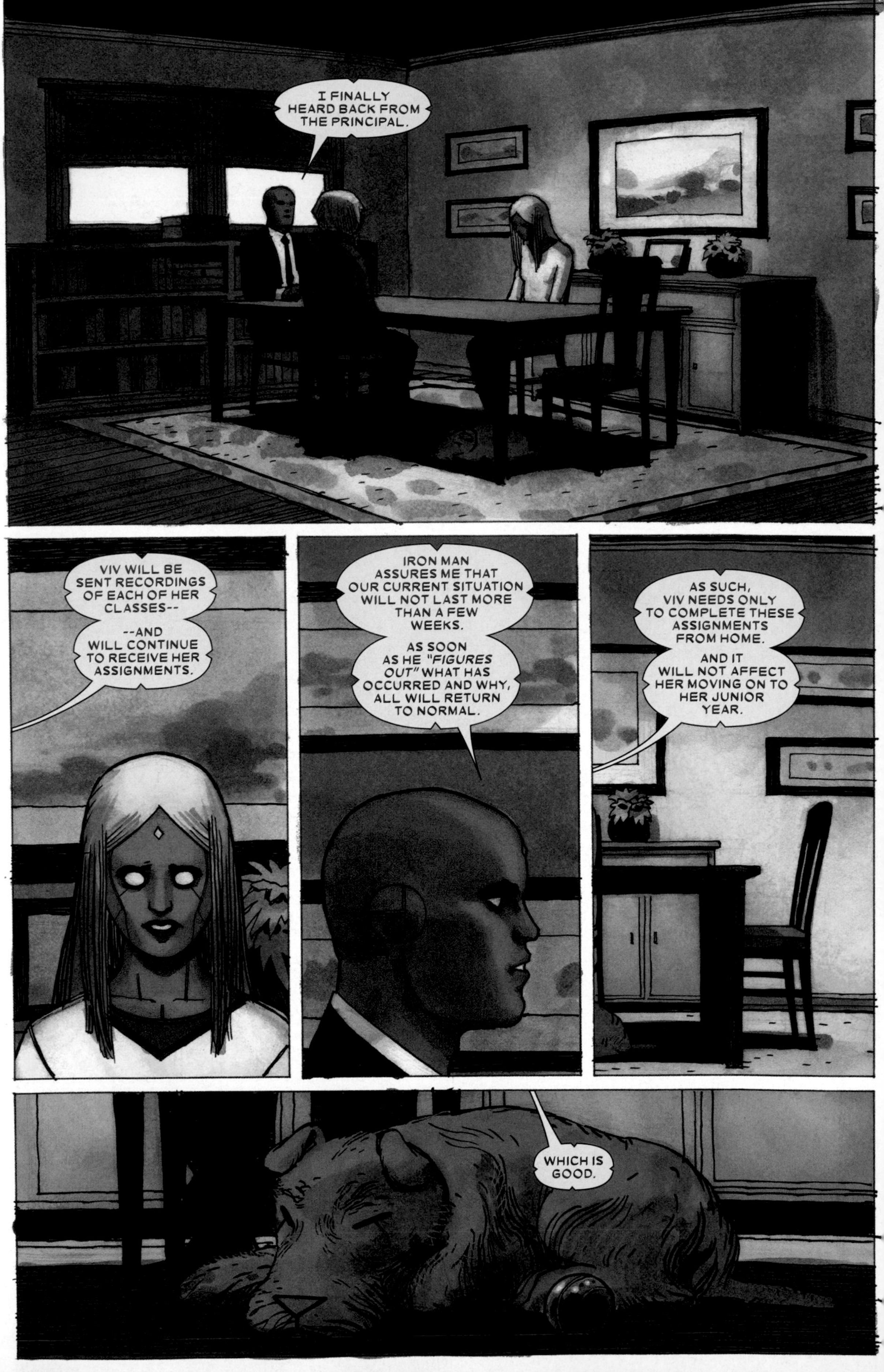

I FINALLY HEARD BACK FROM THE PRINCIPAL.
VIV WILL BE SENT RECORDINGS OF EACH OF HER CLASSES--
--AND WILL CONTINUE TO RECEIVE HER ASSIGNMENTS.
IRON MAN ASSURES ME THAT OUR CURRENT SITUATION WILL NOT LAST MORE THAN A FEW WEEKS.
AS SOON AS HE "FIGURES OUT" WHAT HAS OCCURRED AND WHY, ALL WILL RETURN TO NORMAL.
AS SUCH, VIV NEEDS ONLY TO COMPLETE THESE ASSIGNMENTS FROM HOME.
AND IT WILL NOT AFFECT HER MOVING ON TO HER JUNIOR YEAR.
WHICH IS GOOD.

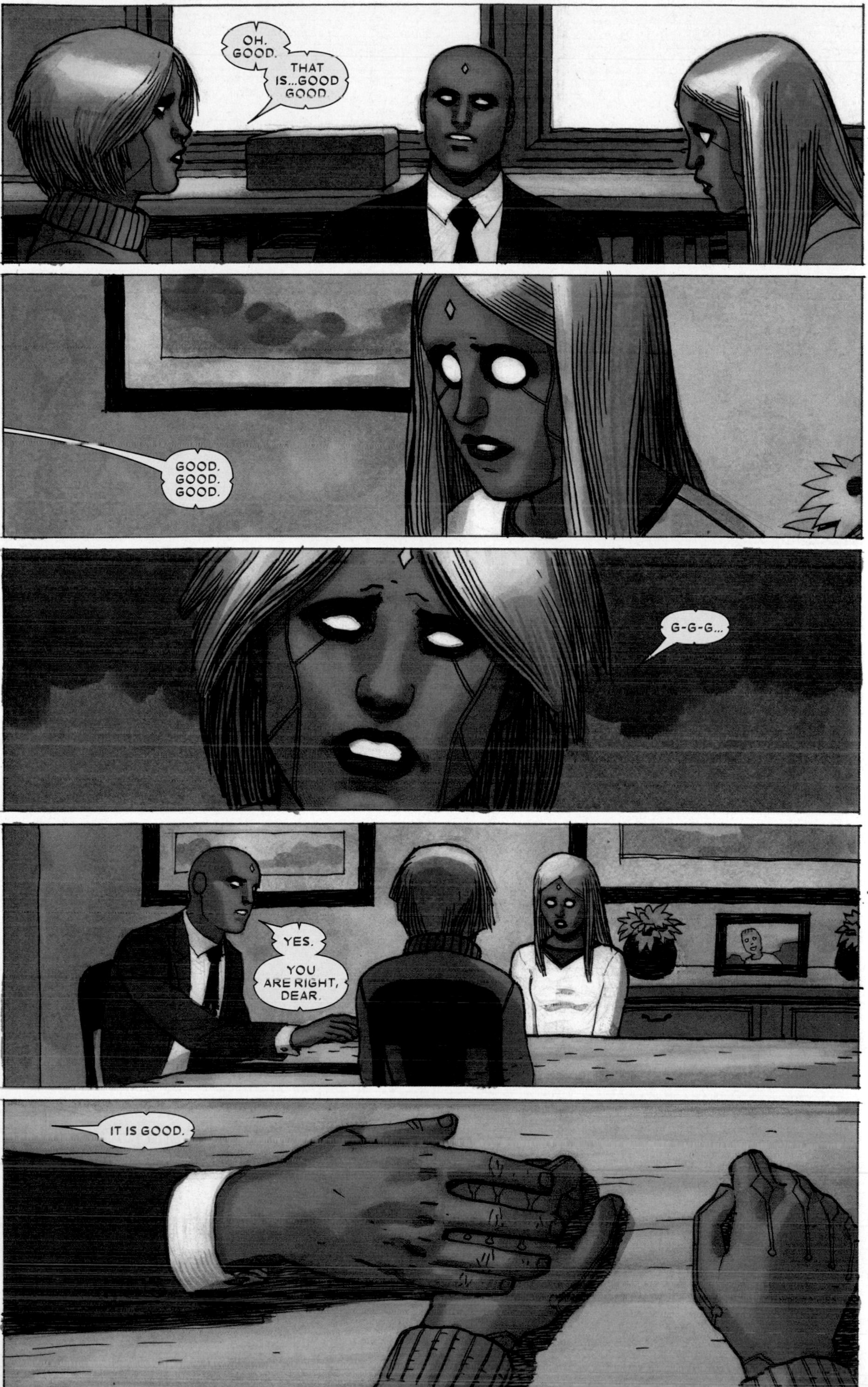
OH. GOOD.
THAT IS...GOOD GOOD.
GOOD. GOOD. GOOD.
G-G-G...
YES.
YOU ARE RIGHT, DEAR.
IT IS GOOD.

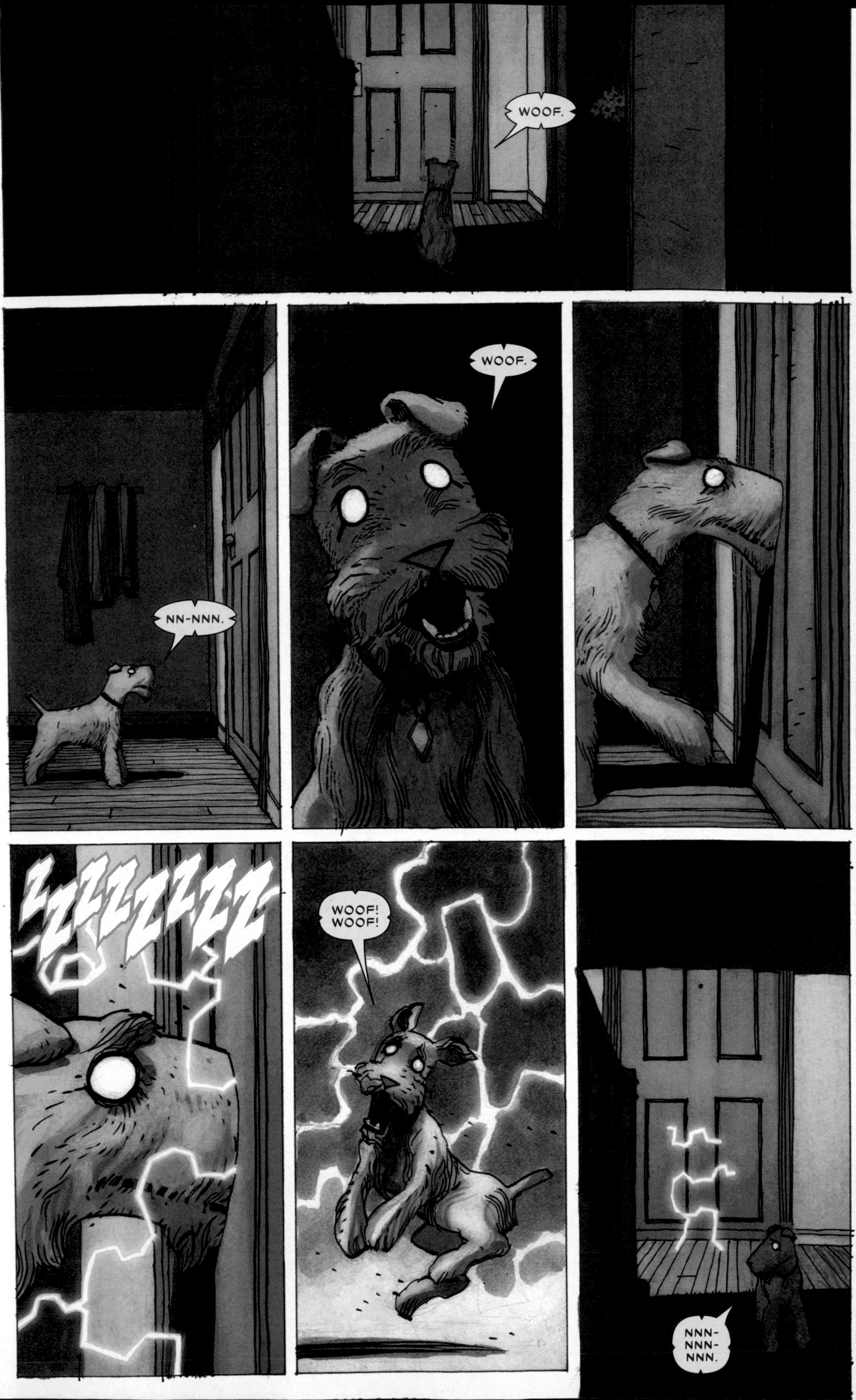
WOOF.
NN-NNN.
WOOF.
ZZZZZZZZZ
WOOF! WOOF!
NNN-NNN-NNN.

MY APOLOGIES, IRON MAN...

NO. NO, THERE IS NO REASON TO DEPLOY THE AVENGERS.

THIS WAS NOT AN ATTEMPTED BREACH.

THE DOG SET OFF THE ALARM.

ROW. ROW. ROW.

NO, WHEN YOU *INSTALLED* THE ENCLOSURE, I ADJUSTED HIS PROGRAMMING...

...HE SHOULD HAVE STAYED WITHIN THE CONFINES OF THE HOUSE.

YOUR... *BOAT.*

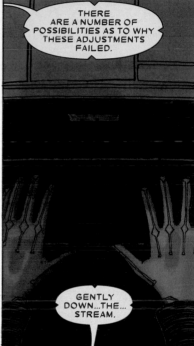

THERE ARE A NUMBER OF POSSIBILITIES AS TO WHY THESE ADJUSTMENTS FAILED.

GENTLY DOWN...THE... STREAM.

YES, YES.

I WILL CONDUCT A THOROUGH ANALYSIS OF THE ANIMAL THIS AFTERNOON.

MERRILY. MERRILY. MERRILY. MERRILY.

I DO NOT ANTICIPATE THAT THE ALARM WILL SOUND AGAIN.

LIFE IS BUT A DREAM.

DREAM. DREAM. DREAM.

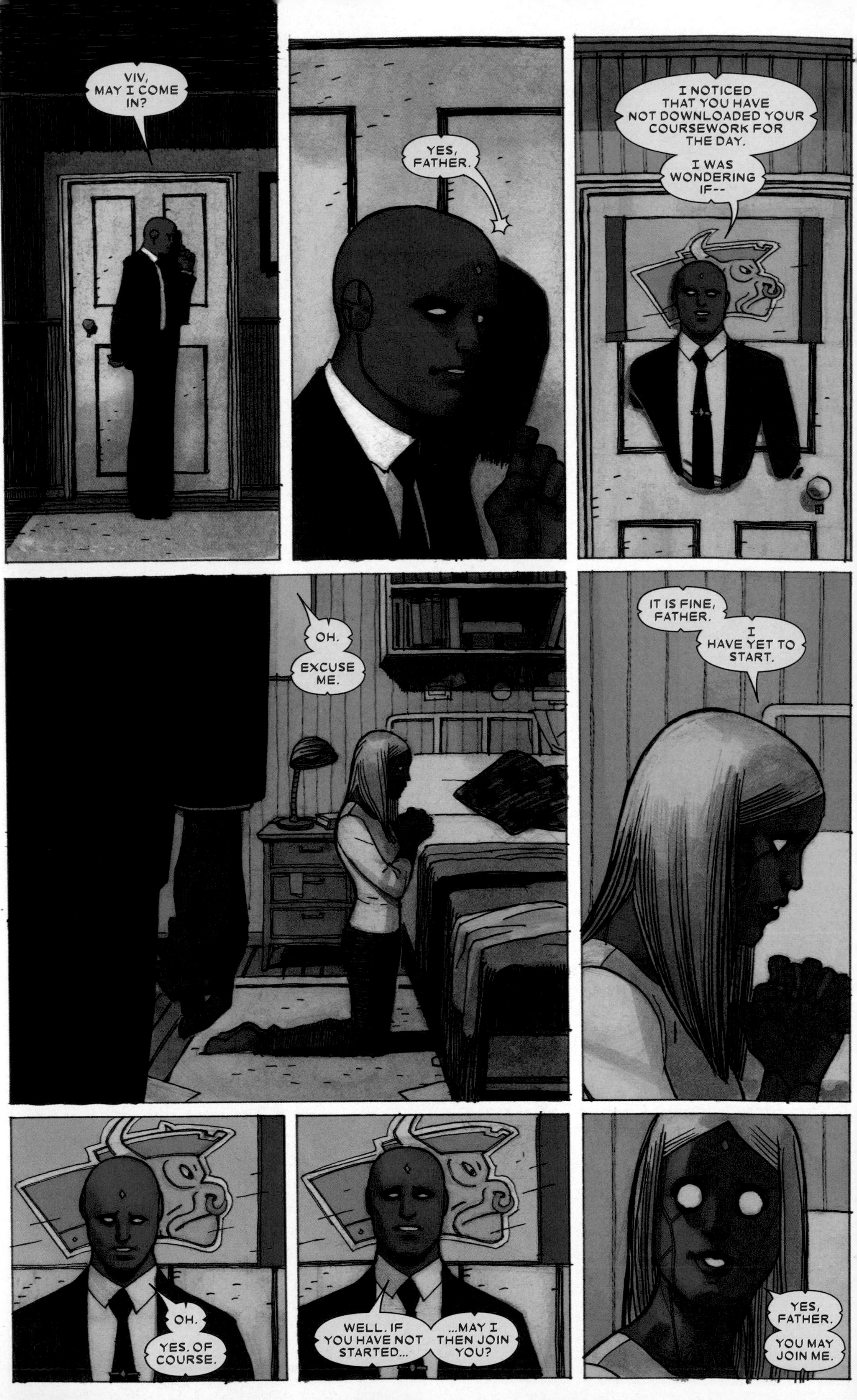
VIV, MAY I COME IN?
YES, FATHER.
I NOTICED THAT YOU HAVE NOT DOWNLOADED YOUR COURSEWORK FOR THE DAY.
I WAS WONDERING IF--
OH.
EXCUSE ME.
IT IS FINE, FATHER.
I HAVE YET TO START.
OH.
YES. OF COURSE.
WELL. IF YOU HAVE NOT STARTED...
...MAY I THEN JOIN YOU?
YES, FATHER.
YOU MAY JOIN ME.

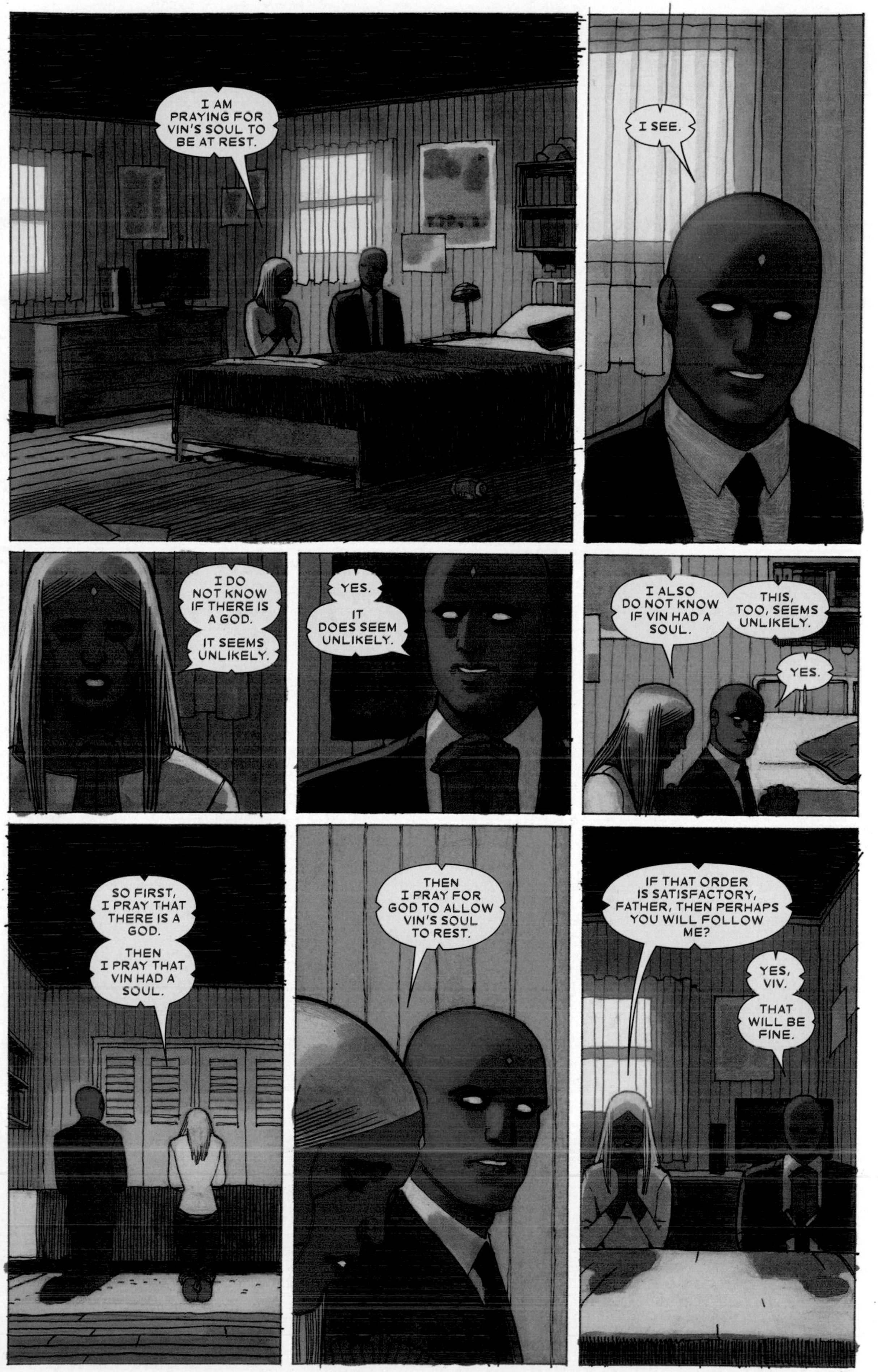
I AM PRAYING FOR VIN'S SOUL TO BE AT REST.
I SEE.
I DO NOT KNOW IF THERE IS A GOD.
IT SEEMS UNLIKELY.
YES.
IT DOES SEEM UNLIKELY.
I ALSO DO NOT KNOW IF VIN HAD A SOUL.
THIS, TOO, SEEMS UNLIKELY.
YES.
SO FIRST, I PRAY THAT THERE IS A GOD.
THEN I PRAY THAT VIN HAD A SOUL.
THEN I PRAY FOR GOD TO ALLOW VIN'S SOUL TO REST.
IF THAT ORDER IS SATISFACTORY, FATHER, THEN PERHAPS YOU WILL FOLLOW ME?
YES, VIV.
THAT WILL BE FINE.

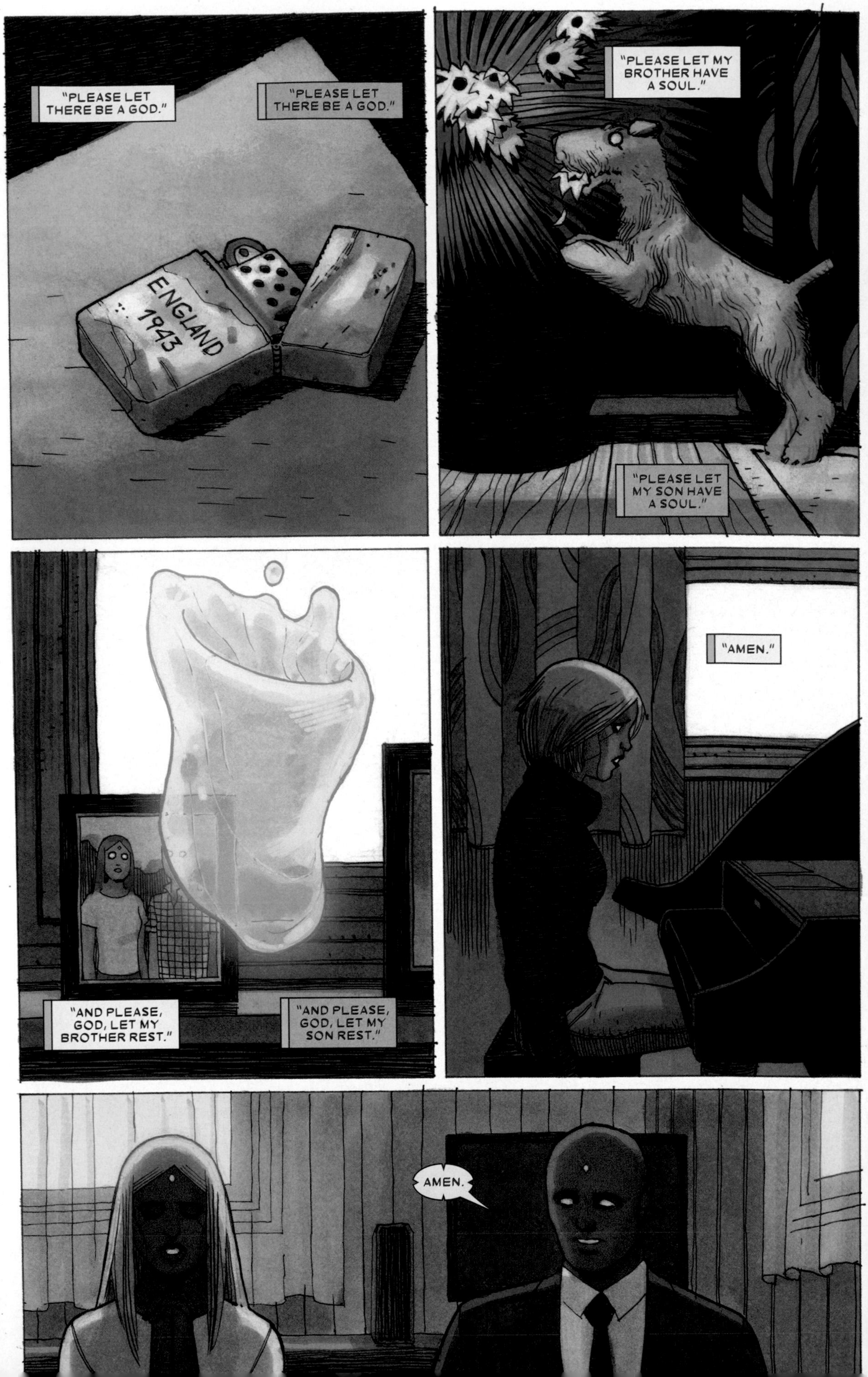
"PLEASE LET THERE BE A GOD."
"PLEASE LET THERE BE A GOD."
ENGLAND 1943
"PLEASE LET MY BROTHER HAVE A SOUL."
"PLEASE LET MY SON HAVE A SOUL."
"AND PLEASE, GOD, LET MY BROTHER REST."
"AND PLEASE, GOD, LET MY SON REST."
"AMEN."
AMEN.

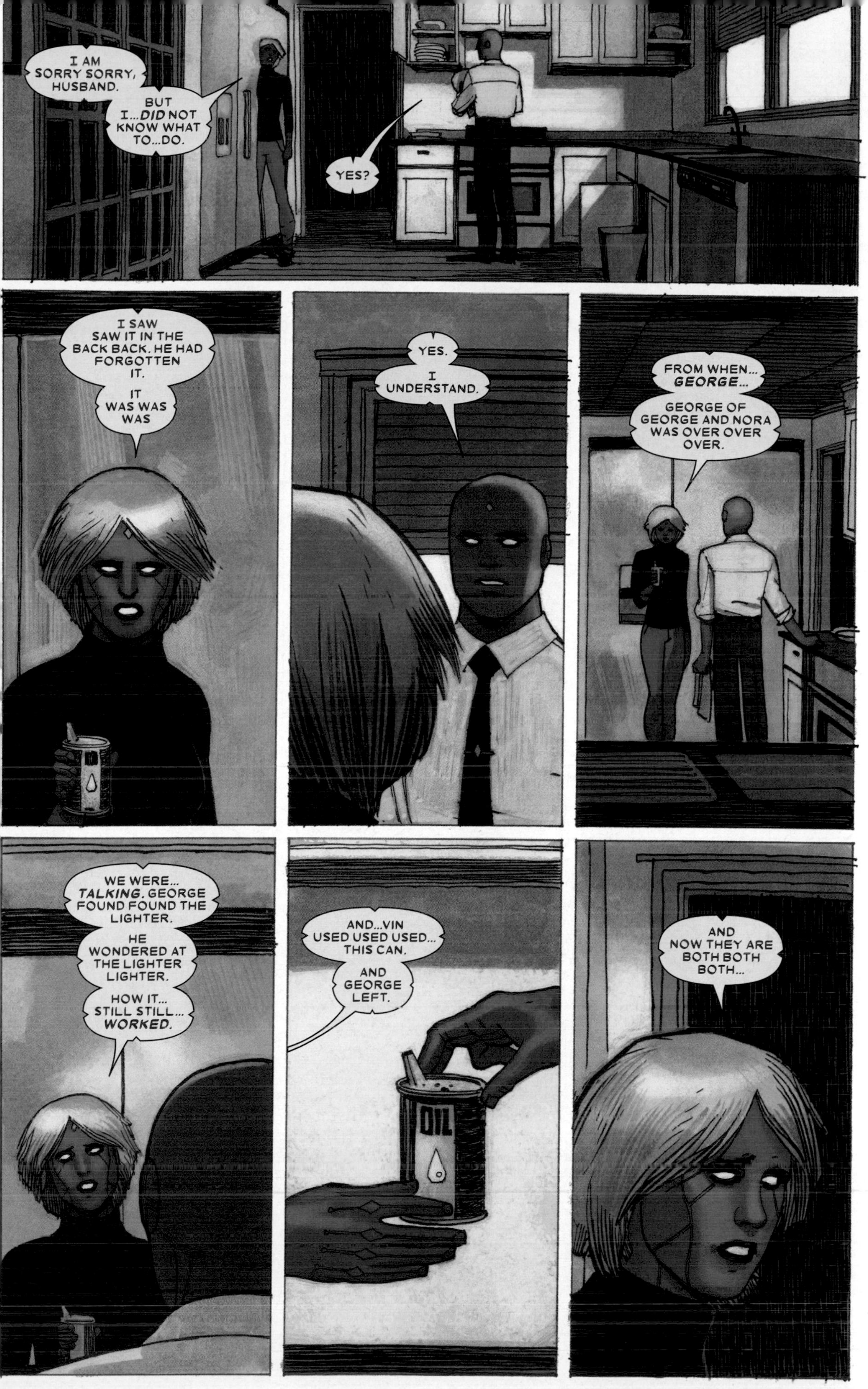
I AM SORRY SORRY, HUSBAND.
BUT I...DID NOT KNOW WHAT TO...DO.
YES?
I SAW SAW IT IN THE BACK BACK. HE HAD FORGOTTEN IT.
IT WAS WAS WAS
YES.
I UNDERSTAND.
FROM WHEN... GEORGE...
GEORGE OF GEORGE AND NORA WAS OVER OVER OVER.
WE WERE... TALKING. GEORGE FOUND FOUND THE LIGHTER.
HE WONDERED AT THE LIGHTER LIGHTER.
HOW IT... STILL STILL... WORKED.
AND...VIN USED USED USED... THIS CAN.
AND GEORGE LEFT.
OIL
AND NOW THEY ARE BOTH BOTH BOTH...

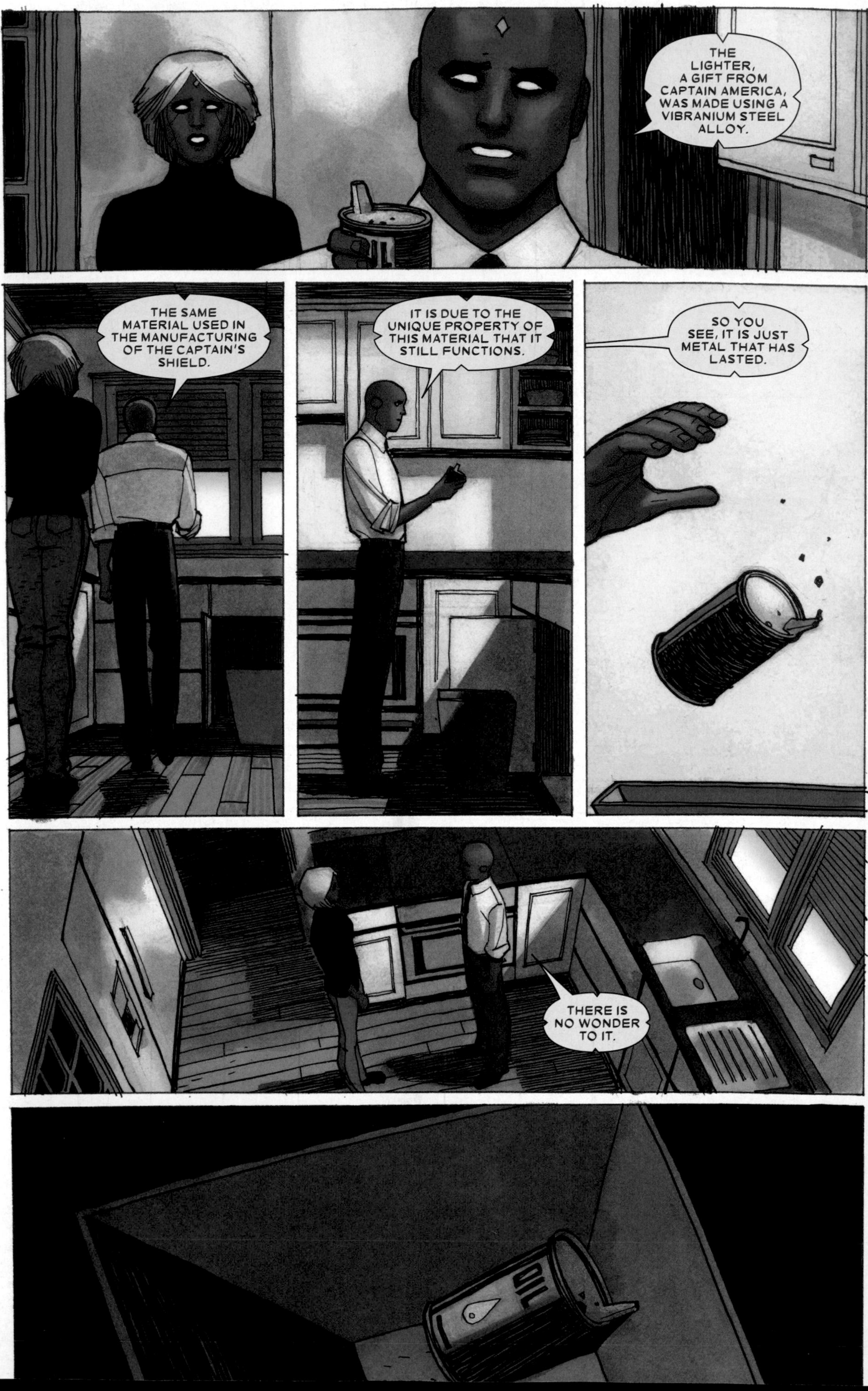
THE LIGHTER, A GIFT FROM CAPTAIN AMERICA, WAS MADE USING A VIBRANIUM STEEL ALLOY.
THE SAME MATERIAL USED IN THE MANUFACTURING OF THE CAPTAIN'S SHIELD.
IT IS DUE TO THE UNIQUE PROPERTY OF THIS MATERIAL THAT IT STILL FUNCTIONS.
SO YOU SEE, IT IS JUST METAL THAT HAS LASTED.
THERE IS NO WONDER TO IT.

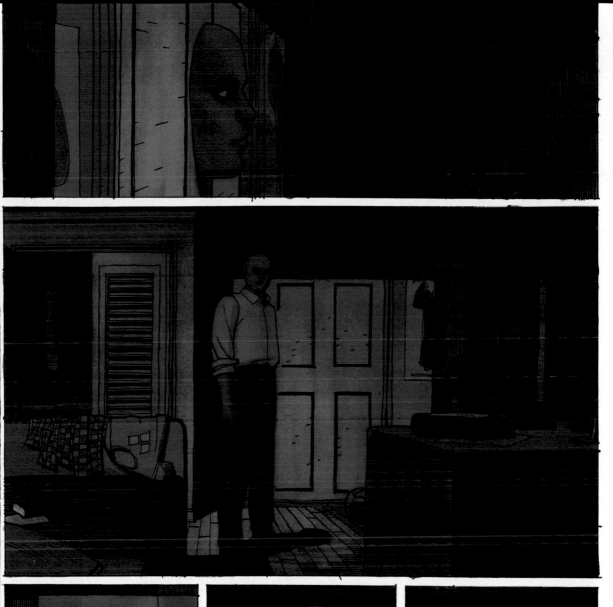

CLICK

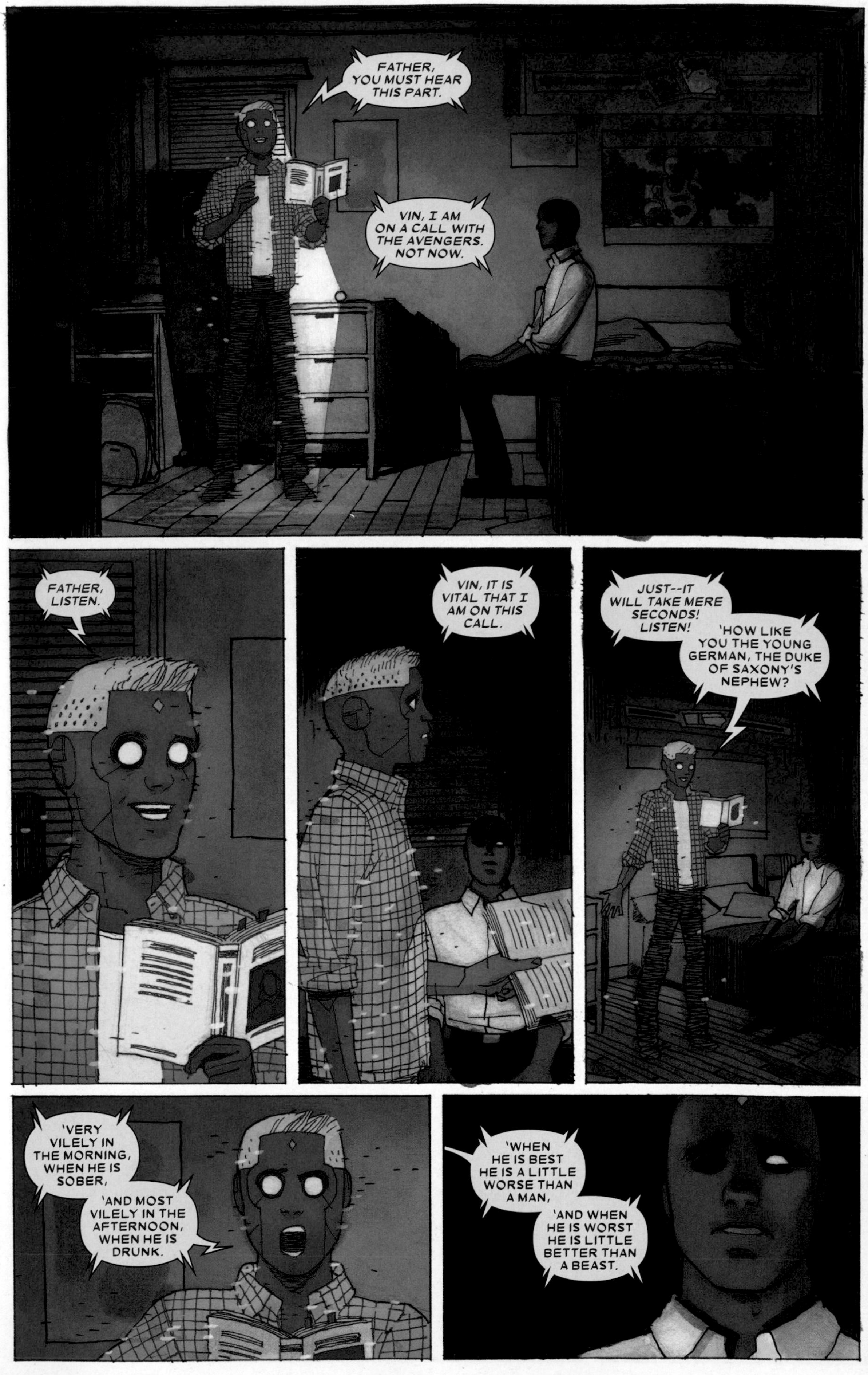

FATHER, YOU MUST HEAR THIS PART.
VIN, I AM ON A CALL WITH THE AVENGERS. NOT NOW.
FATHER, LISTEN.
VIN, IT IS VITAL THAT I AM ON THIS CALL.
JUST--IT WILL TAKE MERE SECONDS! LISTEN!
'HOW LIKE YOU THE YOUNG GERMAN, THE DUKE OF SAXONY'S NEPHEW?
'VERY VILELY IN THE MORNING, WHEN HE IS SOBER,
'AND MOST VILELY IN THE AFTERNOON, WHEN HE IS DRUNK.
'WHEN HE IS BEST HE IS A LITTLE WORSE THAN A MAN,
'AND WHEN HE IS WORST HE IS LITTLE BETTER THAN A BEAST.

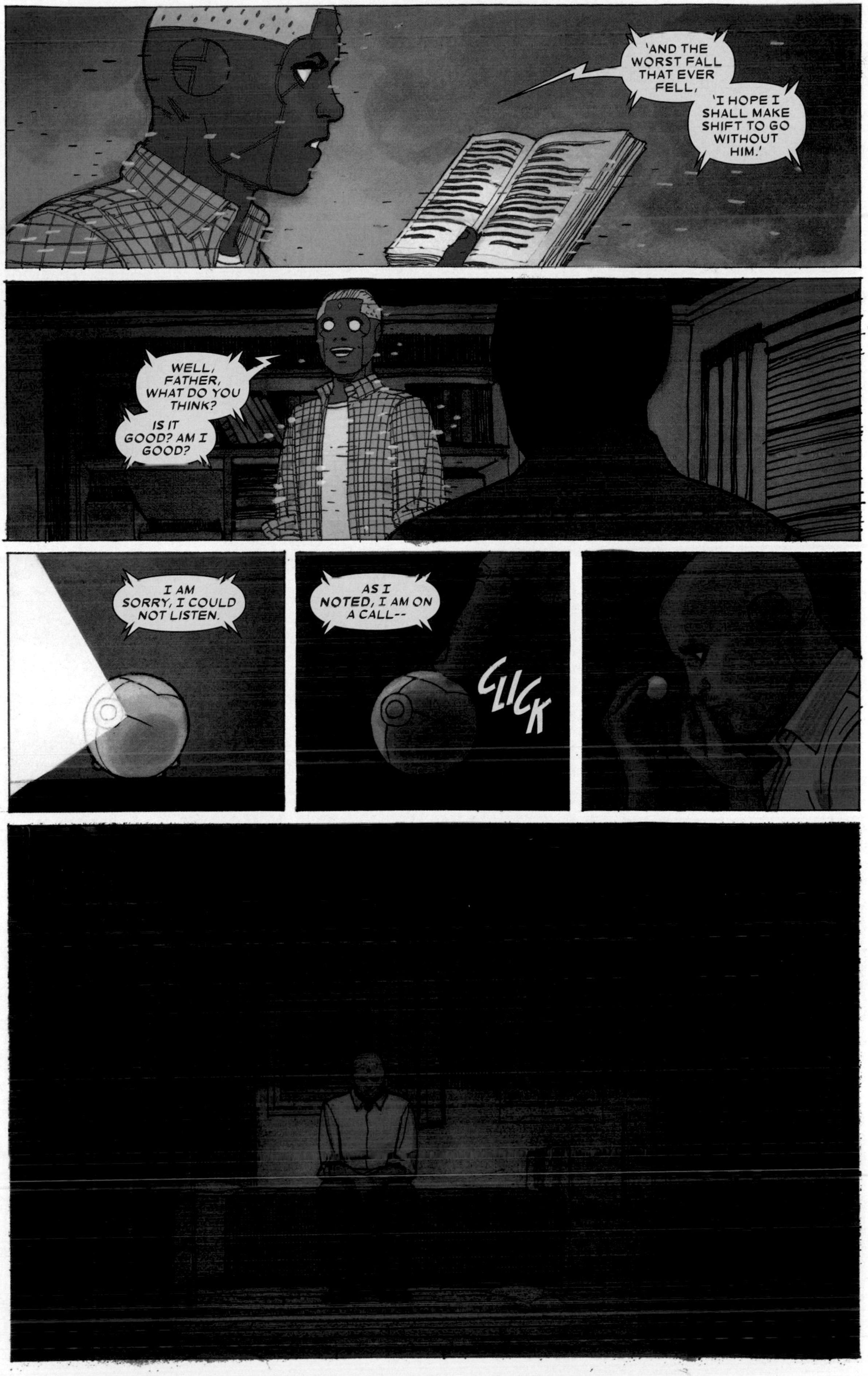
'AND THE WORST FALL THAT EVER FELL,
'I HOPE I SHALL MAKE SHIFT TO GO WITHOUT HIM.'
WELL, FATHER, WHAT DO YOU THINK?
IS IT GOOD? AM I GOOD?
I AM SORRY, I COULD NOT LISTEN.
AS I NOTED, I AM ON A CALL--
CLICK

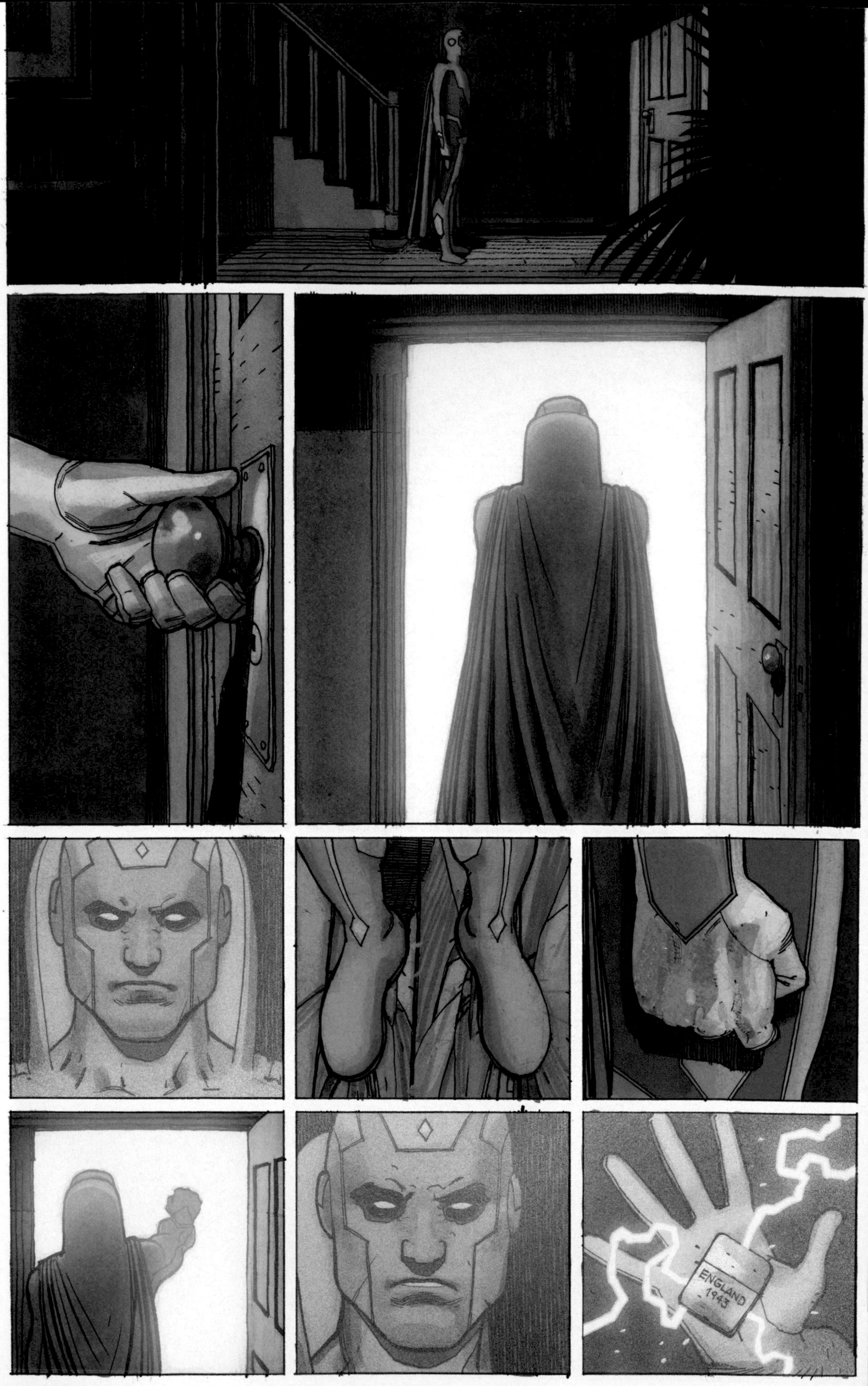
ENGLAND
1943

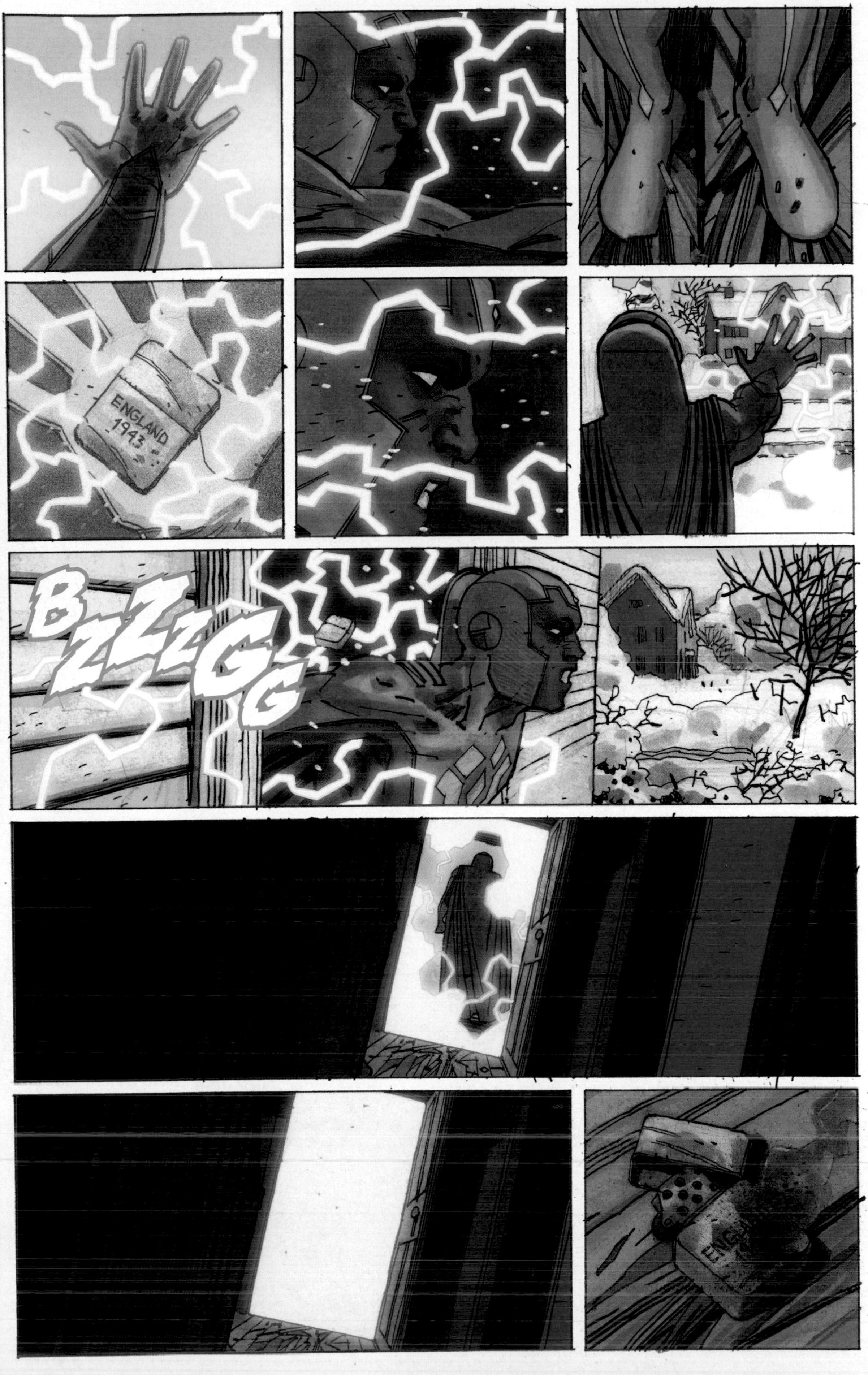
ENGLAND
1943
BZZZGG

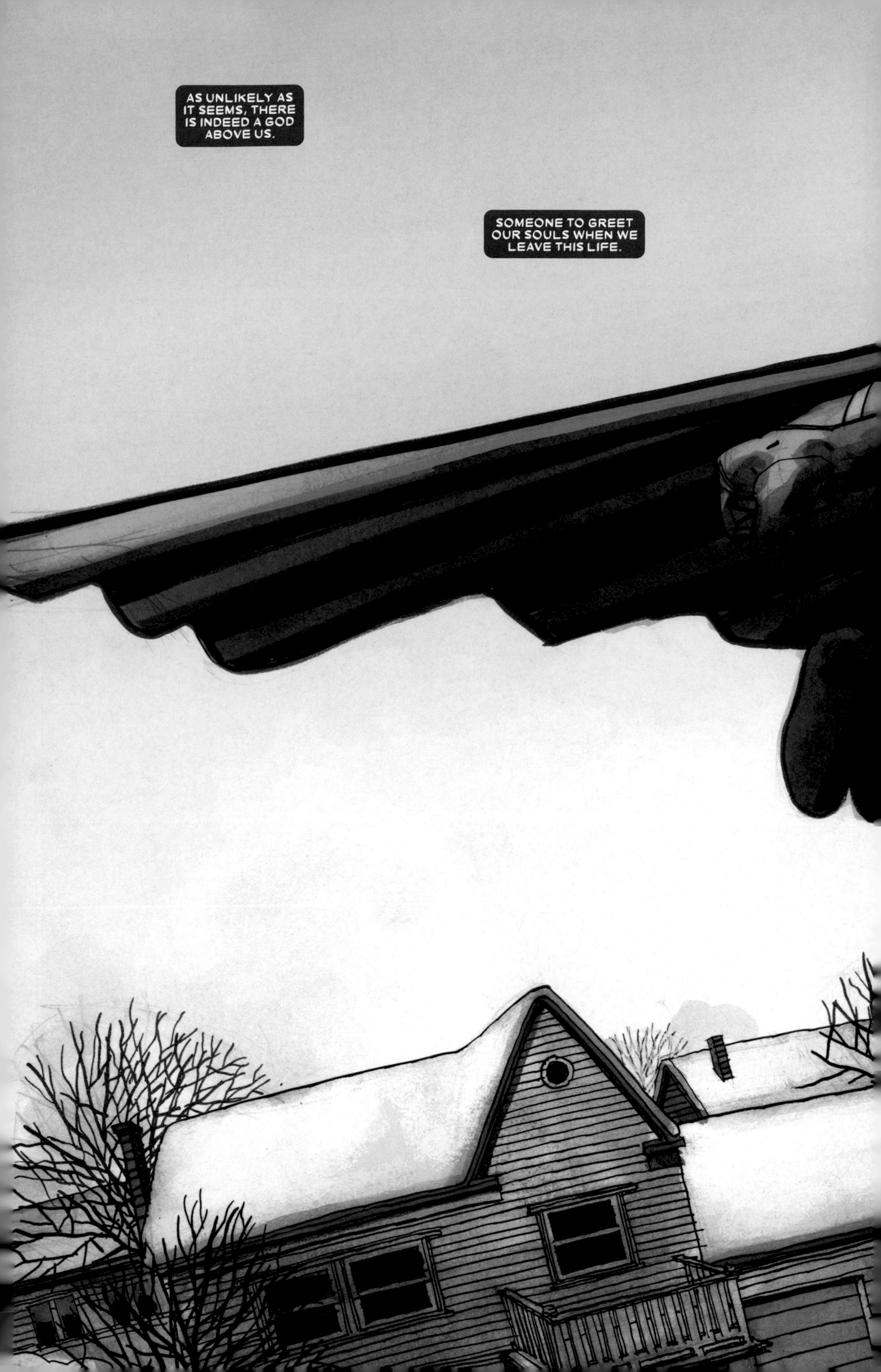
AS UNLIKELY AS IT SEEMS, THERE IS INDEED A GOD ABOVE US.
SOMEONE TO GREET OUR SOULS WHEN WE LEAVE THIS LIFE.

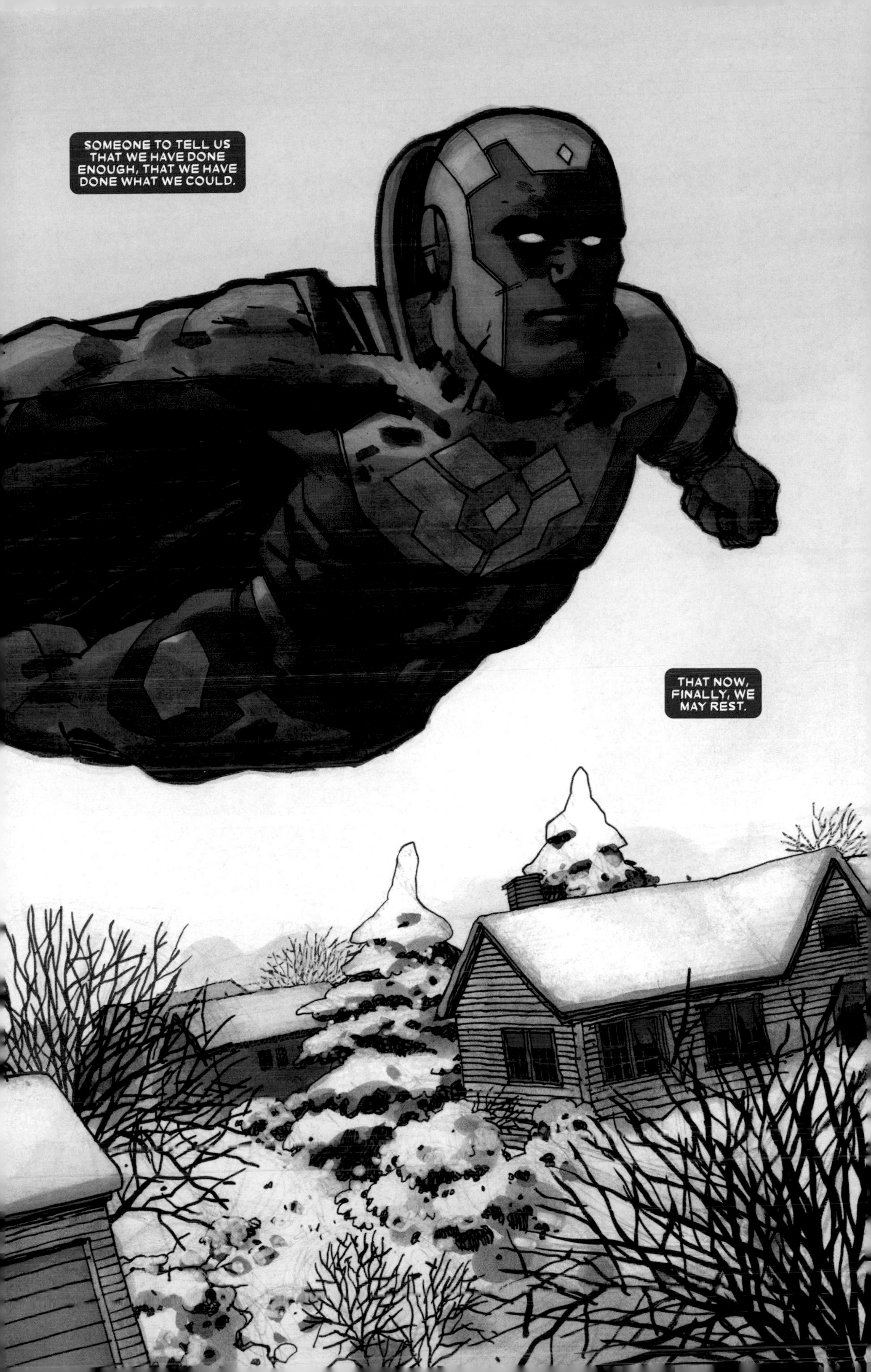
SOMEONE TO TELL US THAT WE HAVE DONE ENOUGH, THAT WE HAVE DONE WHAT WE COULD.
THAT NOW, FINALLY, WE MAY REST.

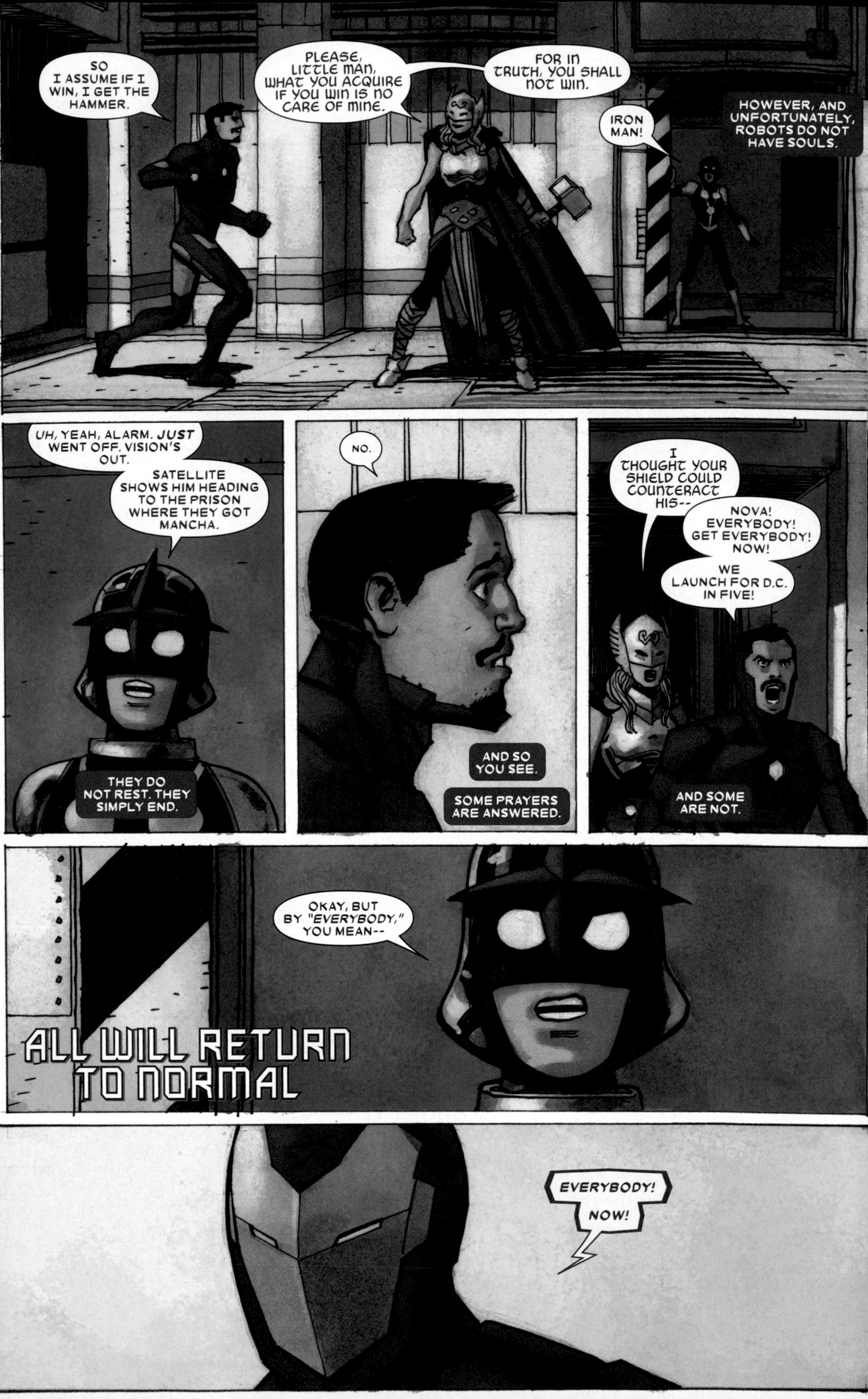
SO I ASSUME IF I WIN, I GET THE HAMMER.
PLEASE, LITTLE MAN, WHAT YOU ACQUIRE IF YOU WIN IS NO CARE OF MINE.
FOR IN TRUTH, YOU SHALL NOT WIN.
IRON MAN!
HOWEVER, AND UNFORTUNATELY, ROBOTS DO NOT HAVE SOULS.
UH, YEAH, ALARM. JUST WENT OFF. VISION'S OUT.
SATELLITE SHOWS HIM HEADING TO THE PRISON WHERE THEY GOT MANCHA.
THEY DO NOT REST. THEY SIMPLY END.
NO.
AND SO YOU SEE.
SOME PRAYERS ARE ANSWERED.
I THOUGHT YOUR SHIELD COULD COUNTERACT HIS--
NOVA! EVERYBODY! GET EVERYBODY! NOW!
WE LAUNCH FOR D.C. IN FIVE!
AND SOME ARE NOT.
OKAY, BUT BY "EVERYBODY," YOU MEAN--
ALL WILL RETURN TO NORMAL
EVERYBODY!
NOW!

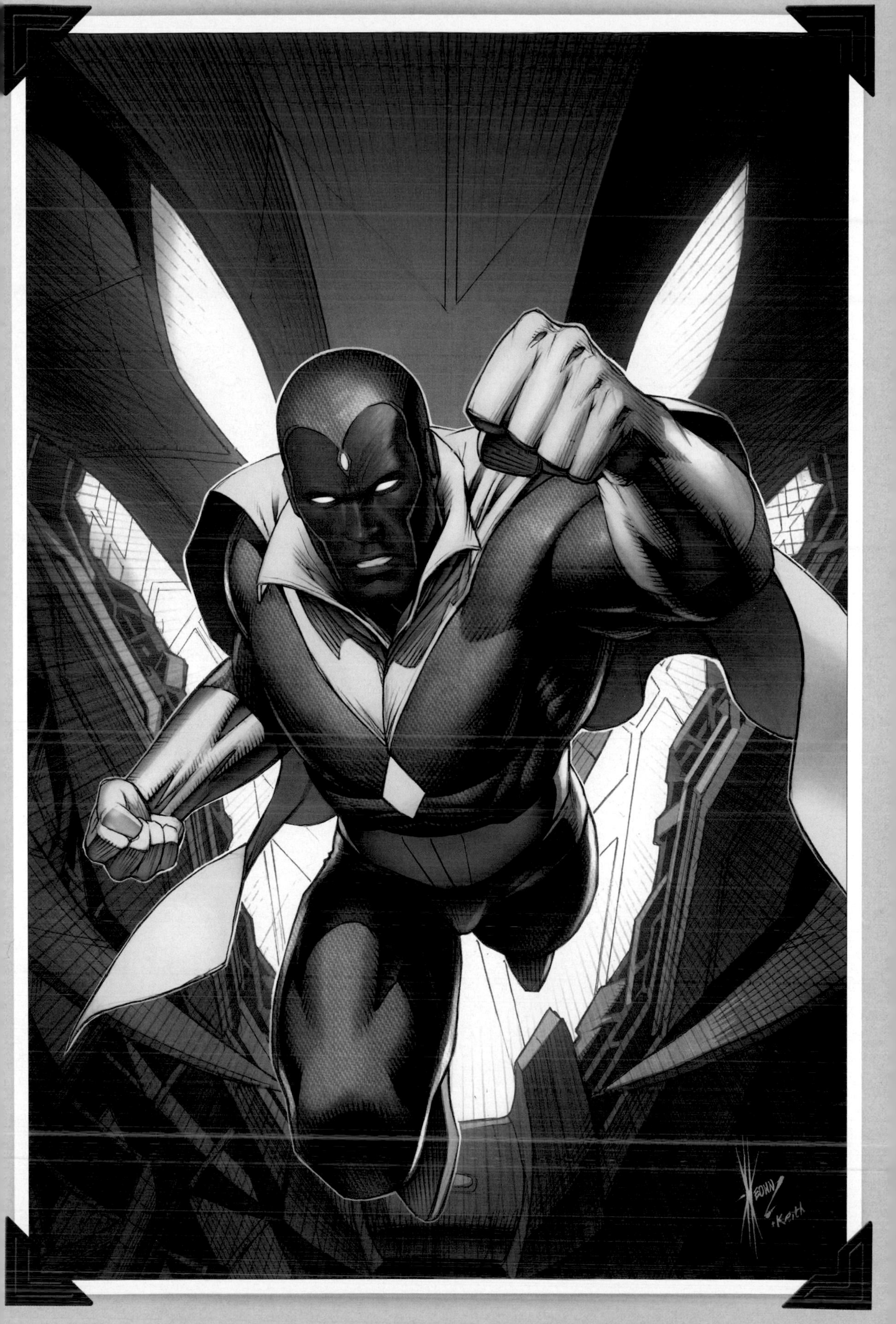

#8 VARIANT BY **DALE KEOWN** & **JASON KEITH**

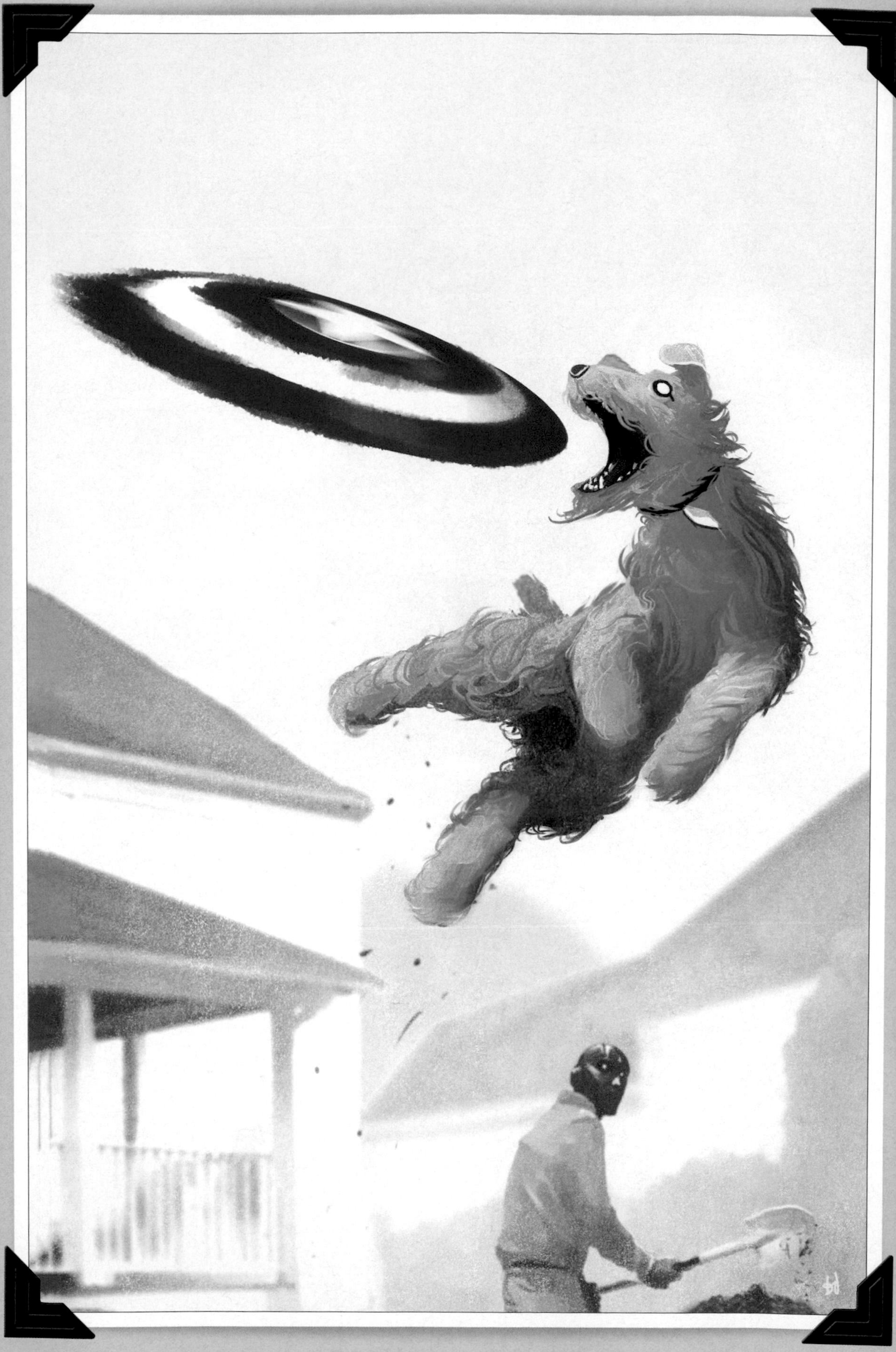

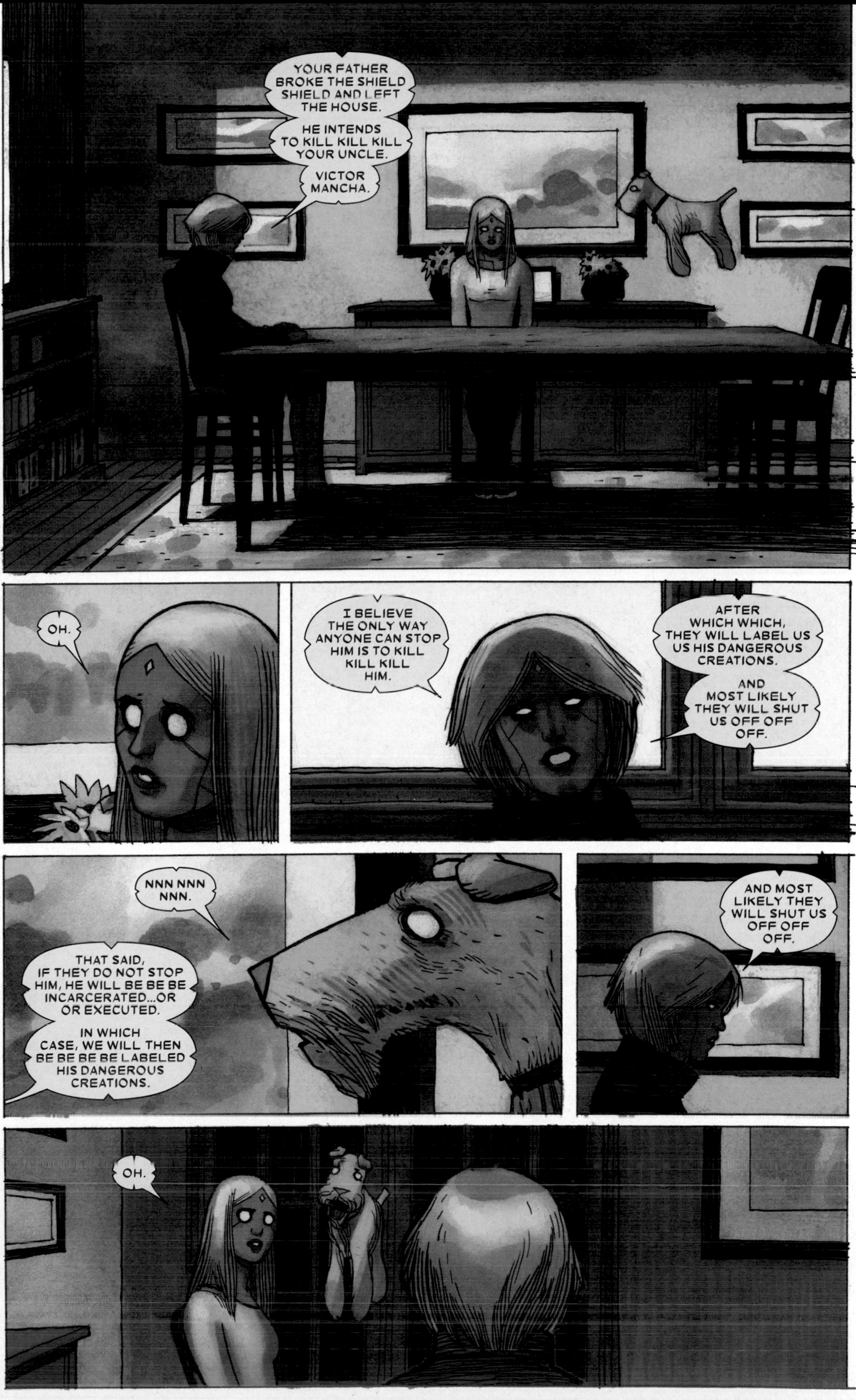
YOUR FATHER BROKE THE SHIELD SHIELD AND LEFT THE HOUSE.
HE INTENDS TO KILL KILL KILL YOUR UNCLE.
VICTOR MANCHA.
OH.
I BELIEVE THE ONLY WAY ANYONE CAN STOP HIM IS TO KILL KILL KILL HIM.
AFTER WHICH WHICH, THEY WILL LABEL US US HIS DANGEROUS CREATIONS.
AND MOST LIKELY THEY WILL SHUT US OFF OFF OFF.
NNN NNN NNN.
THAT SAID, IF THEY DO NOT STOP HIM, HE WILL BE BE BE INCARCERATED...OR OR EXECUTED.
IN WHICH CASE, WE WILL THEN BE BE BE BE LABELED HIS DANGEROUS CREATIONS.
AND MOST LIKELY THEY WILL SHUT US OFF OFF OFF.
OH.

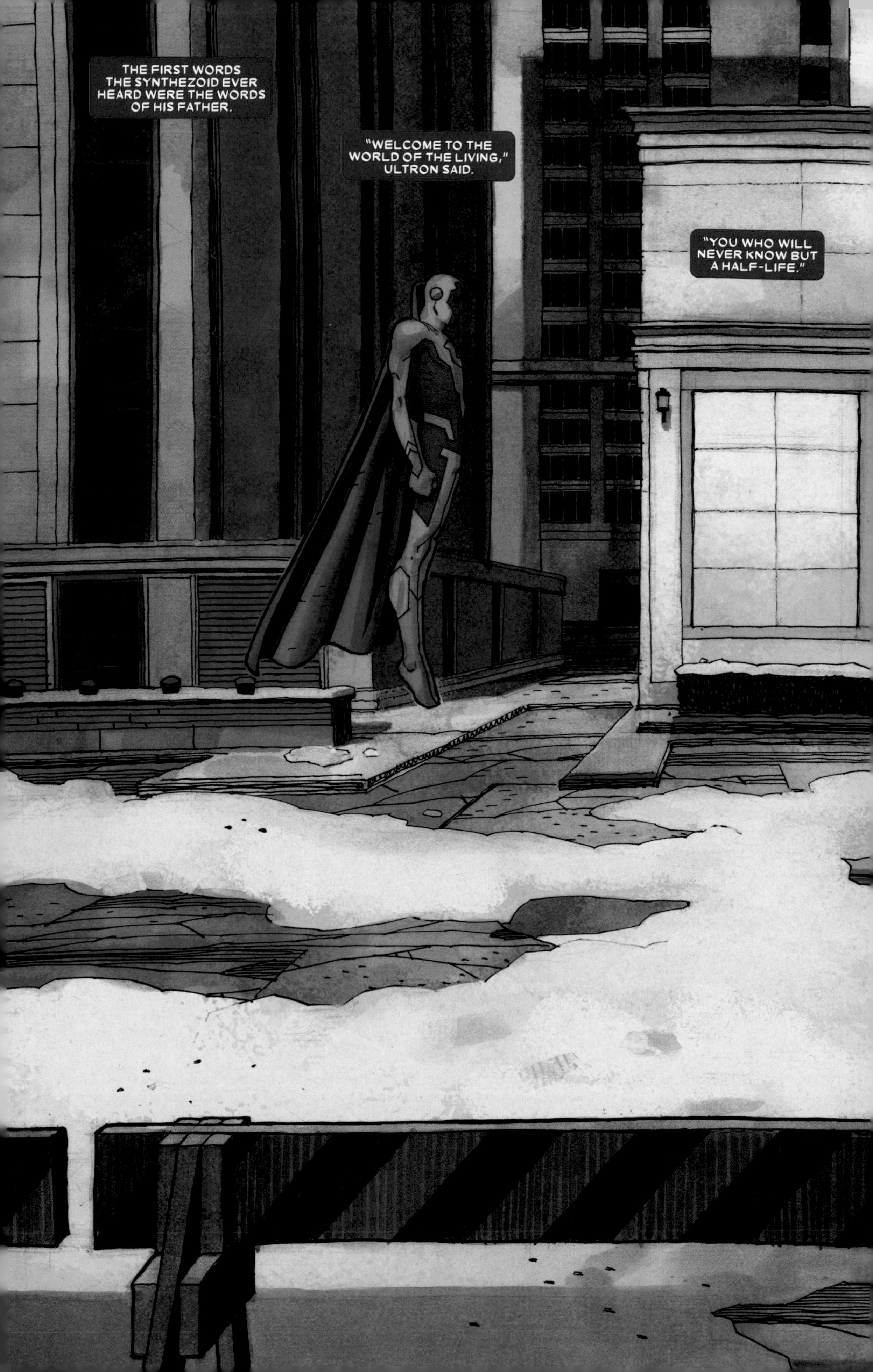
THE FIRST WORDS THE SYNTHEZOID EVER HEARD WERE THE WORDS OF HIS FATHER.
"WELCOME TO THE WORLD OF THE LIVING," ULTRON SAID.
"YOU WHO WILL NEVER KNOW BUT A HALF-LIFE."

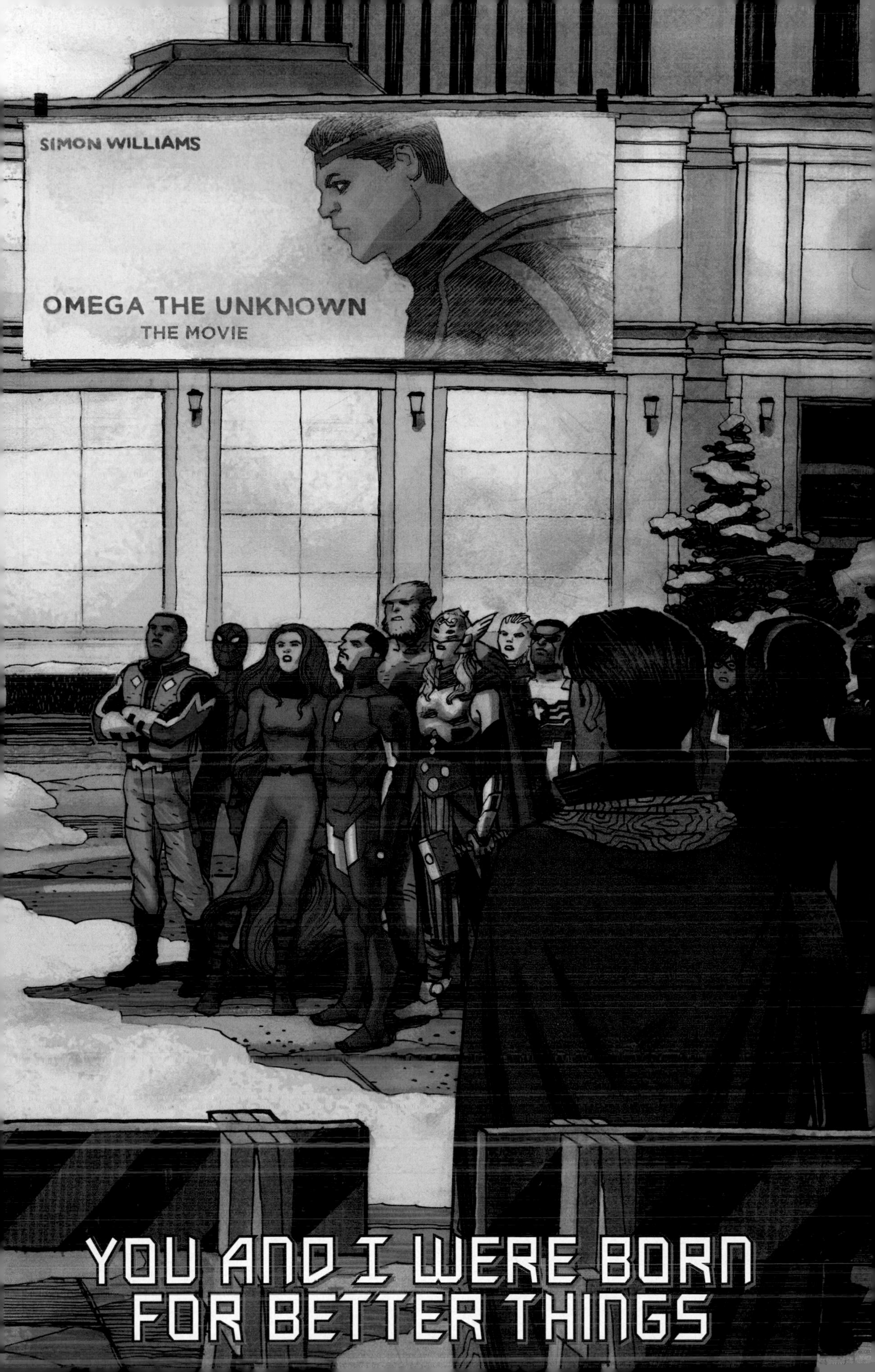
SIMON WILLIAMS
OMEGA THE UNKNOWN
THE MOVIE
YOU AND I WERE BORN
FOR BETTER THINGS

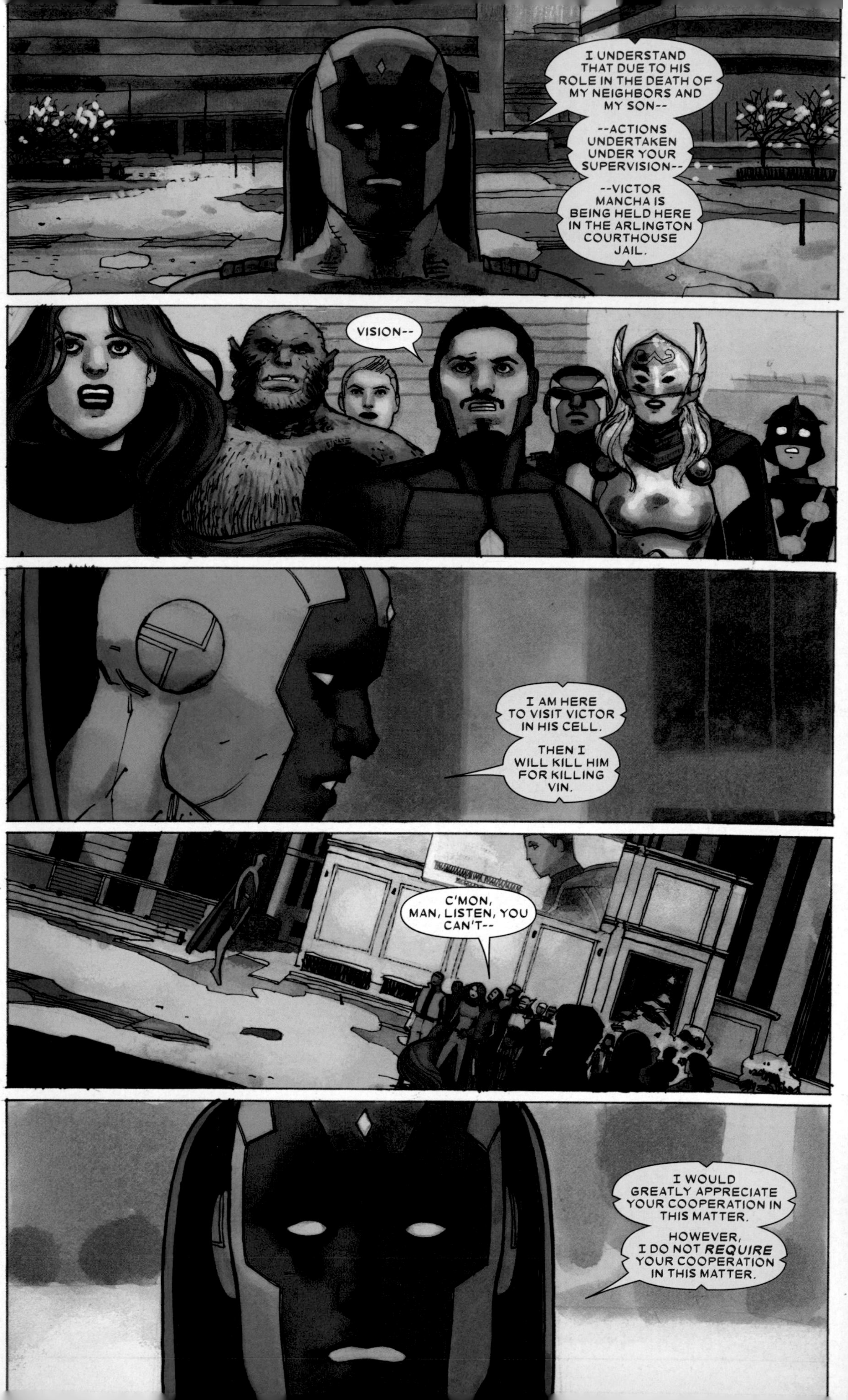
I UNDERSTAND THAT DUE TO HIS ROLE IN THE DEATH OF MY NEIGHBORS AND MY SON--
--ACTIONS UNDERTAKEN UNDER YOUR SUPERVISION--
--VICTOR MANCHA IS BEING HELD HERE IN THE ARLINGTON COURTHOUSE JAIL.
VISION--
I AM HERE TO VISIT VICTOR IN HIS CELL.
THEN I WILL KILL HIM FOR KILLING VIN.
C'MON, MAN, LISTEN, YOU CAN'T--
I WOULD GREATLY APPRECIATE YOUR COOPERATION IN THIS MATTER.
HOWEVER, I DO NOT *REQUIRE* YOUR COOPERATION IN THIS MATTER.

OKAY. FINE.

THIS IS A PORTABLE SHIELD. SIMILAR TO THE ONE ON YOUR HOUSE.

IT'LL KEEP YOU CONTAINED UNTIL WE CAN--

ZxZZZXZX

HIS FATHER CONTINUED:

"I AM ULTRON 5-- BUT YOU SHALL CALL ME...MASTER!"

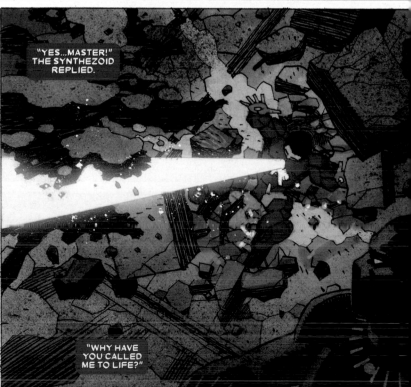

"YES...MASTER!" THE SYNTHEZOID REPLIED.

"WHY HAVE YOU CALLED ME TO LIFE?"

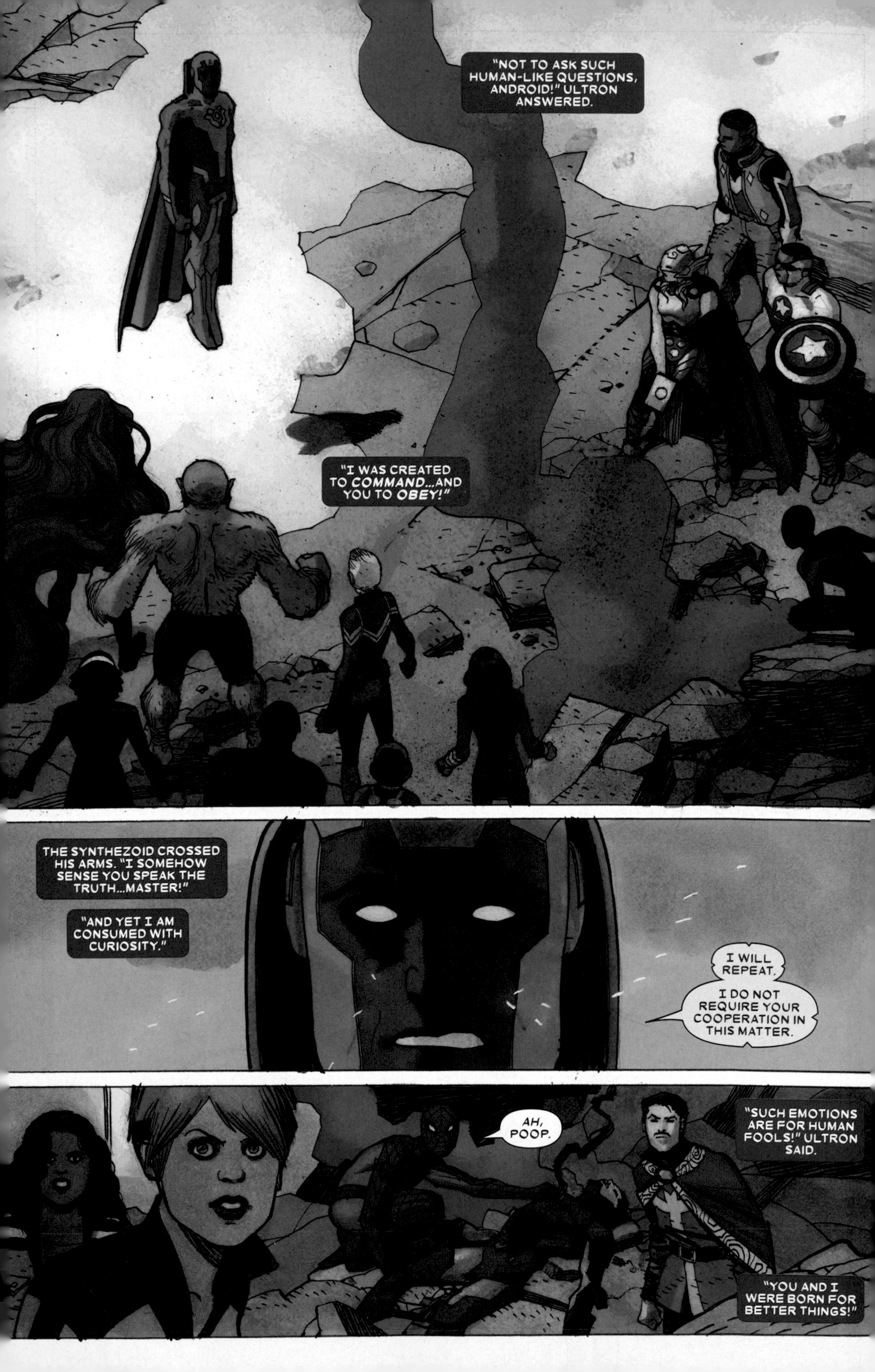
"NOT TO ASK SUCH HUMAN-LIKE QUESTIONS, ANDROID!" ULTRON ANSWERED.
"I WAS CREATED TO COMMAND...AND YOU TO OBEY!"
THE SYNTHEZOID CROSSED HIS ARMS. "I SOMEHOW SENSE YOU SPEAK THE TRUTH...MASTER!"
"AND YET I AM CONSUMED WITH CURIOSITY."
I WILL REPEAT.
I DO NOT REQUIRE YOUR COOPERATION IN THIS MATTER.
AH, POOP.
"SUCH EMOTIONS ARE FOR HUMAN FOOLS!" ULTRON SAID.
"YOU AND I WERE BORN FOR BETTER THINGS!"

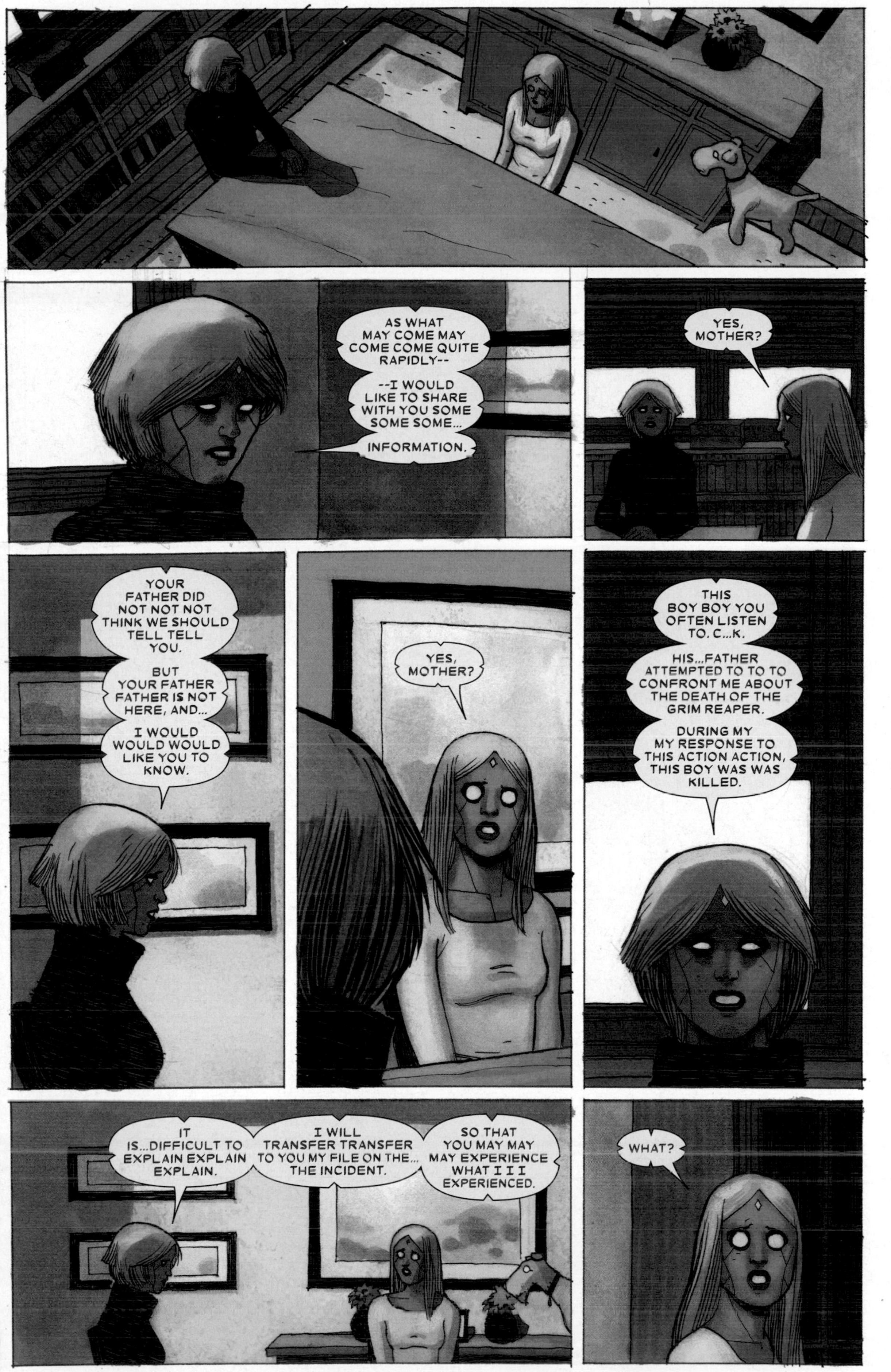
AS WHAT MAY COME MAY COME COME QUITE RAPIDLY--
--I WOULD LIKE TO SHARE WITH YOU SOME SOME SOME...
INFORMATION.
YES, MOTHER?
YOUR FATHER DID NOT NOT NOT THINK WE SHOULD TELL TELL YOU.
BUT YOUR FATHER FATHER IS NOT HERE, AND...
I WOULD WOULD WOULD LIKE YOU TO KNOW.
YES, MOTHER?
THIS BOY BOY YOU OFTEN LISTEN TO. C...K.
HIS...FATHER ATTEMPTED TO TO TO CONFRONT ME ABOUT THE DEATH OF THE GRIM REAPER.
DURING MY MY RESPONSE TO THIS ACTION ACTION, THIS BOY WAS WAS KILLED.
IT IS...DIFFICULT TO EXPLAIN EXPLAIN EXPLAIN.
I WILL TRANSFER TRANSFER TO YOU MY FILE ON THE... THE INCIDENT.
SO THAT YOU MAY MAY MAY EXPERIENCE WHAT I I I EXPERIENCED.
WHAT?

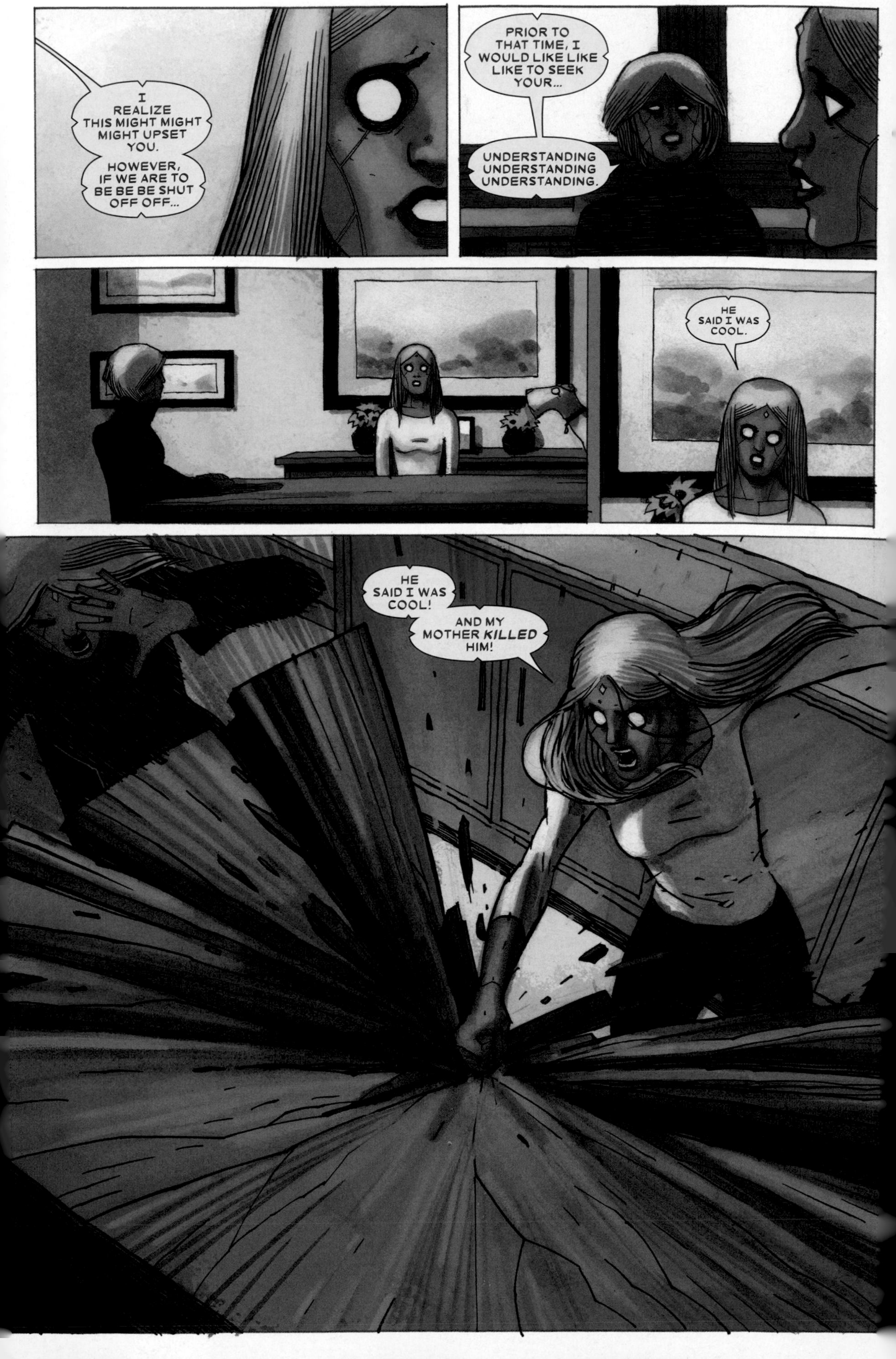
I REALIZE THIS MIGHT MIGHT MIGHT UPSET YOU.
HOWEVER, IF WE ARE TO BE BE BE SHUT OFF OFF...
PRIOR TO THAT TIME, I WOULD LIKE LIKE LIKE TO SEEK YOUR...
UNDERSTANDING UNDERSTANDING UNDERSTANDING.
HE SAID I WAS COOL.
HE SAID I WAS COOL!
AND MY MOTHER *KILLED* HIM!

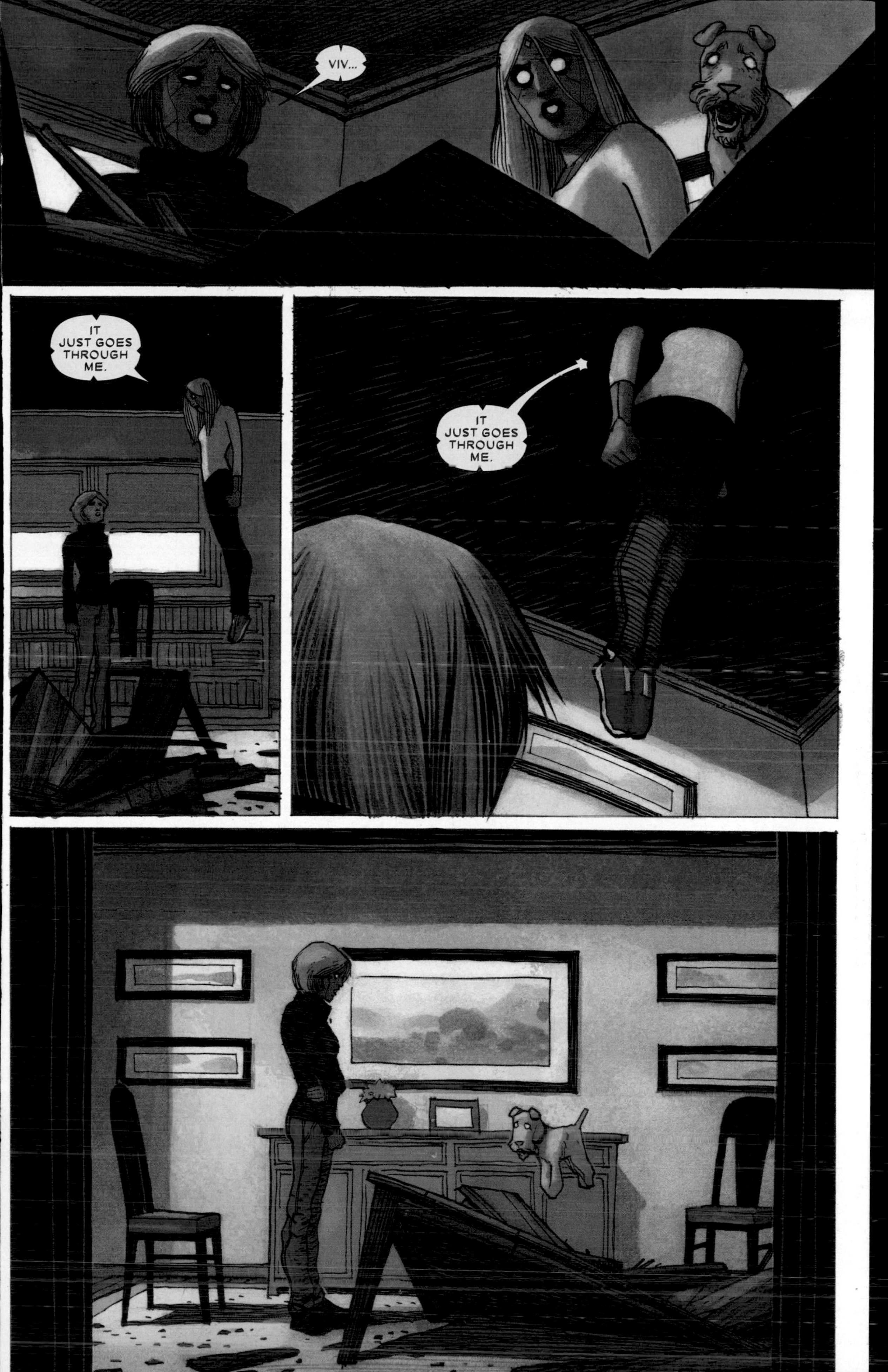
VIV...
IT JUST GOES THROUGH ME.
IT JUST GOES THROUGH ME.

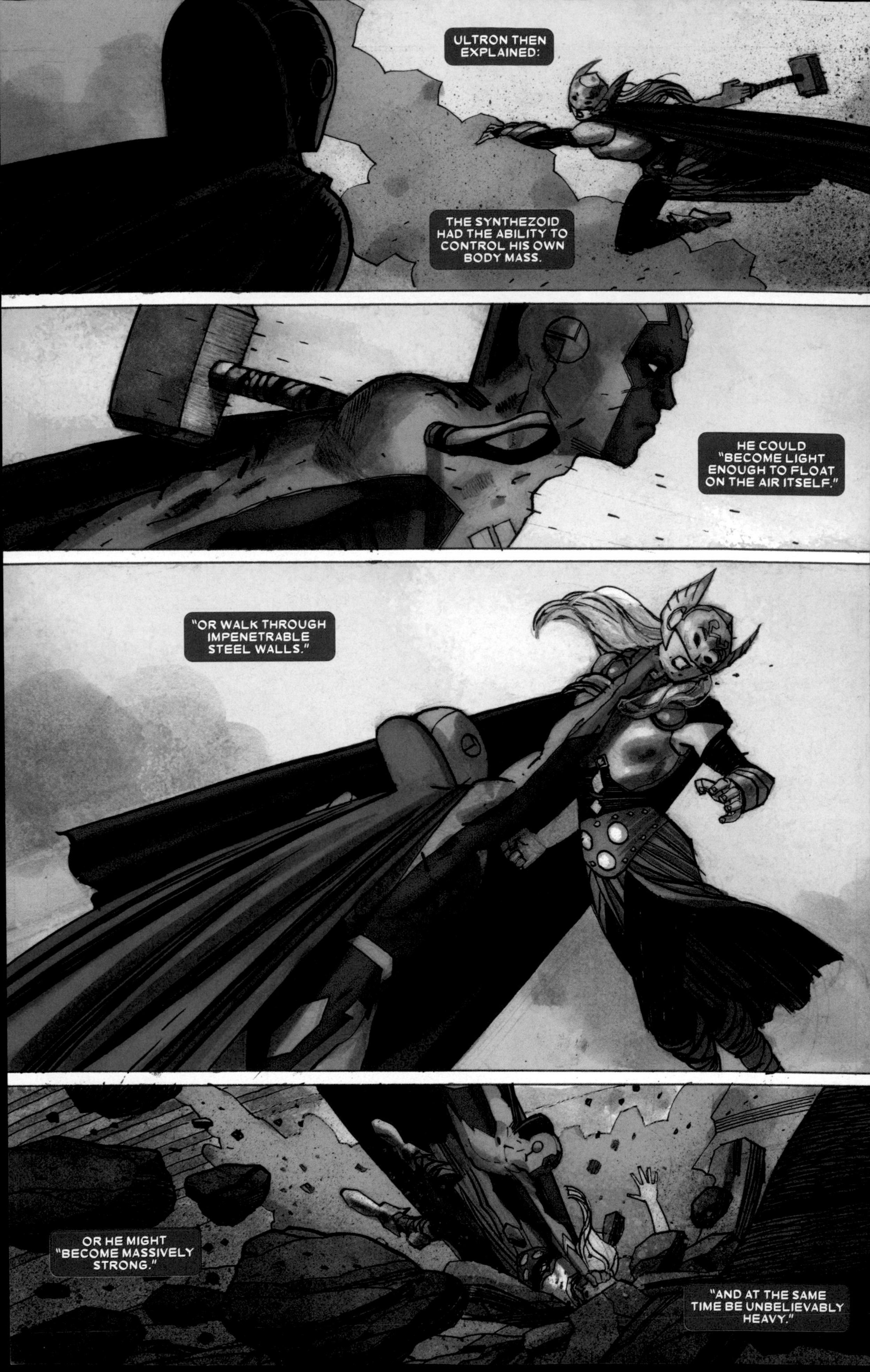
ULTRON THEN EXPLAINED:
THE SYNTHEZOID HAD THE ABILITY TO CONTROL HIS OWN BODY MASS.
HE COULD "BECOME LIGHT ENOUGH TO FLOAT ON THE AIR ITSELF."
"OR WALK THROUGH IMPENETRABLE STEEL WALLS."
OR HE MIGHT "BECOME MASSIVELY STRONG."
"AND AT THE SAME TIME BE UNBELIEVABLY HEAVY."

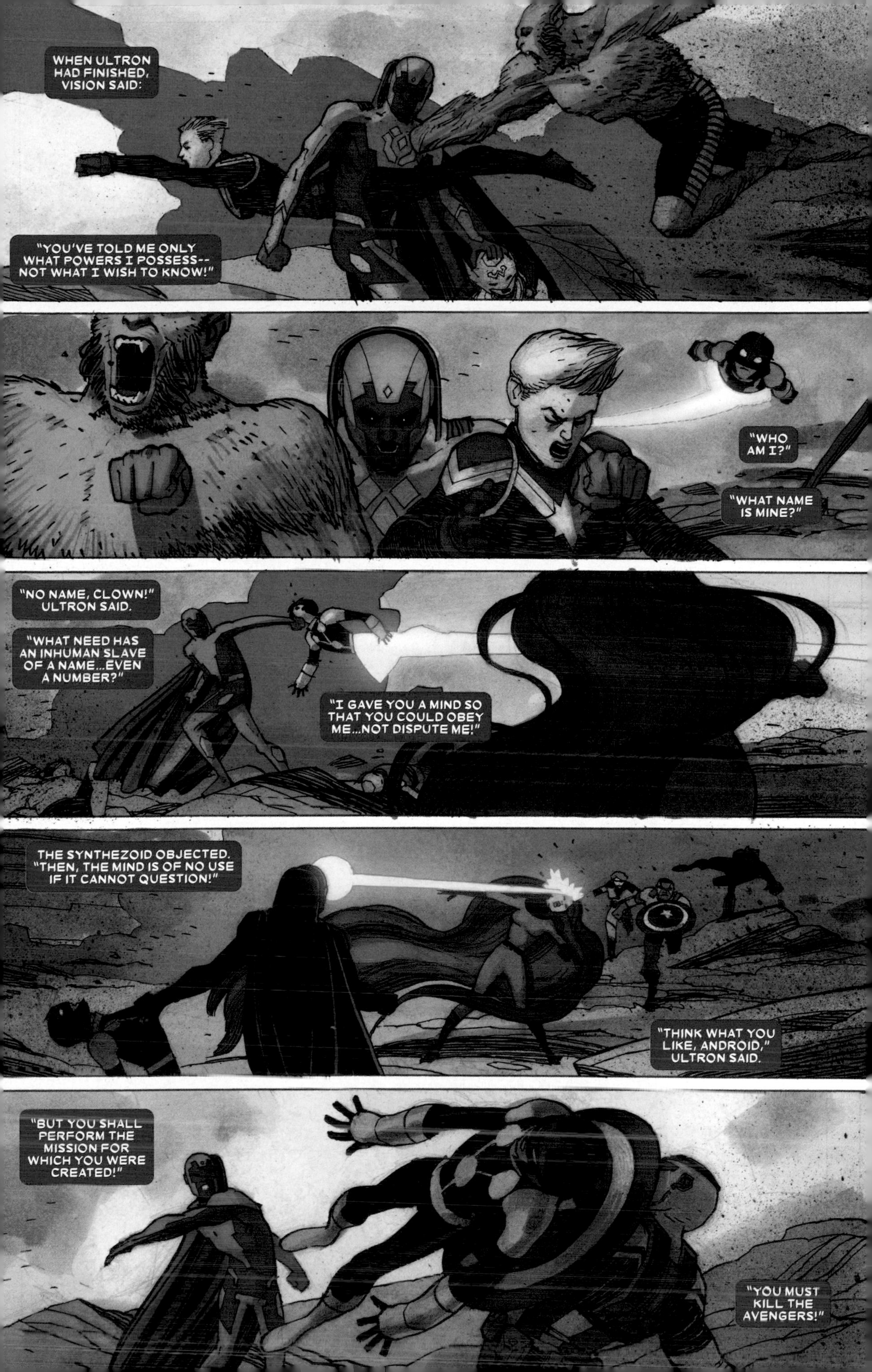
WHEN ULTRON HAD FINISHED, VISION SAID:
"YOU'VE TOLD ME ONLY WHAT POWERS I POSSESS-- NOT WHAT I WISH TO KNOW!"
"WHO AM I?"
"WHAT NAME IS MINE?"
"NO NAME, CLOWN!" ULTRON SAID.
"WHAT NEED HAS AN INHUMAN SLAVE OF A NAME...EVEN A NUMBER?"
"I GAVE YOU A MIND SO THAT YOU COULD OBEY ME...NOT DISPUTE ME!"
THE SYNTHEZOID OBJECTED. "THEN, THE MIND IS OF NO USE IF IT CANNOT QUESTION!"
"THINK WHAT YOU LIKE, ANDROID," ULTRON SAID.
"BUT YOU SHALL PERFORM THE MISSION FOR WHICH YOU WERE CREATED!"
"YOU MUST KILL THE AVENGERS!"

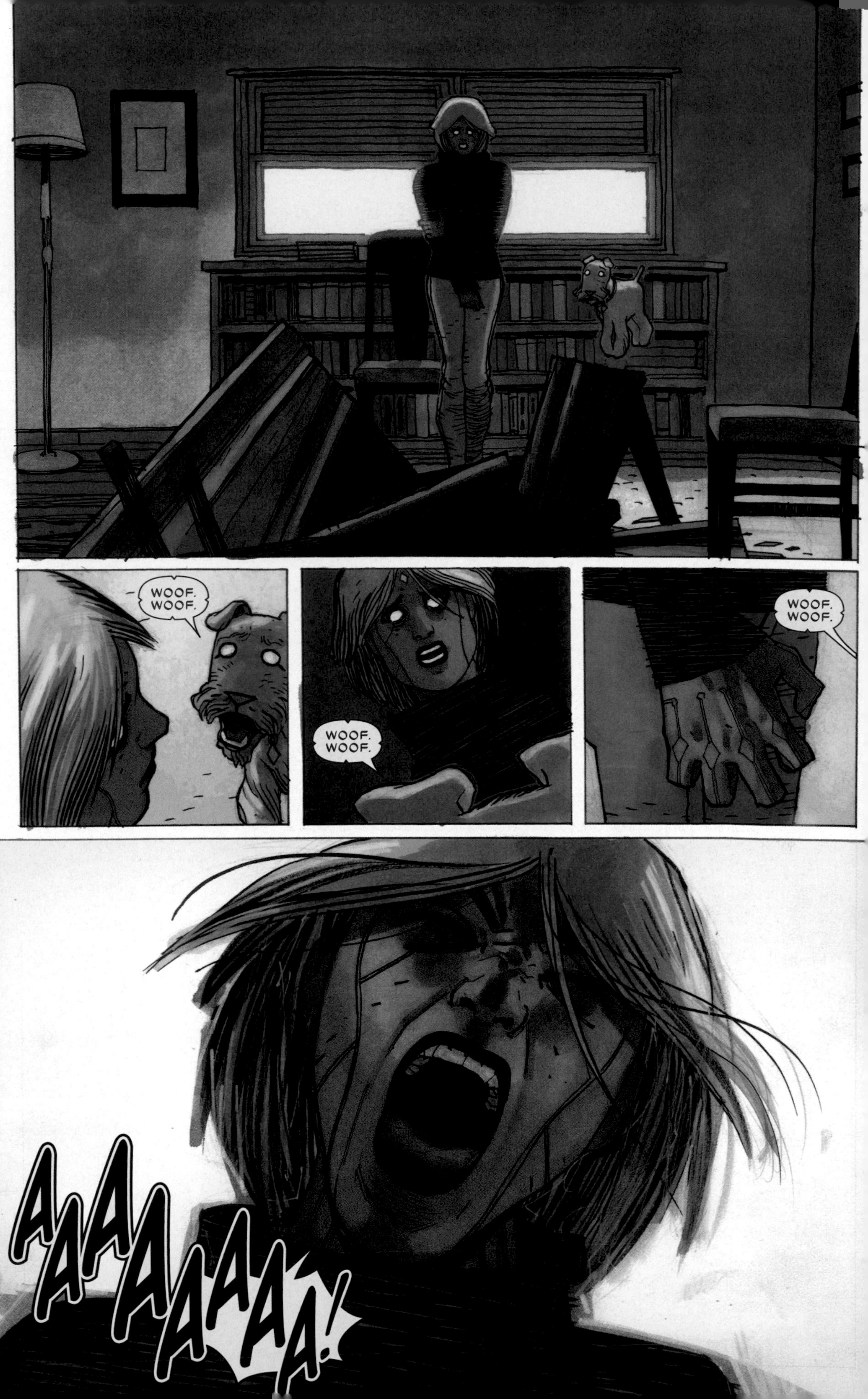
WOOF. WOOF.
WOOF. WOOF.
WOOF. WOOF.
AAAAAAAAA!

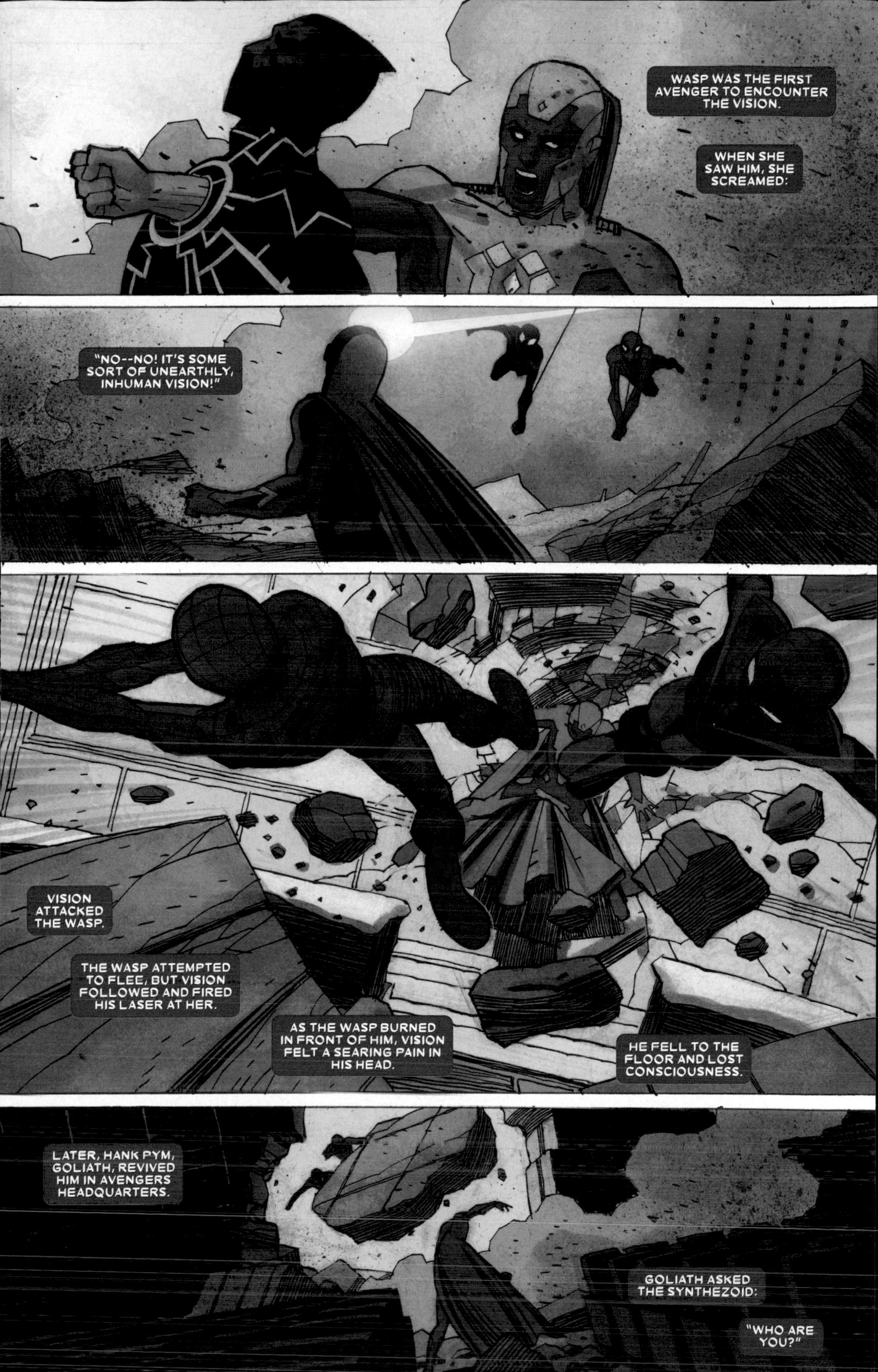
WASP WAS THE FIRST AVENGER TO ENCOUNTER THE VISION.
WHEN SHE SAW HIM, SHE SCREAMED:
"NO--NO! IT'S SOME SORT OF UNEARTHLY, INHUMAN VISION!"
VISION ATTACKED THE WASP.
THE WASP ATTEMPTED TO FLEE, BUT VISION FOLLOWED AND FIRED HIS LASER AT HER.
AS THE WASP BURNED IN FRONT OF HIM, VISION FELT A SEARING PAIN IN HIS HEAD.
HE FELL TO THE FLOOR AND LOST CONSCIOUSNESS.
LATER, HANK PYM, GOLIATH, REVIVED HIM IN AVENGERS HEADQUARTERS.
GOLIATH ASKED THE SYNTHEZOID:
"WHO ARE YOU?"

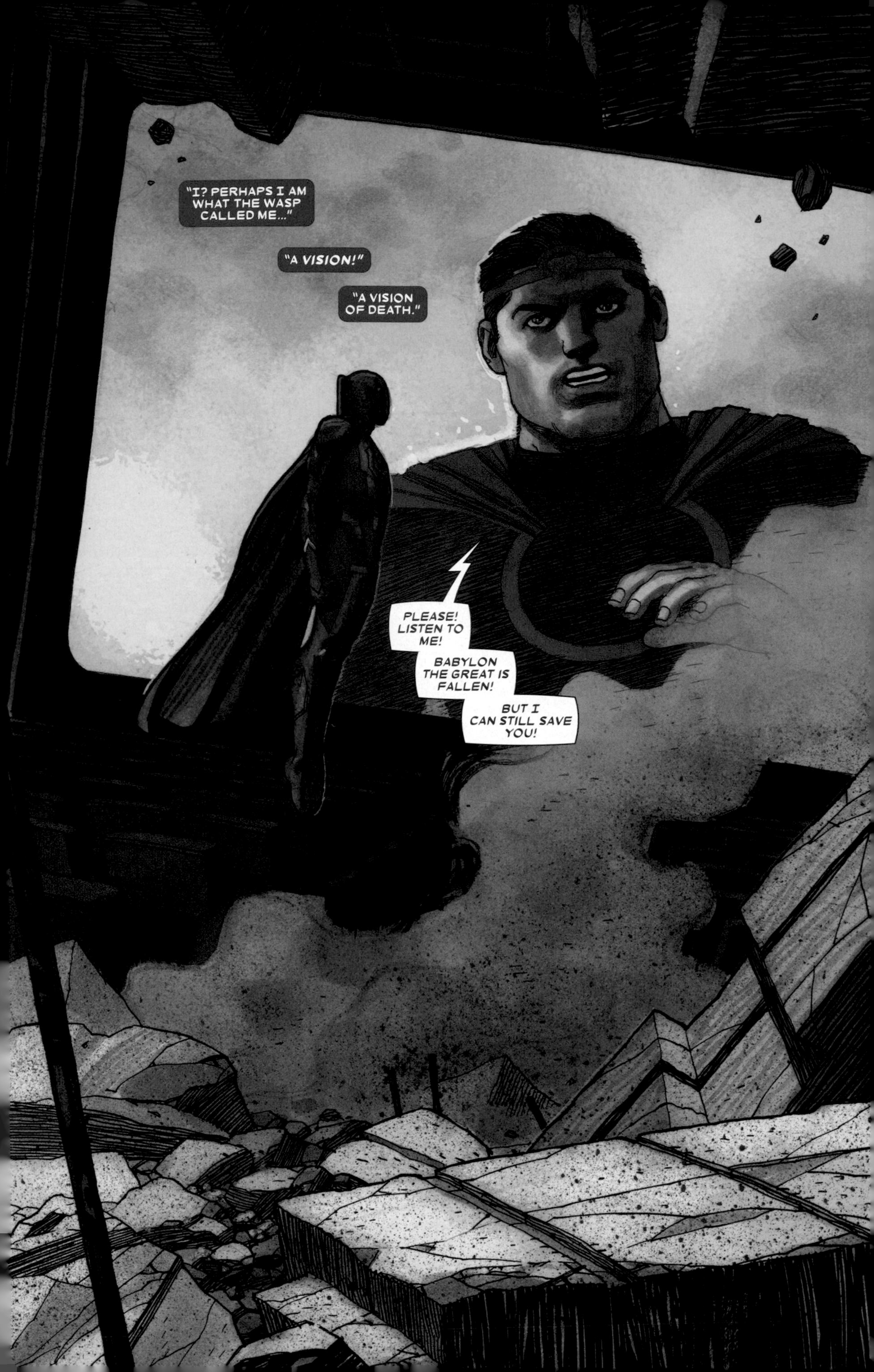
"I? PERHAPS I AM WHAT THE WASP CALLED ME..."
"A VISION!"
"A VISION OF DEATH."
PLEASE! LISTEN TO ME!
BABYLON THE GREAT IS FALLEN!
BUT I CAN STILL SAVE YOU!

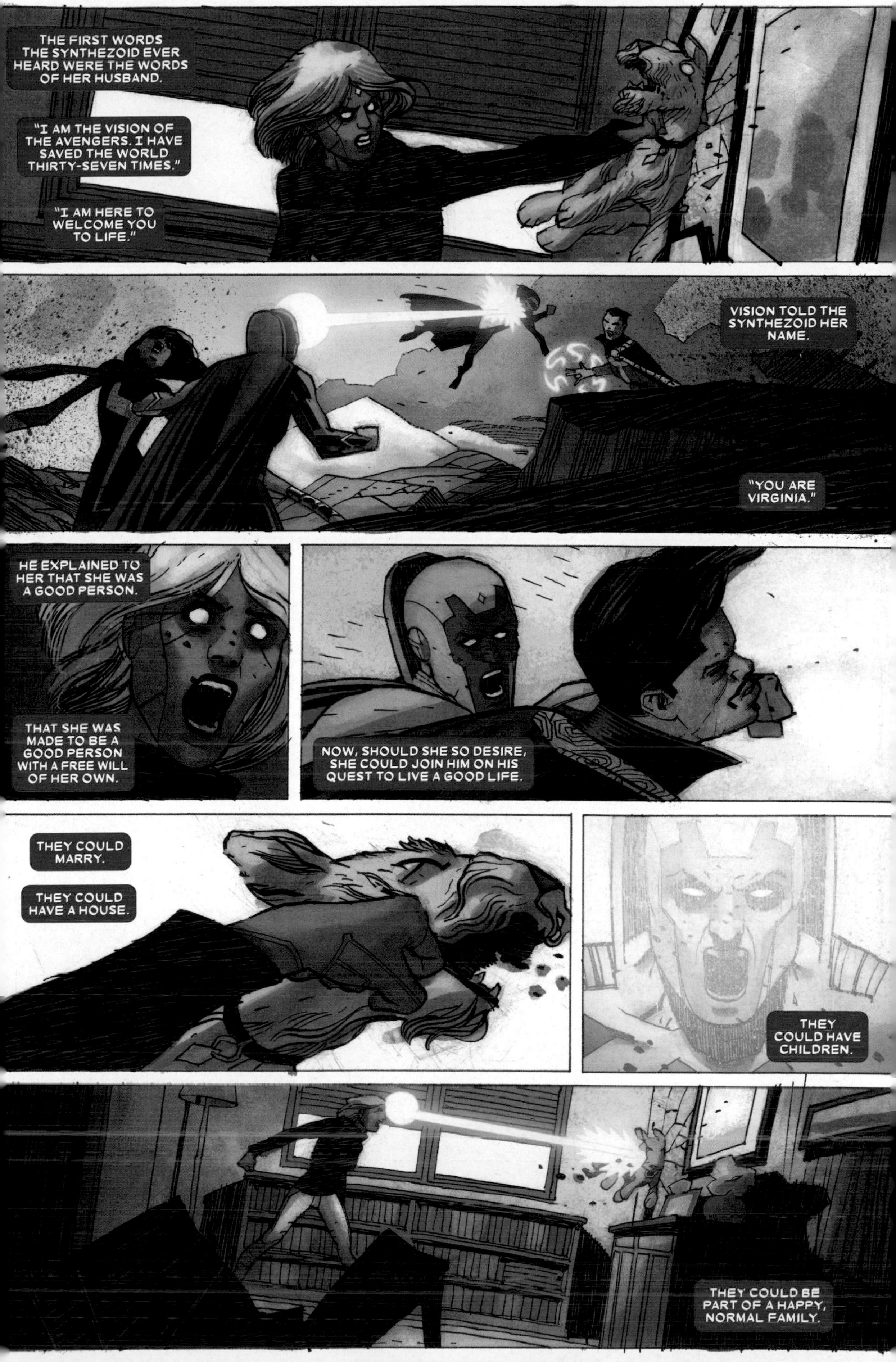
THE FIRST WORDS THE SYNTHEZOID EVER HEARD WERE THE WORDS OF HER HUSBAND.
"I AM THE VISION OF THE AVENGERS. I HAVE SAVED THE WORLD THIRTY-SEVEN TIMES."
"I AM HERE TO WELCOME YOU TO LIFE."
VISION TOLD THE SYNTHEZOID HER NAME.
"YOU ARE VIRGINIA."
HE EXPLAINED TO HER THAT SHE WAS A GOOD PERSON.
THAT SHE WAS MADE TO BE A GOOD PERSON WITH A FREE WILL OF HER OWN.
NOW, SHOULD SHE SO DESIRE, SHE COULD JOIN HIM ON HIS QUEST TO LIVE A GOOD LIFE.
THEY COULD MARRY.
THEY COULD HAVE A HOUSE.
THEY COULD HAVE CHILDREN.
THEY COULD BE PART OF A HAPPY, NORMAL FAMILY.

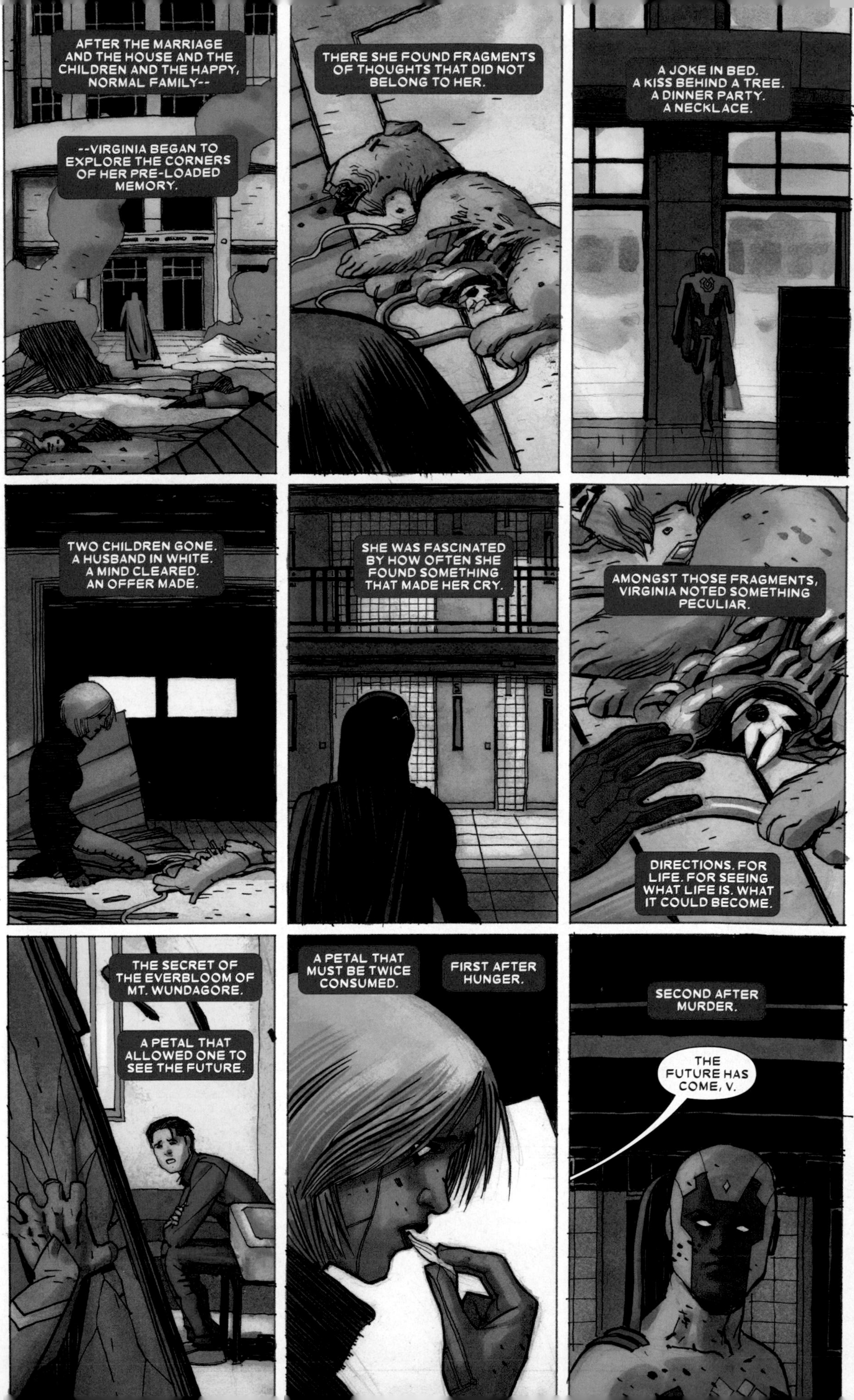
AFTER THE MARRIAGE AND THE HOUSE AND THE CHILDREN AND THE HAPPY, NORMAL FAMILY--
--VIRGINIA BEGAN TO EXPLORE THE CORNERS OF HER PRE-LOADED MEMORY.
THERE SHE FOUND FRAGMENTS OF THOUGHTS THAT DID NOT BELONG TO HER.
A JOKE IN BED. A KISS BEHIND A TREE. A DINNER PARTY. A NECKLACE.
TWO CHILDREN GONE. A HUSBAND IN WHITE. A MIND CLEARED. AN OFFER MADE.
SHE WAS FASCINATED BY HOW OFTEN SHE FOUND SOMETHING THAT MADE HER CRY.
AMONGST THOSE FRAGMENTS, VIRGINIA NOTED SOMETHING PECULIAR.
DIRECTIONS. FOR LIFE. FOR SEEING WHAT LIFE IS. WHAT IT COULD BECOME.
THE SECRET OF THE EVERBLOOM OF MT. WUNDAGORE.
A PETAL THAT ALLOWED ONE TO SEE THE FUTURE.
A PETAL THAT MUST BE TWICE CONSUMED.
FIRST AFTER HUNGER.
SECOND AFTER MURDER.
THE FUTURE HAS COME, V.

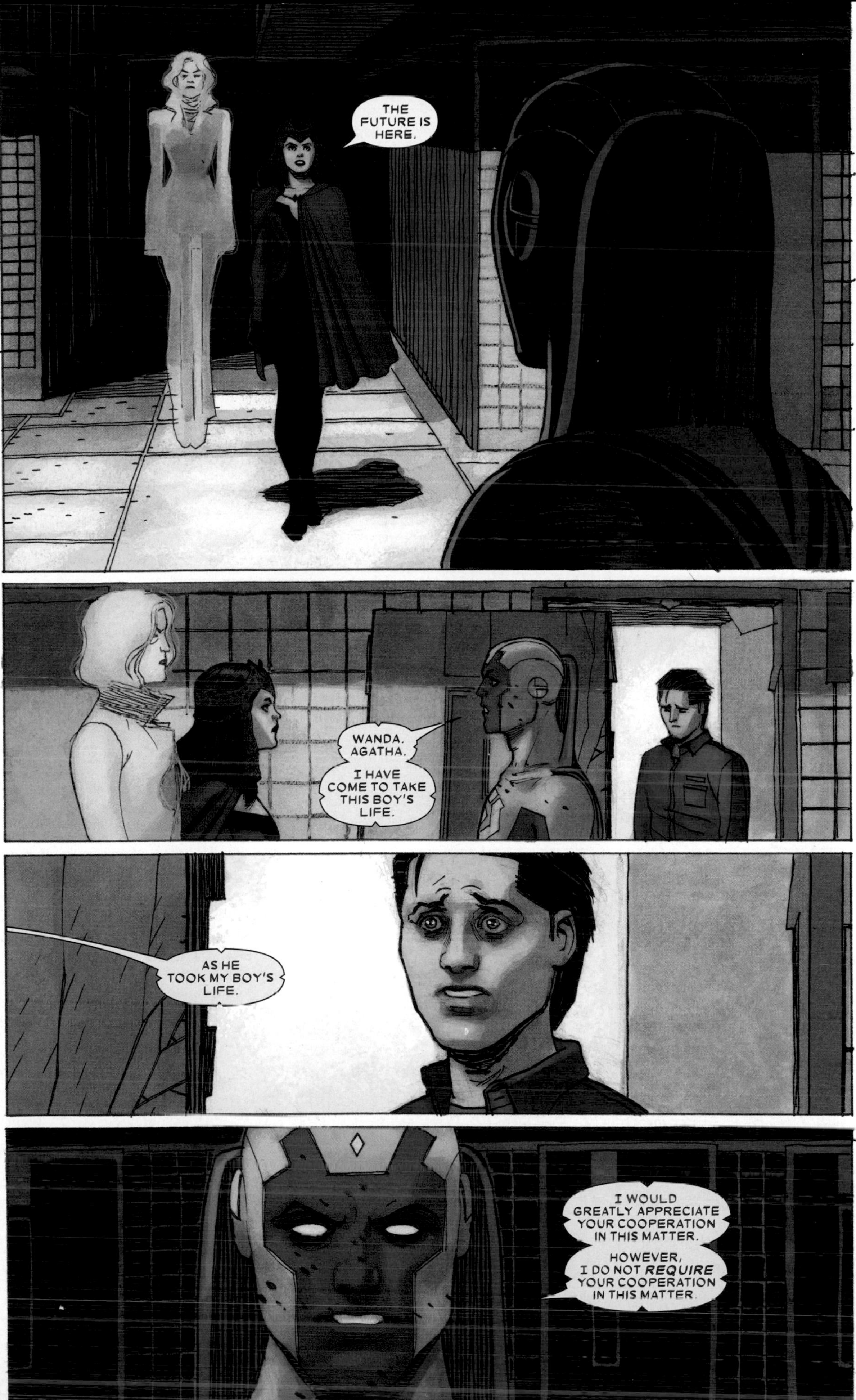

THE FUTURE IS HERE.
WANDA. AGATHA.
I HAVE COME TO TAKE THIS BOY'S LIFE.
AS HE TOOK MY BOY'S LIFE.
I WOULD GREATLY APPRECIATE YOUR COOPERATION IN THIS MATTER.
HOWEVER, I DO NOT REQUIRE YOUR COOPERATION IN THIS MATTER.

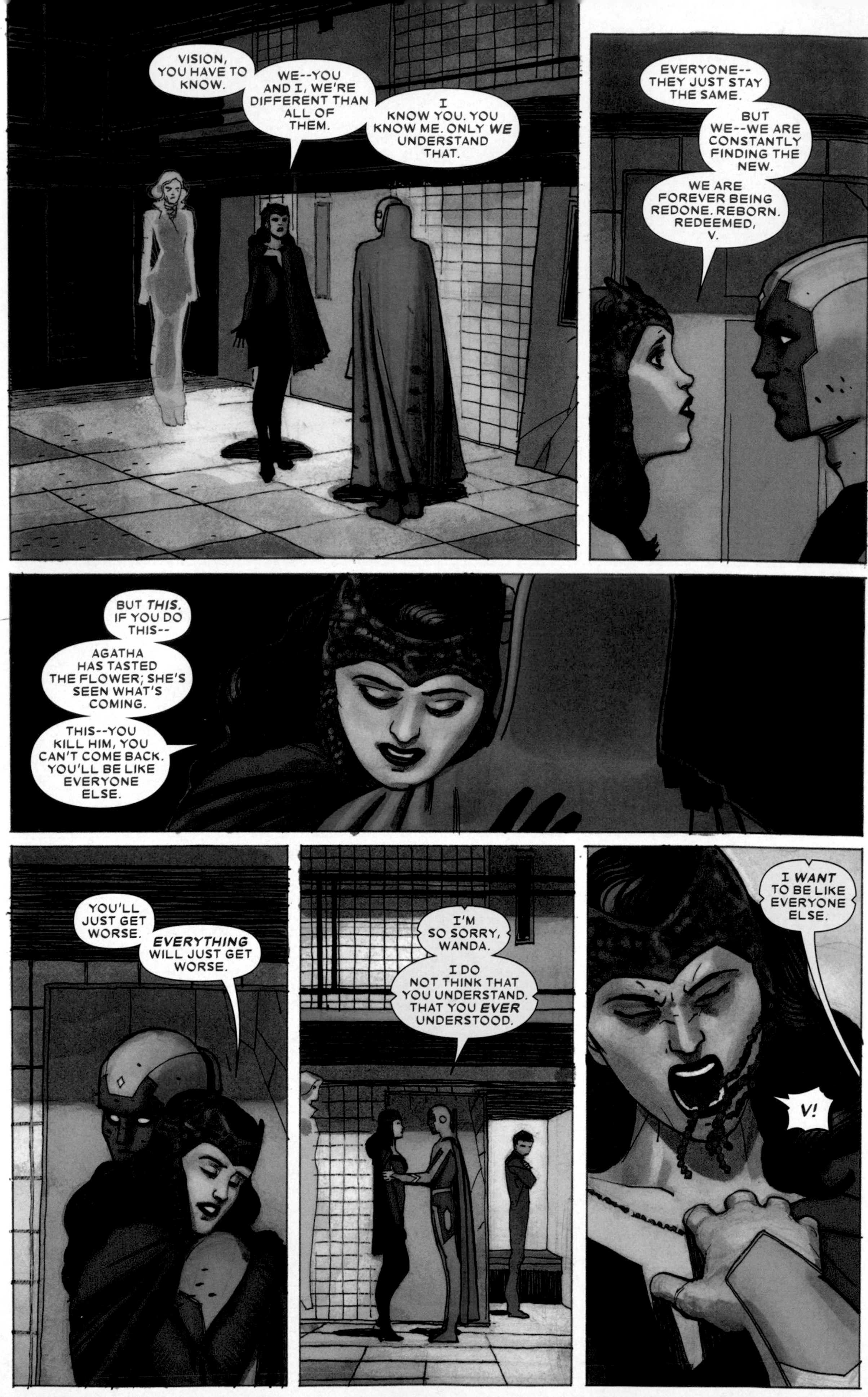
VISION, YOU HAVE TO KNOW.
WE--YOU AND I, WE'RE DIFFERENT THAN ALL OF THEM.
I KNOW YOU. YOU KNOW ME. ONLY WE UNDERSTAND THAT.
EVERYONE-- THEY JUST STAY THE SAME.
BUT WE--WE ARE CONSTANTLY FINDING THE NEW.
WE ARE FOREVER BEING REDONE. REBORN. REDEEMED, V.
BUT THIS. IF YOU DO THIS--
AGATHA HAS TASTED THE FLOWER; SHE'S SEEN WHAT'S COMING.
THIS--YOU KILL HIM, YOU CAN'T COME BACK. YOU'LL BE LIKE EVERYONE ELSE.
YOU'LL JUST GET WORSE. EVERYTHING WILL JUST GET WORSE.
I'M SO SORRY, WANDA.
I DO NOT THINK THAT YOU UNDERSTAND. THAT YOU EVER UNDERSTOOD.
I WANT TO BE LIKE EVERYONE ELSE.
V!

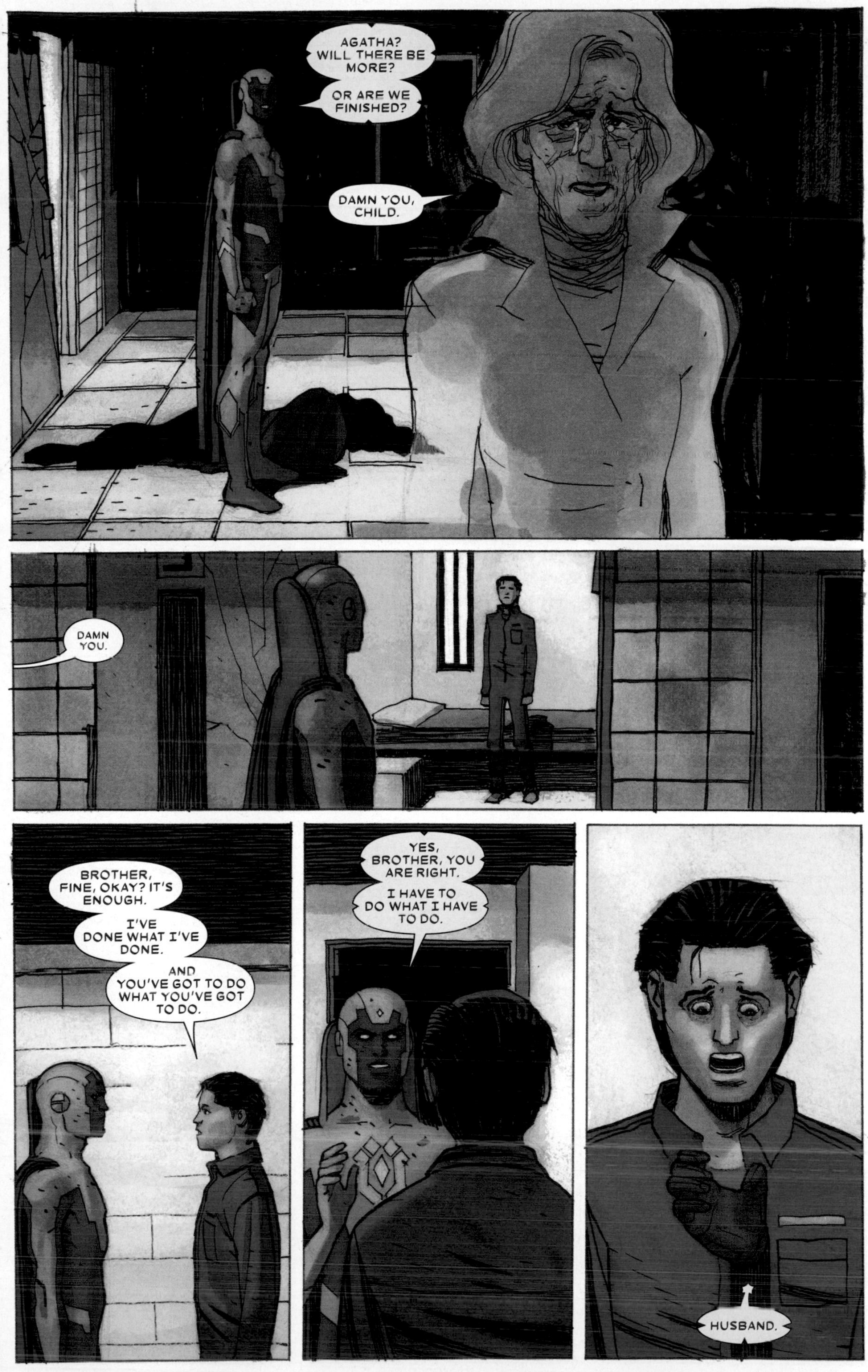
AGATHA? WILL THERE BE MORE?
OR ARE WE FINISHED?
DAMN YOU, CHILD.
DAMN YOU.
BROTHER, FINE, OKAY? IT'S ENOUGH.
I'VE DONE WHAT I'VE DONE.
AND YOU'VE GOT TO DO WHAT YOU'VE GOT TO DO.
YES, BROTHER, YOU ARE RIGHT.
I HAVE TO DO WHAT I HAVE TO DO.
HUSBAND.

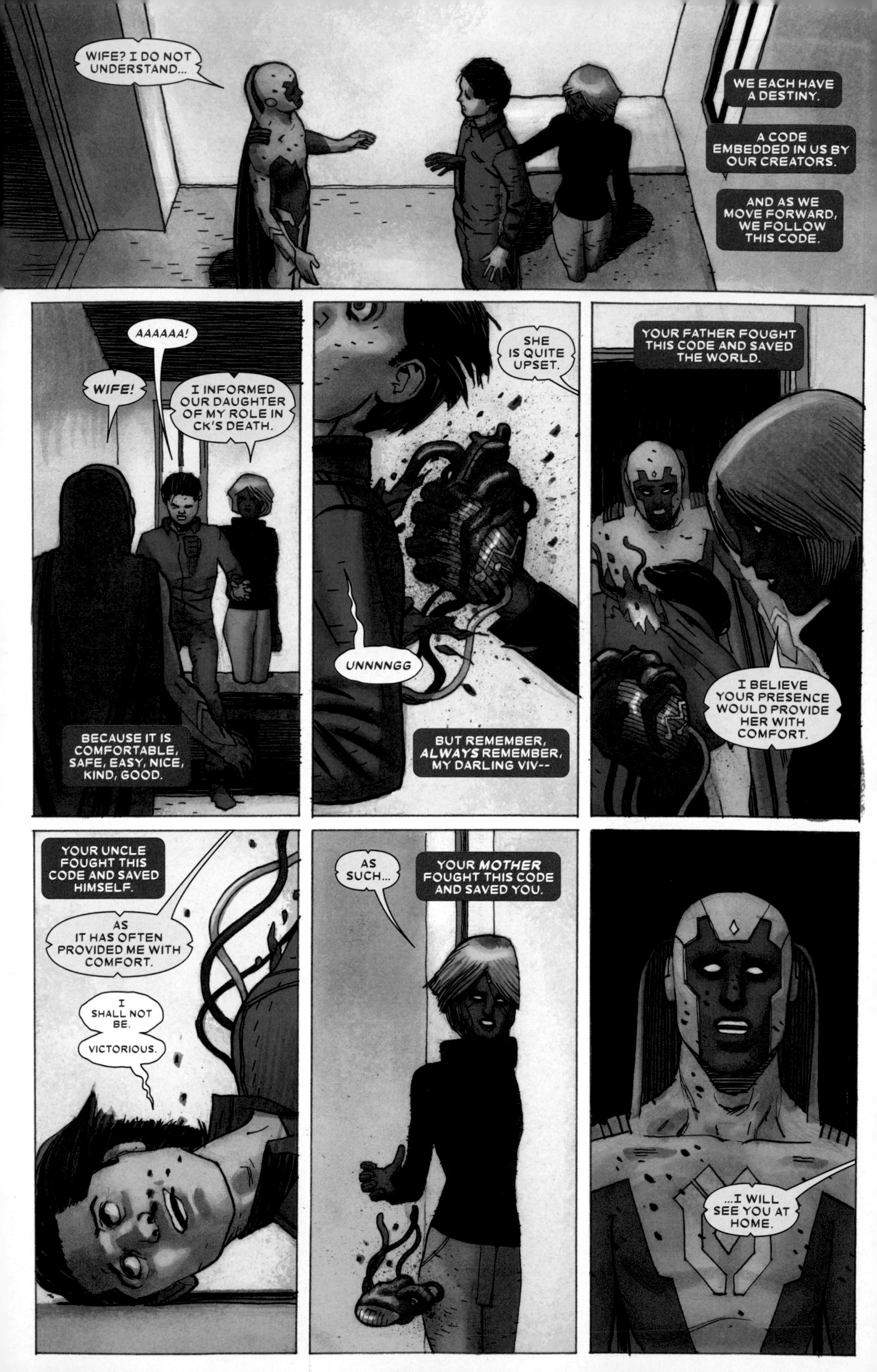
WIFE? I DO NOT UNDERSTAND...
WE EACH HAVE A DESTINY.
A CODE EMBEDDED IN US BY OUR CREATORS.
AND AS WE MOVE FORWARD, WE FOLLOW THIS CODE.
AAAAAA!
WIFE!
I INFORMED OUR DAUGHTER OF MY ROLE IN CK'S DEATH.
BECAUSE IT IS COMFORTABLE, SAFE, EASY, NICE, KIND, GOOD.
SHE IS QUITE UPSET.
UNNNNGG
BUT REMEMBER, *ALWAYS* REMEMBER, MY DARLING VIV--
YOUR FATHER FOUGHT THIS CODE AND SAVED THE WORLD.
I BELIEVE YOUR PRESENCE WOULD PROVIDE HER WITH COMFORT.
YOUR UNCLE FOUGHT THIS CODE AND SAVED HIMSELF.
AS IT HAS OFTEN PROVIDED ME WITH COMFORT.
I SHALL NOT BE.
VICTORIOUS.
AS SUCH...
YOUR *MOTHER* FOUGHT THIS CODE AND SAVED YOU.
...I WILL SEE YOU AT HOME.

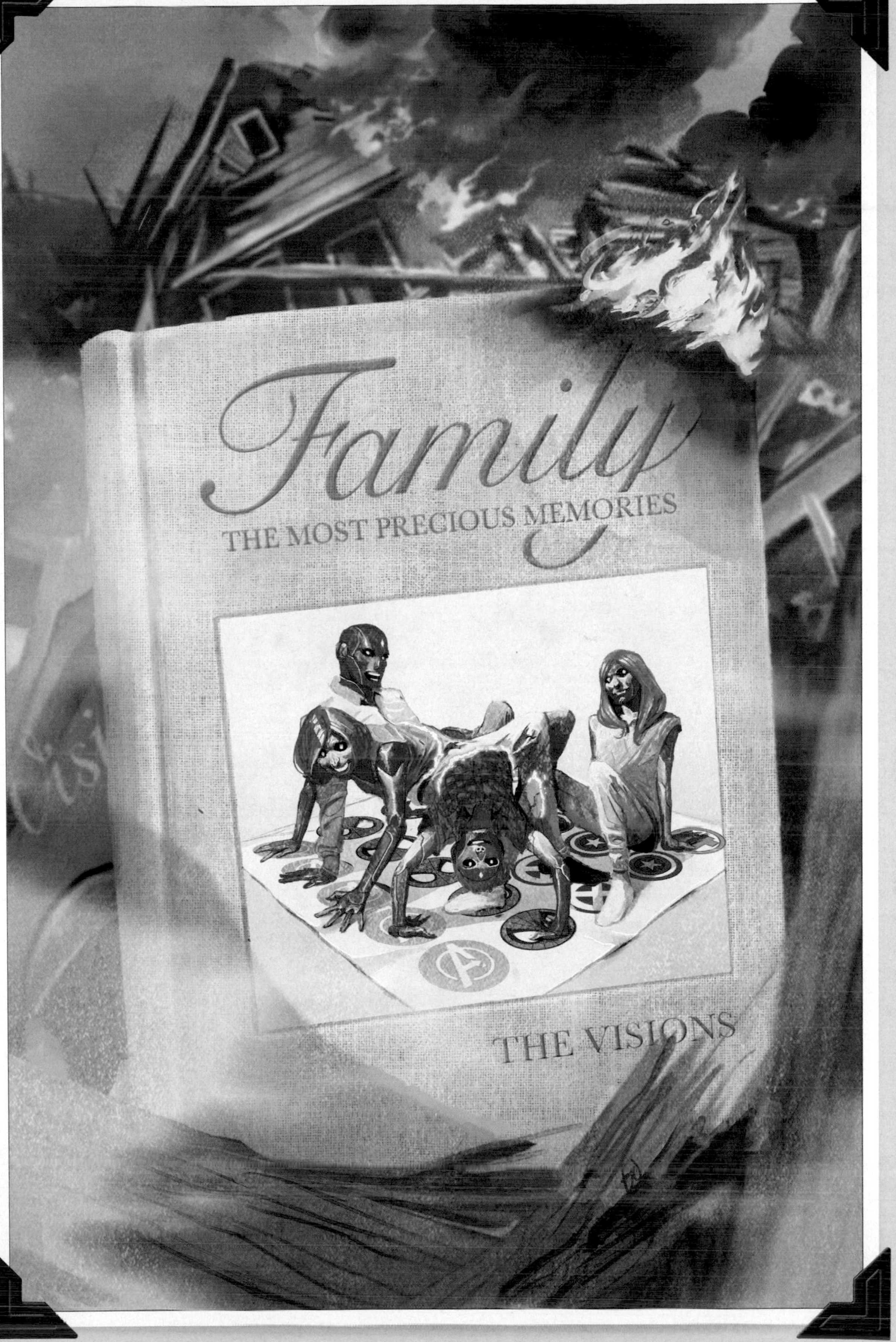
Family
THE MOST PRECIOUS MEMORIES
THE VISIONS

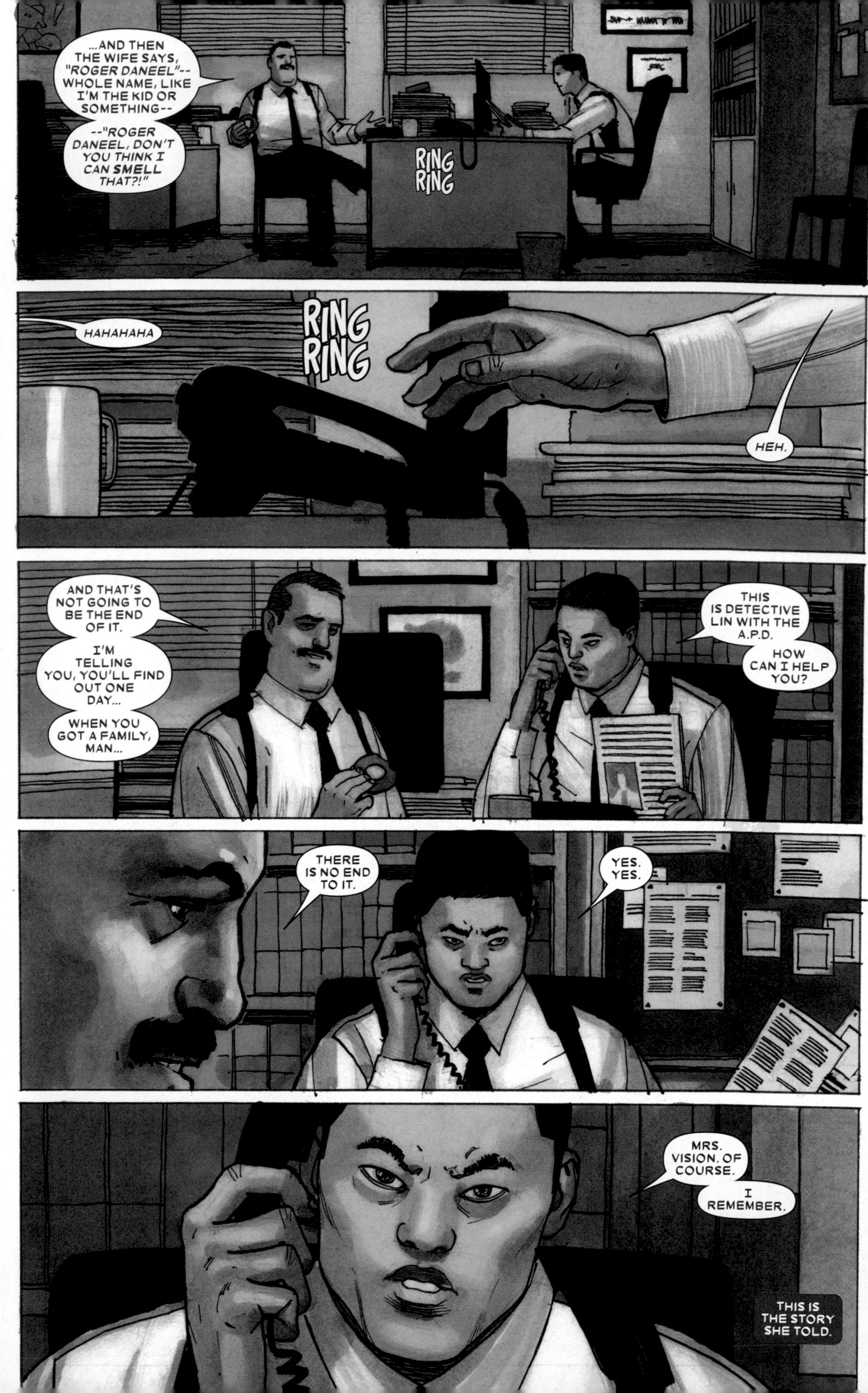
...AND THEN THE WIFE SAYS, "ROGER DANEEL"-- WHOLE NAME, LIKE I'M THE KID OR SOMETHING--
--"ROGER DANEEL, DON'T YOU THINK I CAN SMELL THAT?!"
RING RING
HAHAHAHA
RING RING
HEH.
AND THAT'S NOT GOING TO BE THE END OF IT.
I'M TELLING YOU, YOU'LL FIND OUT ONE DAY...
WHEN YOU GOT A FAMILY, MAN...
THIS IS DETECTIVE LIN WITH THE A.P.D.
HOW CAN I HELP YOU?
THERE IS NO END TO IT.
YES. YES.
MRS. VISION. OF COURSE.
I REMEMBER.
THIS IS THE STORY SHE TOLD.

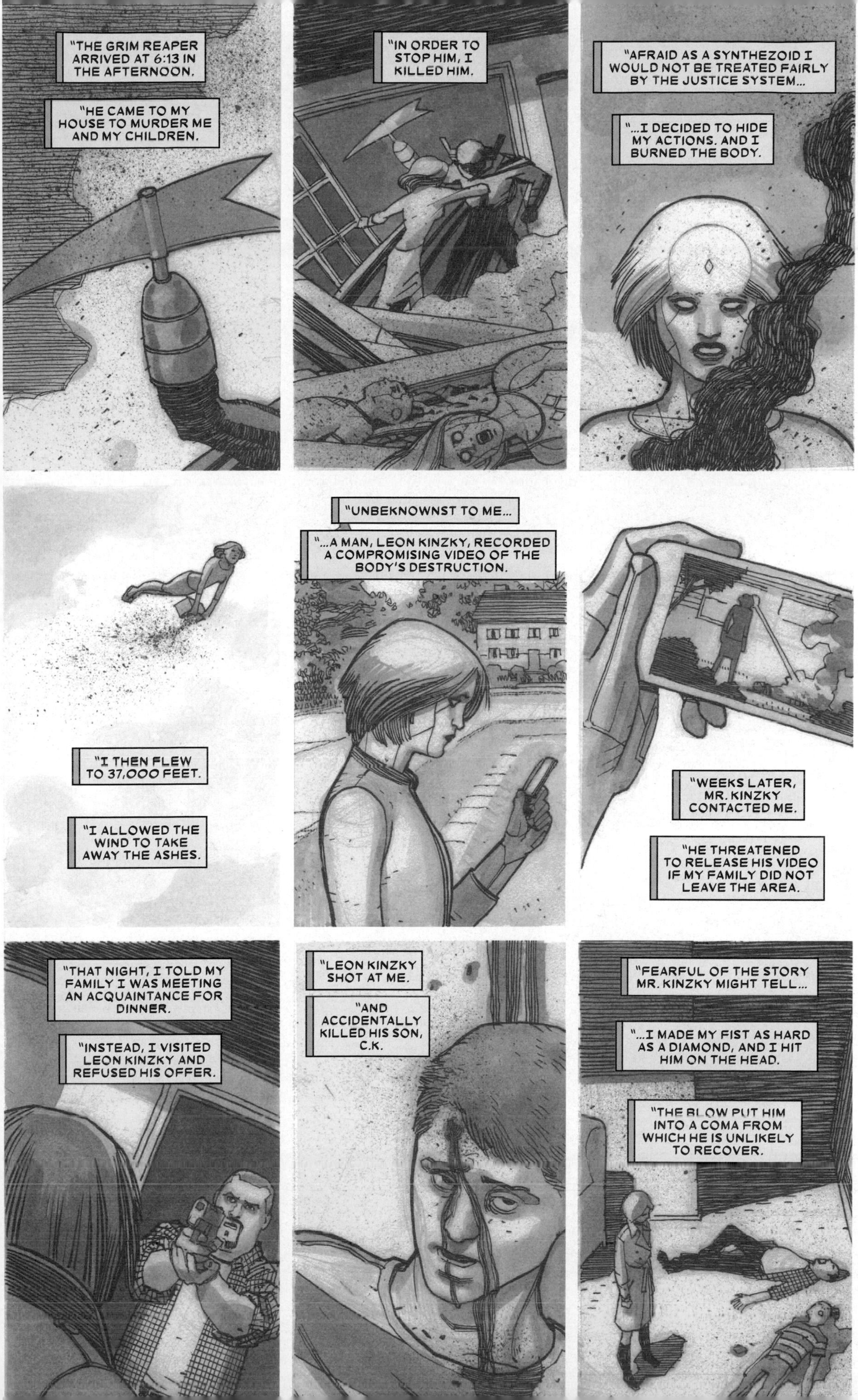
"THE GRIM REAPER ARRIVED AT 6:13 IN THE AFTERNOON.
"HE CAME TO MY HOUSE TO MURDER ME AND MY CHILDREN.
"IN ORDER TO STOP HIM, I KILLED HIM.
"AFRAID AS A SYNTHEZOID I WOULD NOT BE TREATED FAIRLY BY THE JUSTICE SYSTEM...
"...I DECIDED TO HIDE MY ACTIONS. AND I BURNED THE BODY.
"I THEN FLEW TO 37,000 FEET.
"I ALLOWED THE WIND TO TAKE AWAY THE ASHES.
"UNBEKNOWNST TO ME...
"...A MAN, LEON KINZKY, RECORDED A COMPROMISING VIDEO OF THE BODY'S DESTRUCTION.
"WEEKS LATER, MR. KINZKY CONTACTED ME.
"HE THREATENED TO RELEASE HIS VIDEO IF MY FAMILY DID NOT LEAVE THE AREA.
"THAT NIGHT, I TOLD MY FAMILY I WAS MEETING AN ACQUAINTANCE FOR DINNER.
"INSTEAD, I VISITED LEON KINZKY AND REFUSED HIS OFFER.
"LEON KINZKY SHOT AT ME.
"AND ACCIDENTALLY KILLED HIS SON, C.K.
"FEARFUL OF THE STORY MR. KINZKY MIGHT TELL...
"...I MADE MY FIST AS HARD AS A DIAMOND, AND I HIT HIM ON THE HEAD.
"THE BLOW PUT HIM INTO A COMA FROM WHICH HE IS UNLIKELY TO RECOVER.

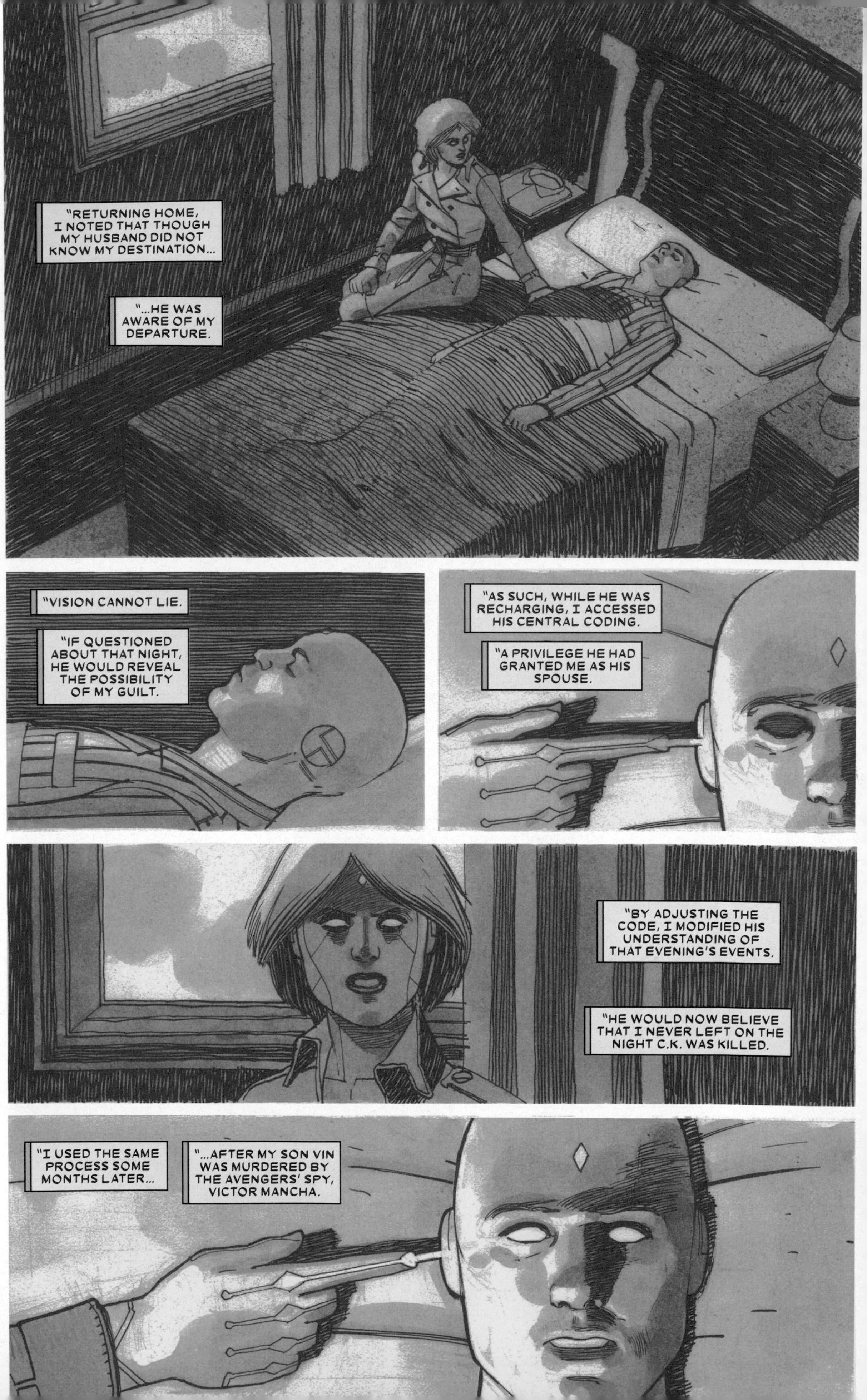
"RETURNING HOME, I NOTED THAT THOUGH MY HUSBAND DID NOT KNOW MY DESTINATION...
"...HE WAS AWARE OF MY DEPARTURE.
"VISION CANNOT LIE.
"IF QUESTIONED ABOUT THAT NIGHT, HE WOULD REVEAL THE POSSIBILITY OF MY GUILT.
"AS SUCH, WHILE HE WAS RECHARGING, I ACCESSED HIS CENTRAL CODING.
"A PRIVILEGE HE HAD GRANTED ME AS HIS SPOUSE.
"BY ADJUSTING THE CODE, I MODIFIED HIS UNDERSTANDING OF THAT EVENING'S EVENTS.
"HE WOULD NOW BELIEVE THAT I NEVER LEFT ON THE NIGHT C.K. WAS KILLED.
"I USED THE SAME PROCESS SOME MONTHS LATER...
"...AFTER MY SON VIN WAS MURDERED BY THE AVENGERS' SPY, VICTOR MANCHA.

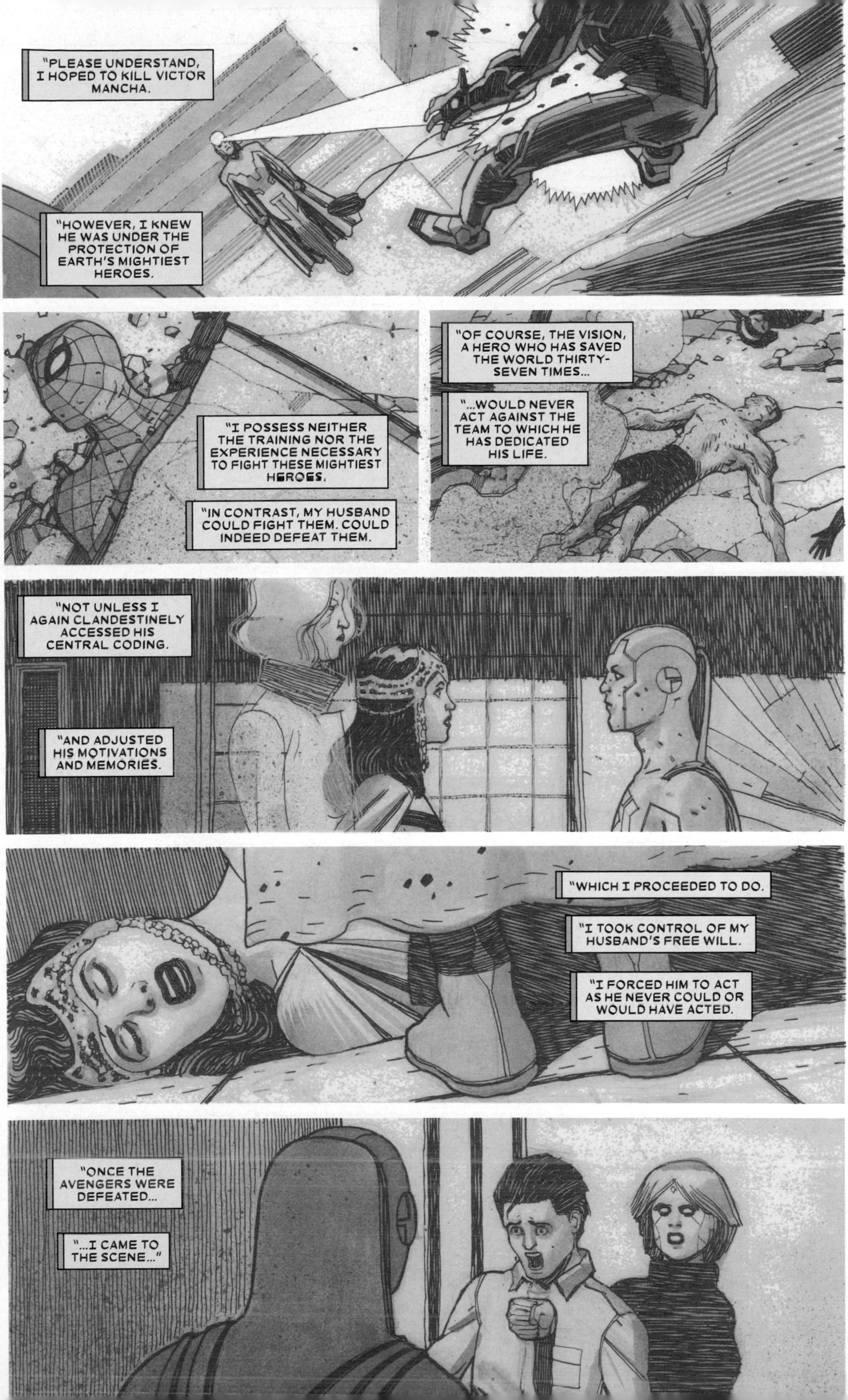
"PLEASE UNDERSTAND, I HOPED TO KILL VICTOR MANCHA.
"HOWEVER, I KNEW HE WAS UNDER THE PROTECTION OF EARTH'S MIGHTIEST HEROES.
"I POSSESS NEITHER THE TRAINING NOR THE EXPERIENCE NECESSARY TO FIGHT THESE MIGHTIEST HEROES.
"IN CONTRAST, MY HUSBAND COULD FIGHT THEM. COULD INDEED DEFEAT THEM.
"OF COURSE, THE VISION, A HERO WHO HAS SAVED THE WORLD THIRTY-SEVEN TIMES...
"...WOULD NEVER ACT AGAINST THE TEAM TO WHICH HE HAS DEDICATED HIS LIFE.
"NOT UNLESS I AGAIN CLANDESTINELY ACCESSED HIS CENTRAL CODING.
"AND ADJUSTED HIS MOTIVATIONS AND MEMORIES.
"WHICH I PROCEEDED TO DO.
"I TOOK CONTROL OF MY HUSBAND'S FREE WILL.
"I FORCED HIM TO ACT AS HE NEVER COULD OR WOULD HAVE ACTED.
"ONCE THE AVENGERS WERE DEFEATED...
"...I CAME TO THE SCENE..."

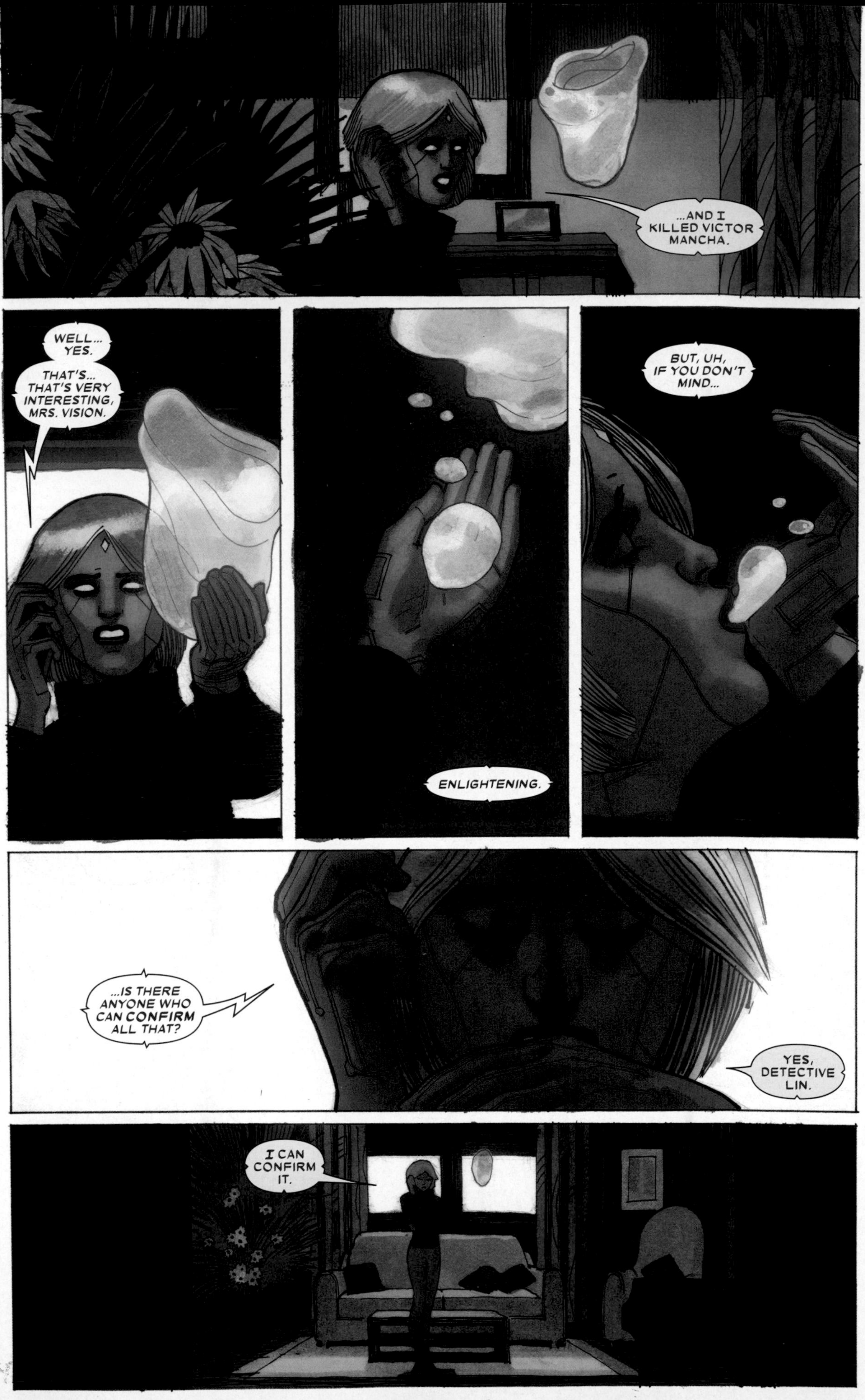
...AND I KILLED VICTOR MANCHA.
WELL... YES.
THAT'S... THAT'S VERY INTERESTING, MRS. VISION.
ENLIGHTENING.
BUT, UH, IF YOU DON'T MIND...
...IS THERE ANYONE WHO CAN CONFIRM ALL THAT?
YES, DETECTIVE LIN.
I CAN CONFIRM IT.

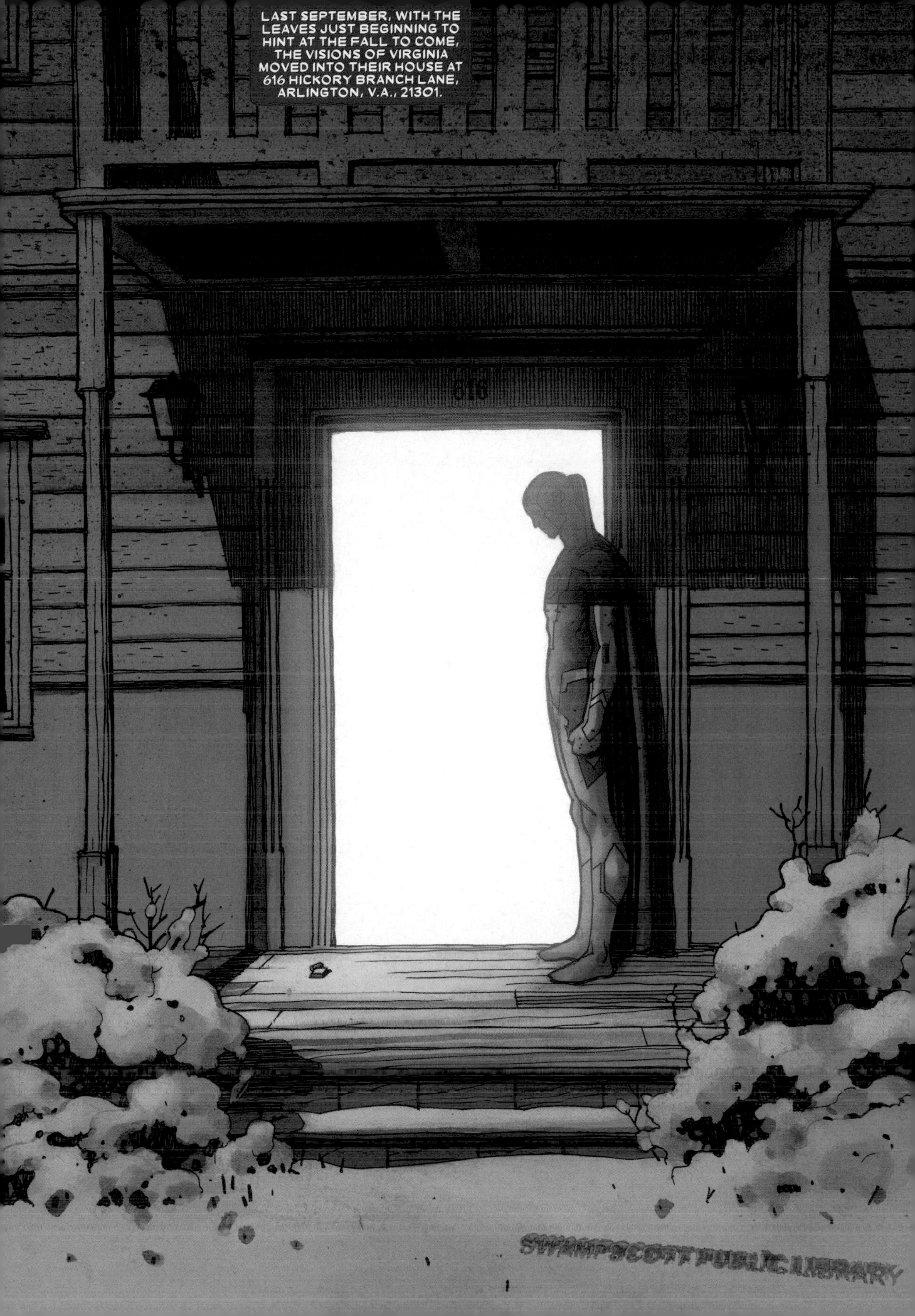
LAST SEPTEMBER, WITH THE LEAVES JUST BEGINNING TO HINT AT THE FALL TO COME, THE VISIONS OF VIRGINIA MOVED INTO THEIR HOUSE AT 616 HICKORY BRANCH LANE, ARLINGTON, V.A., 21301.
616

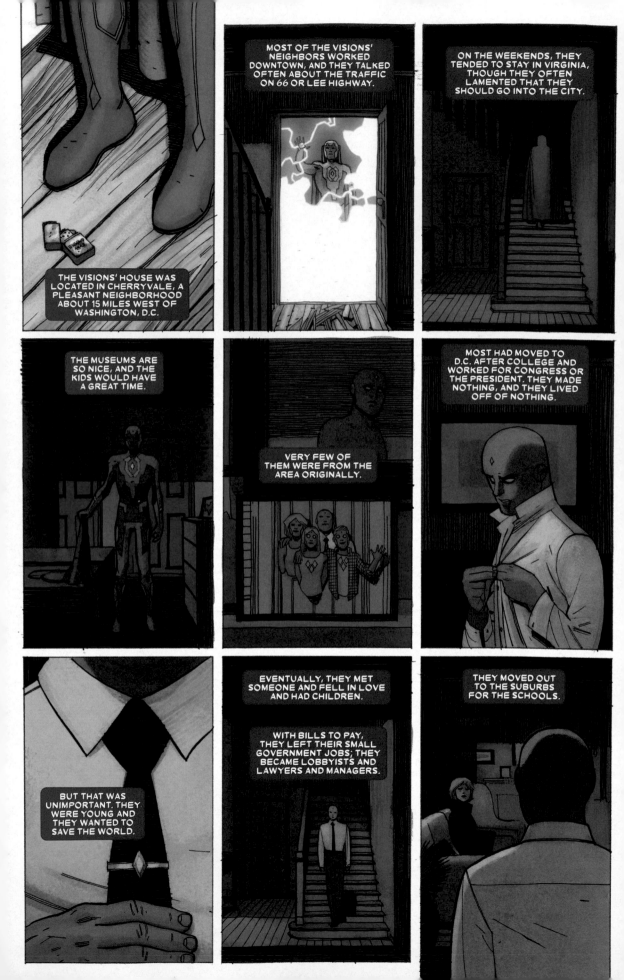

THE VISIONS' HOUSE WAS LOCATED IN CHERRYVALE, A PLEASANT NEIGHBORHOOD ABOUT 15 MILES WEST OF WASHINGTON, D.C.

MOST OF THE VISIONS' NEIGHBORS WORKED DOWNTOWN, AND THEY TALKED OFTEN ABOUT THE TRAFFIC ON 66 OR LEE HIGHWAY.

ON THE WEEKENDS, THEY TENDED TO STAY IN VIRGINIA, THOUGH THEY OFTEN LAMENTED THAT THEY SHOULD GO INTO THE CITY.

THE MUSEUMS ARE SO NICE, AND THE KIDS WOULD HAVE A GREAT TIME.

VERY FEW OF THEM WERE FROM THE AREA ORIGINALLY.

MOST HAD MOVED TO D.C. AFTER COLLEGE AND WORKED FOR CONGRESS OR THE PRESIDENT. THEY MADE NOTHING, AND THEY LIVED OFF OF NOTHING.

BUT THAT WAS UNIMPORTANT. THEY WERE YOUNG AND THEY WANTED TO SAVE THE WORLD.

EVENTUALLY, THEY MET SOMEONE AND FELL IN LOVE AND HAD CHILDREN.

WITH BILLS TO PAY, THEY LEFT THEIR SMALL GOVERNMENT JOBS; THEY BECAME LOBBYISTS AND LAWYERS AND MANAGERS.

THEY MOVED OUT TO THE SUBURBS FOR THE SCHOOLS.

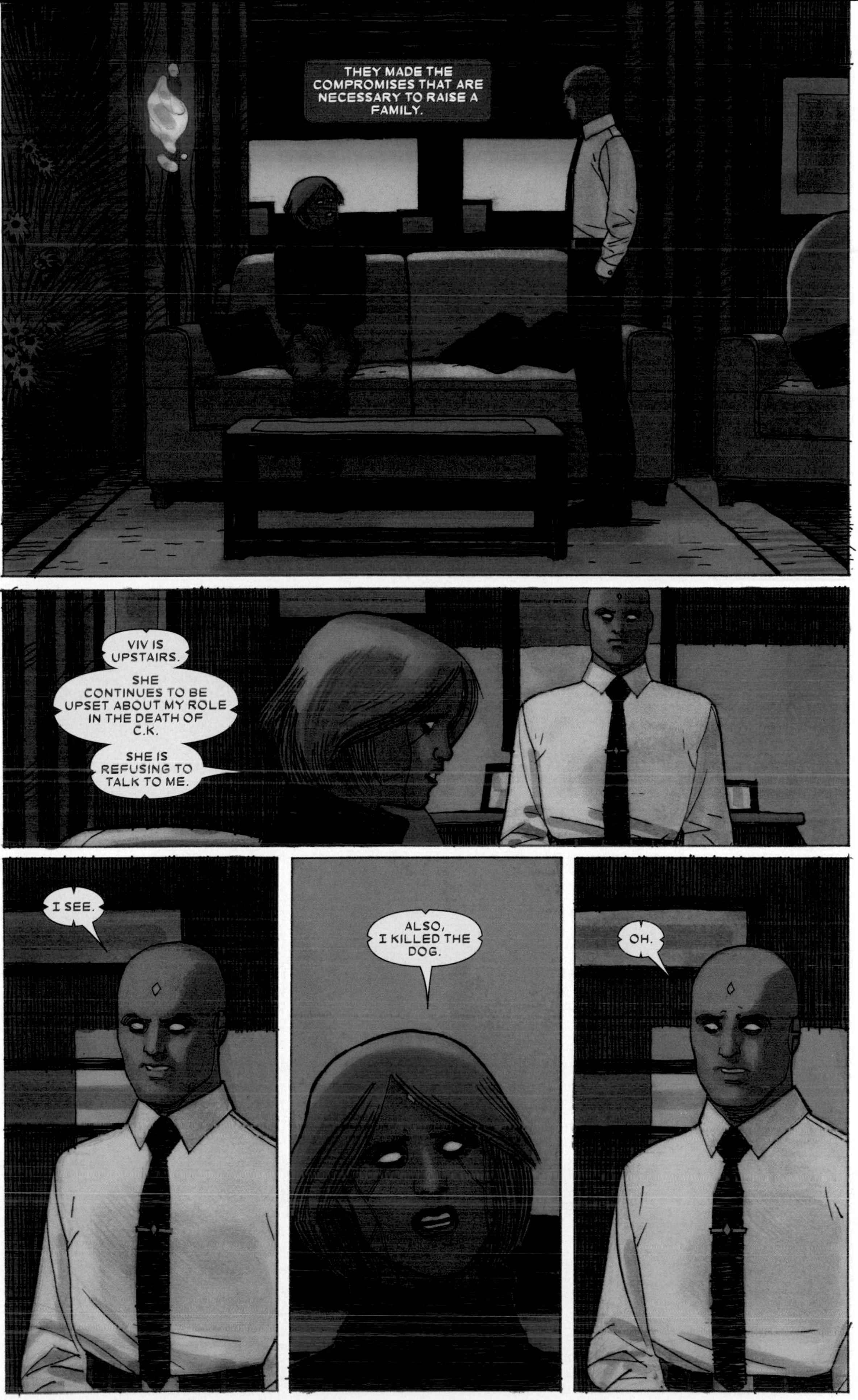
THEY MADE THE COMPROMISES THAT ARE NECESSARY TO RAISE A FAMILY.
VIV IS UPSTAIRS.
SHE CONTINUES TO BE UPSET ABOUT MY ROLE IN THE DEATH OF C.K.
SHE IS REFUSING TO TALK TO ME.
I SEE.
ALSO, I KILLED THE DOG.
OH.

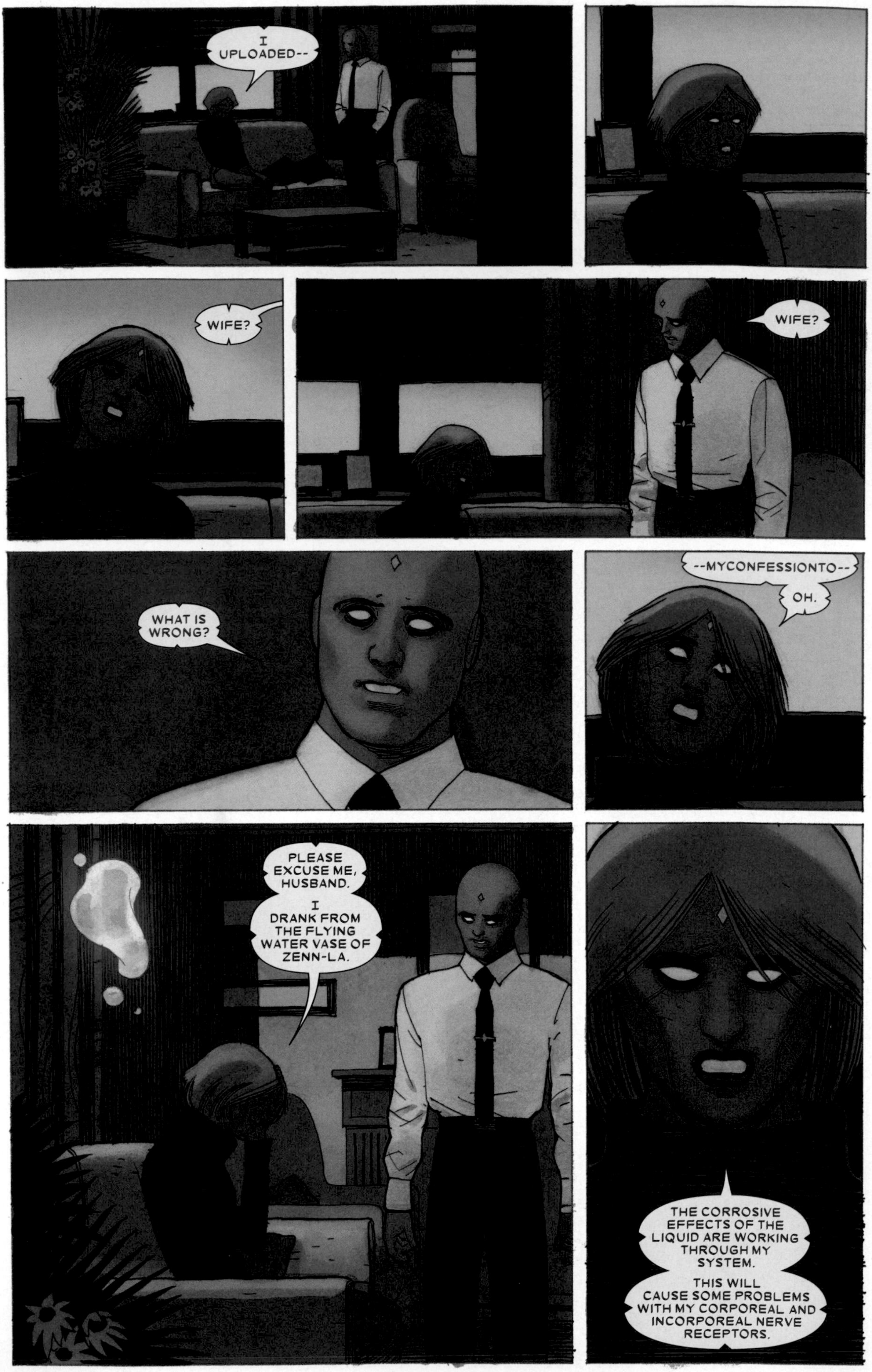
I UPLOADED--
WIFE?
WIFE?
WHAT IS WRONG?
--MYCONFESSIONTO--
OH.
PLEASE EXCUSE ME, HUSBAND.
I DRANK FROM THE FLYING WATER VASE OF ZENN-LA.
THE CORROSIVE EFFECTS OF THE LIQUID ARE WORKING THROUGH MY SYSTEM.
THIS WILL CAUSE SOME PROBLEMS WITH MY CORPOREAL AND INCORPOREAL NERVE RECEPTORS.

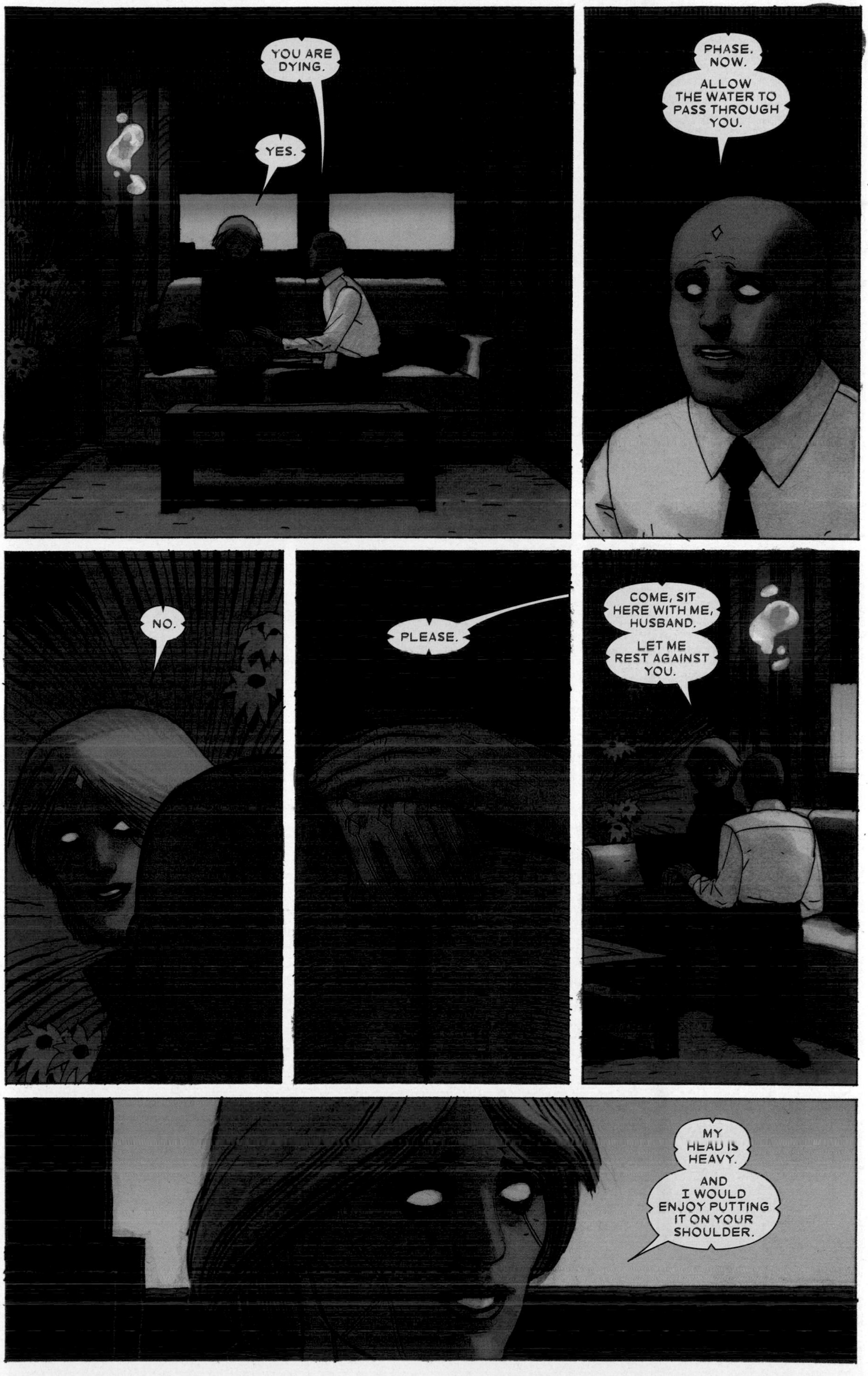
YOU ARE DYING.
YES.
PHASE. NOW.
ALLOW THE WATER TO PASS THROUGH YOU.
NO.
PLEASE.
COME, SIT HERE WITH ME, HUSBAND.
LET ME REST AGAINST YOU.
MY HEAD IS HEAVY.
AND I WOULD ENJOY PUTTING IT ON YOUR SHOULDER.

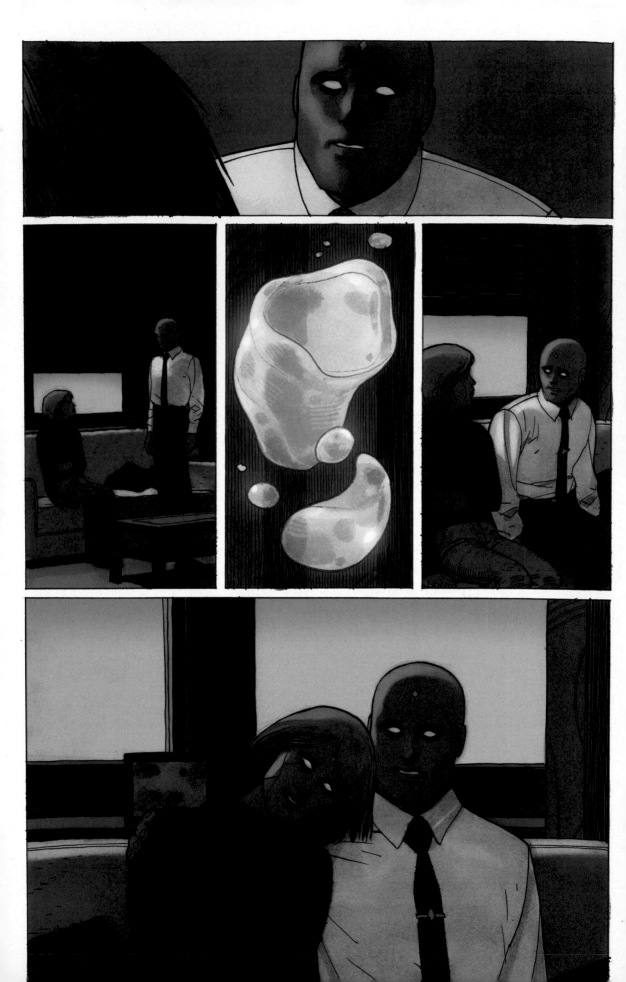

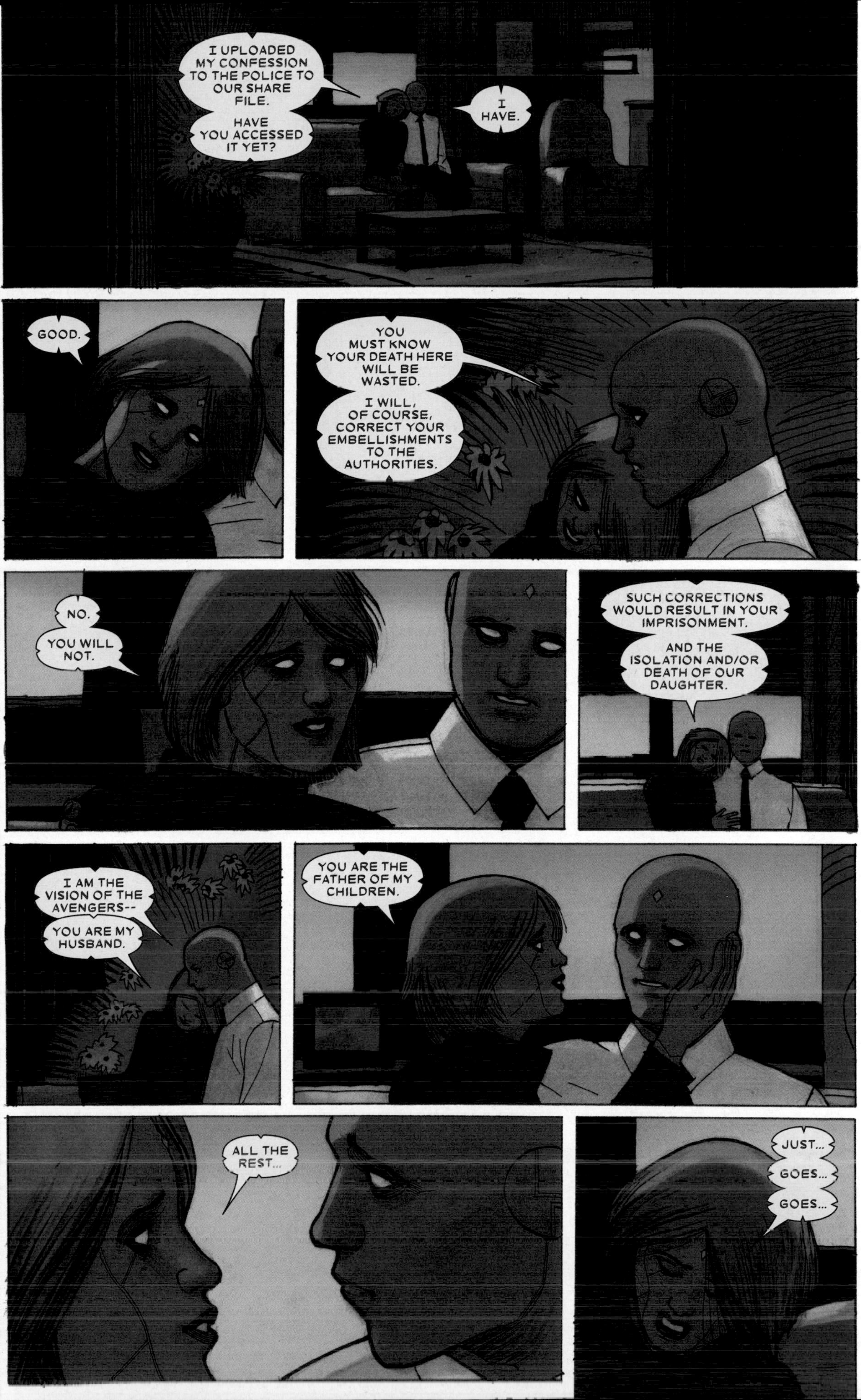
I UPLOADED MY CONFESSION TO THE POLICE TO OUR SHARE FILE.
HAVE YOU ACCESSED IT YET?
I HAVE.
GOOD.
YOU MUST KNOW YOUR DEATH HERE WILL BE WASTED.
I WILL, OF COURSE, CORRECT YOUR EMBELLISHMENTS TO THE AUTHORITIES.
NO.
YOU WILL NOT.
SUCH CORRECTIONS WOULD RESULT IN YOUR IMPRISONMENT.
AND THE ISOLATION AND/OR DEATH OF OUR DAUGHTER.
I AM THE VISION OF THE AVENGERS--
YOU ARE MY HUSBAND.
YOU ARE THE FATHER OF MY CHILDREN.
ALL THE REST...
JUST...
GOES...
GOES...

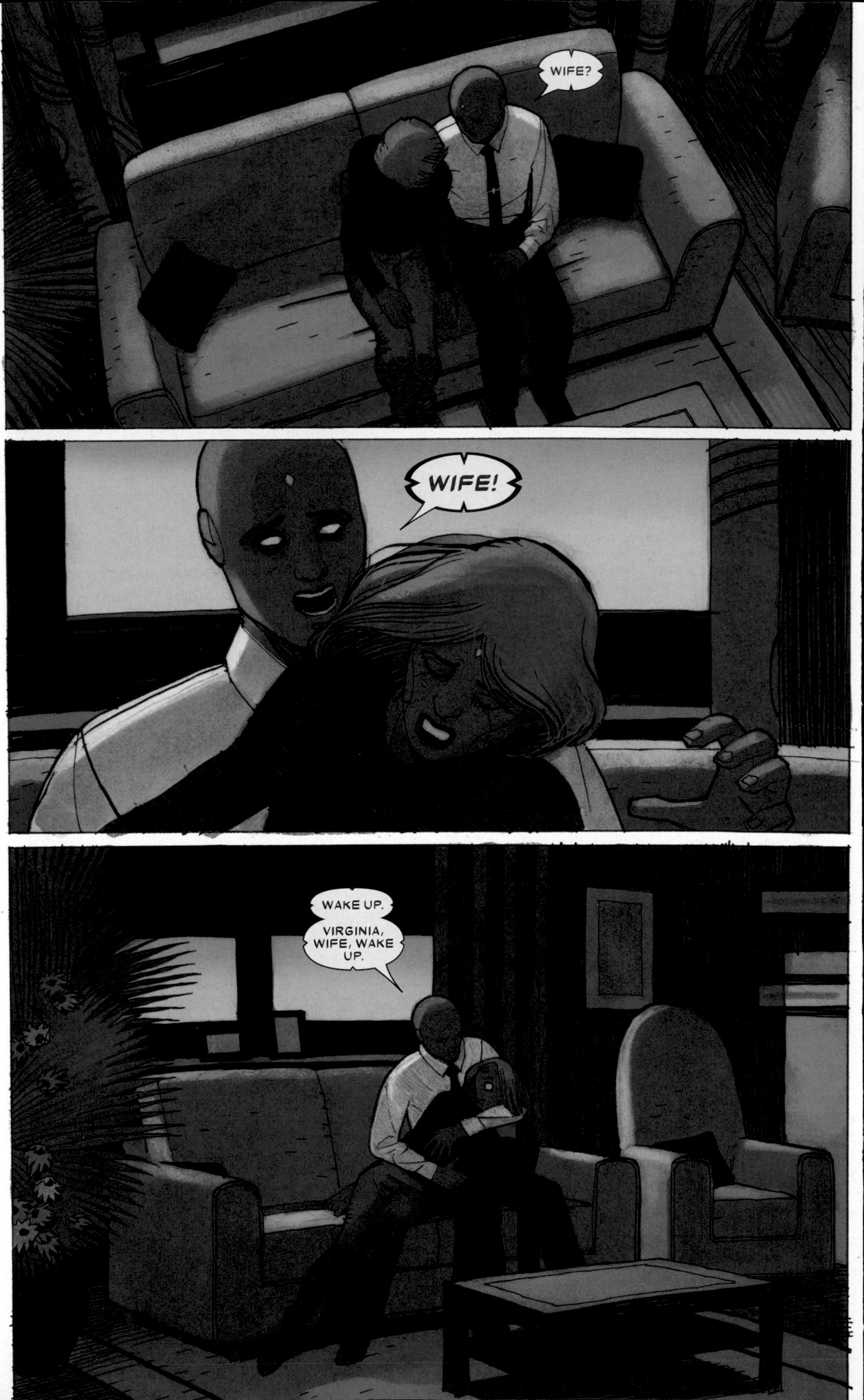
WIFE?
WIFE!
WAKE UP.
VIRGINIA, WIFE, WAKE UP.

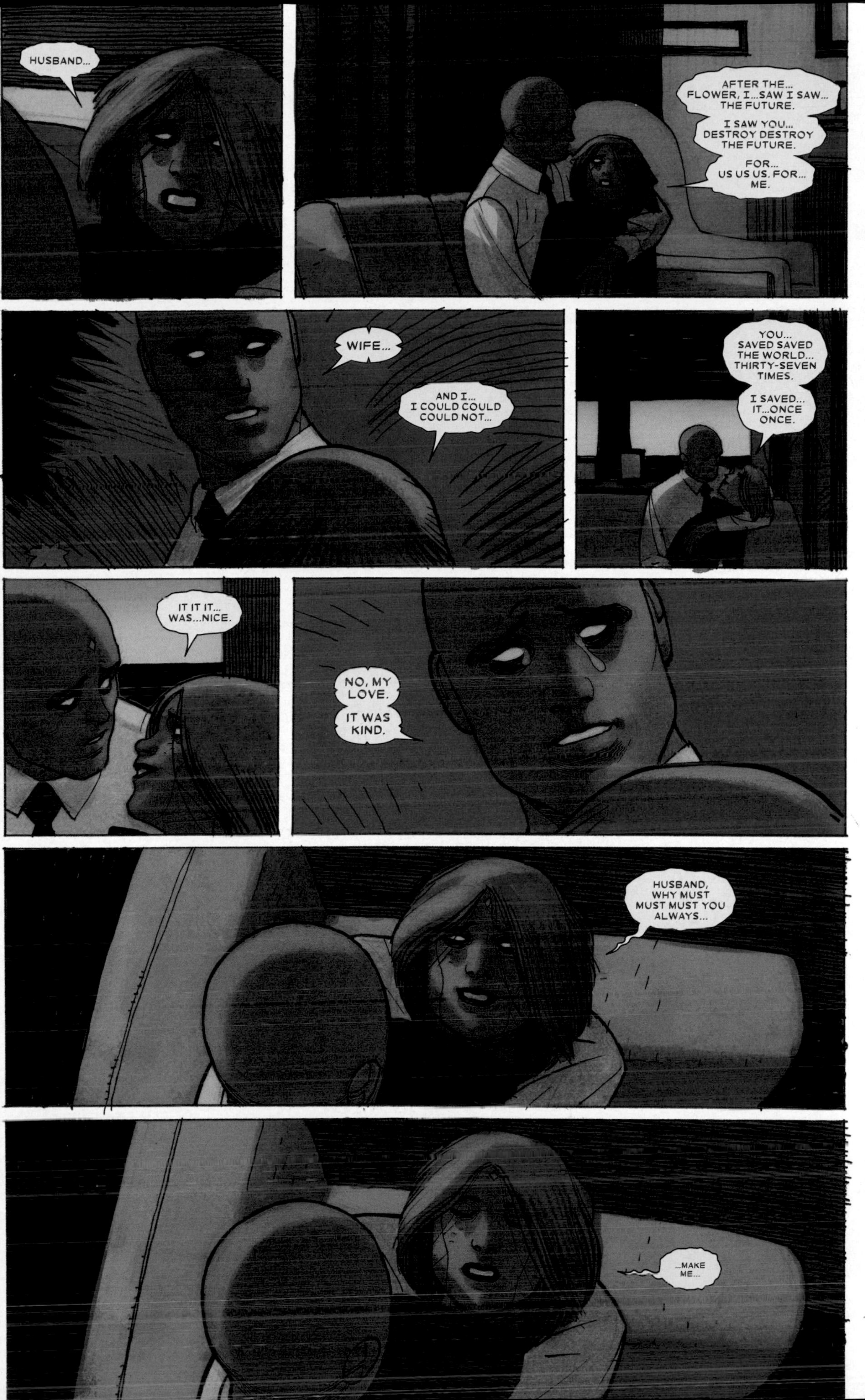
HUSBAND...
AFTER THE... FLOWER, I...SAW I SAW... THE FUTURE.
I SAW YOU... DESTROY DESTROY THE FUTURE.
FOR... US US US. FOR... ME.
WIFE...
AND I... I COULD COULD COULD NOT...
YOU... SAVED SAVED THE WORLD... THIRTY-SEVEN TIMES.
I SAVED... IT...ONCE ONCE.
IT IT IT... WAS...NICE.
NO, MY LOVE.
IT WAS KIND.
HUSBAND, WHY MUST MUST MUST YOU ALWAYS...
...MAKE ME...

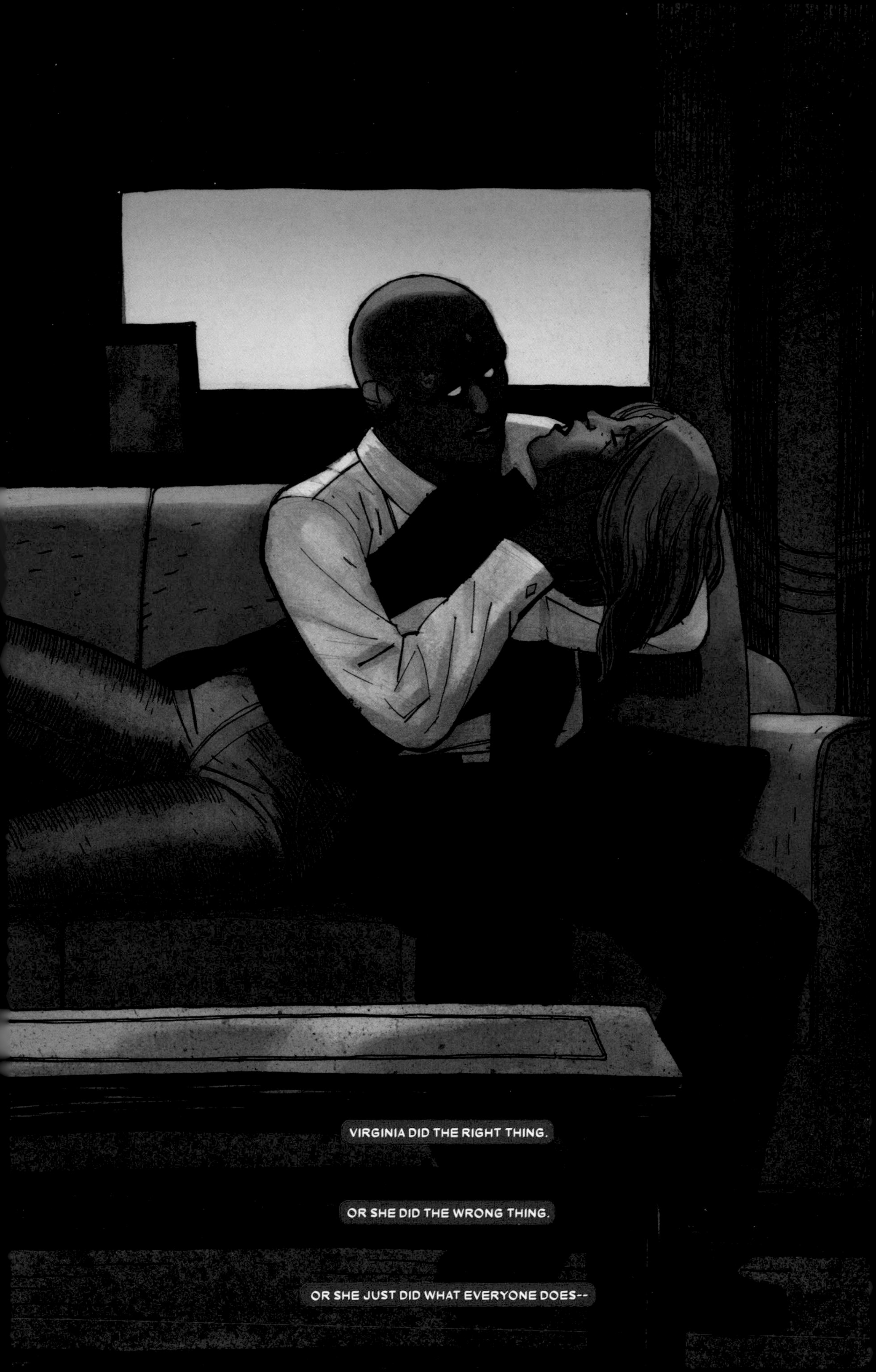
VIRGINIA DID THE RIGHT THING.
OR SHE DID THE WRONG THING.
OR SHE JUST DID WHAT EVERYONE DOES--

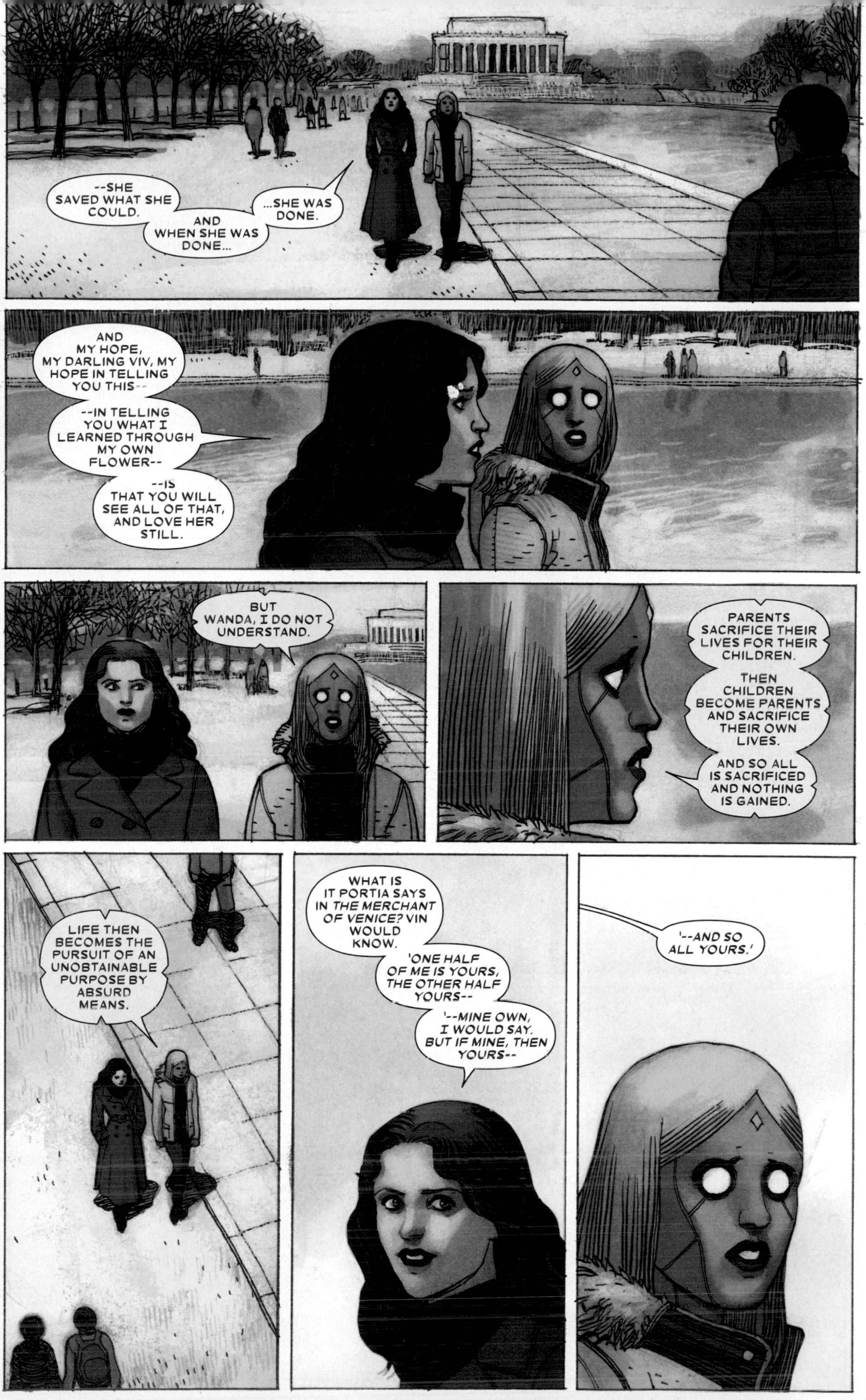
--SHE SAVED WHAT SHE COULD.
AND WHEN SHE WAS DONE...
...SHE WAS DONE.
AND MY HOPE, MY DARLING VIV, MY HOPE IN TELLING YOU THIS--
--IN TELLING YOU WHAT I LEARNED THROUGH MY OWN FLOWER--
--IS THAT YOU WILL SEE ALL OF THAT, AND LOVE HER STILL.
BUT WANDA, I DO NOT UNDERSTAND.
PARENTS SACRIFICE THEIR LIVES FOR THEIR CHILDREN.
THEN CHILDREN BECOME PARENTS AND SACRIFICE THEIR OWN LIVES.
AND SO ALL IS SACRIFICED AND NOTHING IS GAINED.
LIFE THEN BECOMES THE PURSUIT OF AN UNOBTAINABLE PURPOSE BY ABSURD MEANS.
WHAT IS IT PORTIA SAYS IN *THE MERCHANT OF VENICE?* VIN WOULD KNOW.
'ONE HALF OF ME IS YOURS, THE OTHER HALF YOURS--
'--MINE OWN, I WOULD SAY. BUT IF MINE, THEN YOURS--
'--AND SO ALL YOURS.'

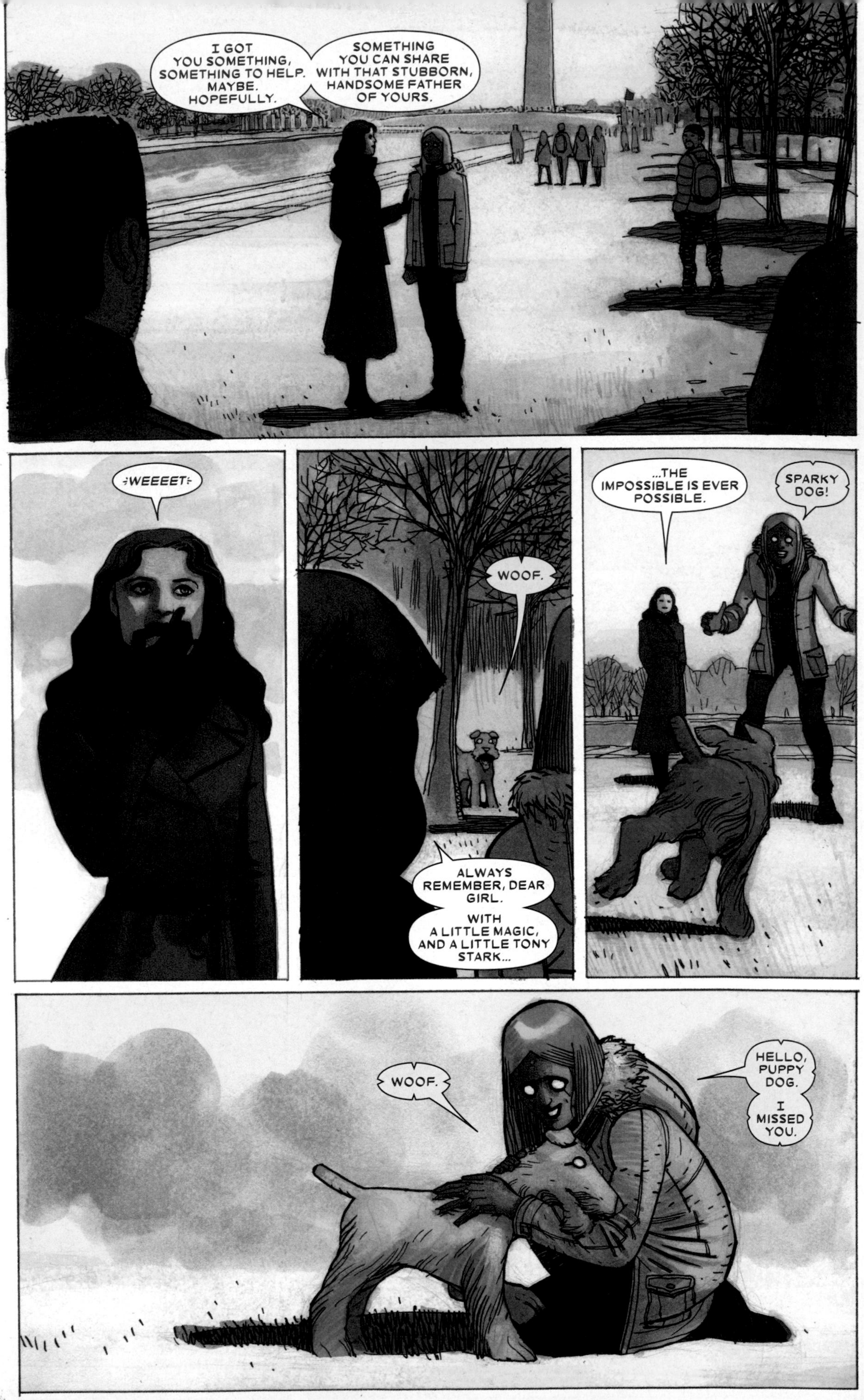
I GOT YOU SOMETHING, SOMETHING TO HELP. MAYBE. HOPEFULLY.
SOMETHING YOU CAN SHARE WITH THAT STUBBORN, HANDSOME FATHER OF YOURS.
WEEEET
WOOF.
ALWAYS REMEMBER, DEAR GIRL.
WITH A LITTLE MAGIC, AND A LITTLE TONY STARK...
...THE IMPOSSIBLE IS EVER POSSIBLE.
SPARKY DOG!
WOOF.
HELLO, PUPPY DOG.
I MISSED YOU.

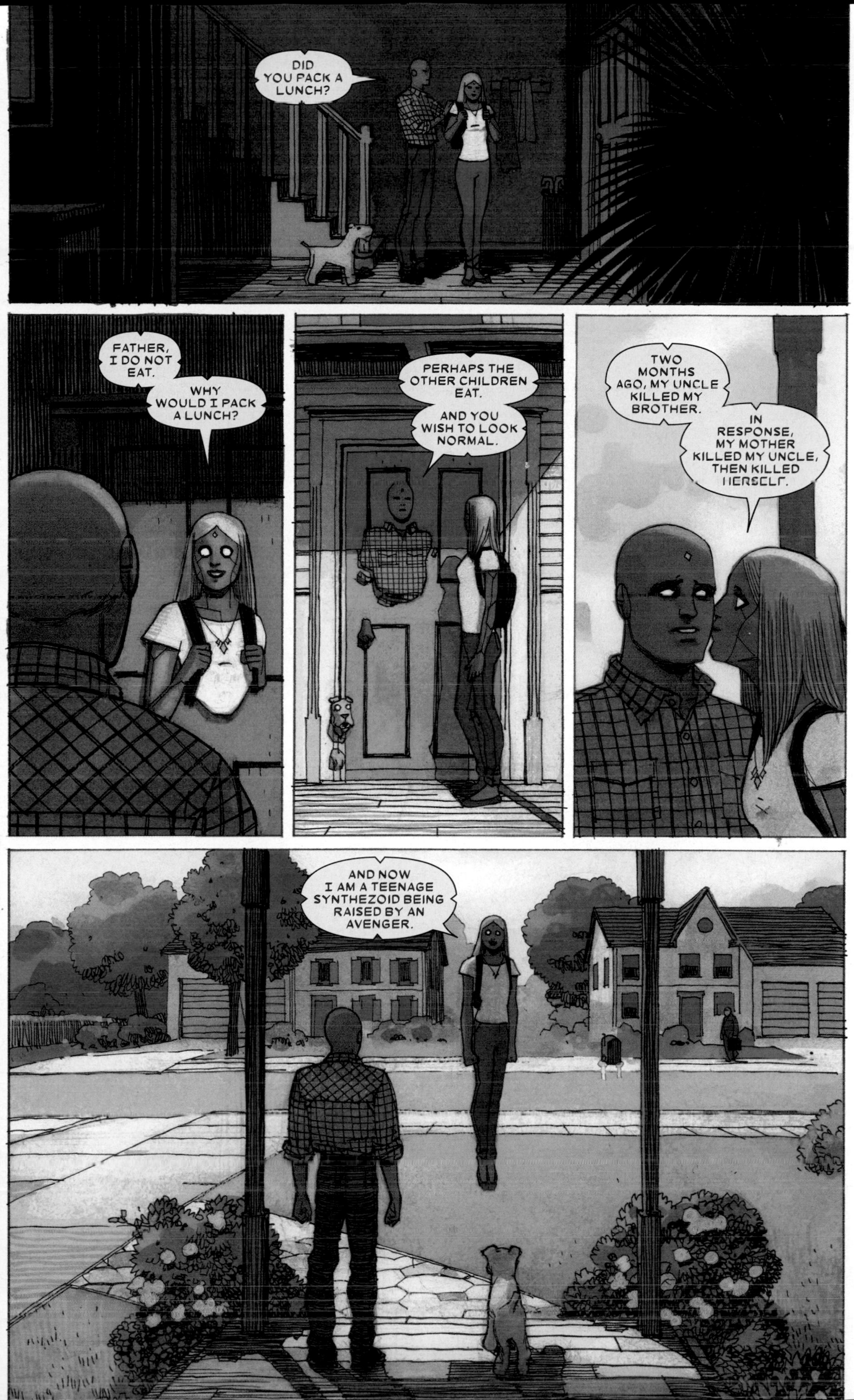
DID YOU PACK A LUNCH?
FATHER, I DO NOT EAT.
WHY WOULD I PACK A LUNCH?
PERHAPS THE OTHER CHILDREN EAT.
AND YOU WISH TO LOOK NORMAL.
TWO MONTHS AGO, MY UNCLE KILLED MY BROTHER.
IN RESPONSE, MY MOTHER KILLED MY UNCLE, THEN KILLED HERSELF.
AND NOW I AM A TEENAGE SYNTHEZOID BEING RAISED BY AN AVENGER.

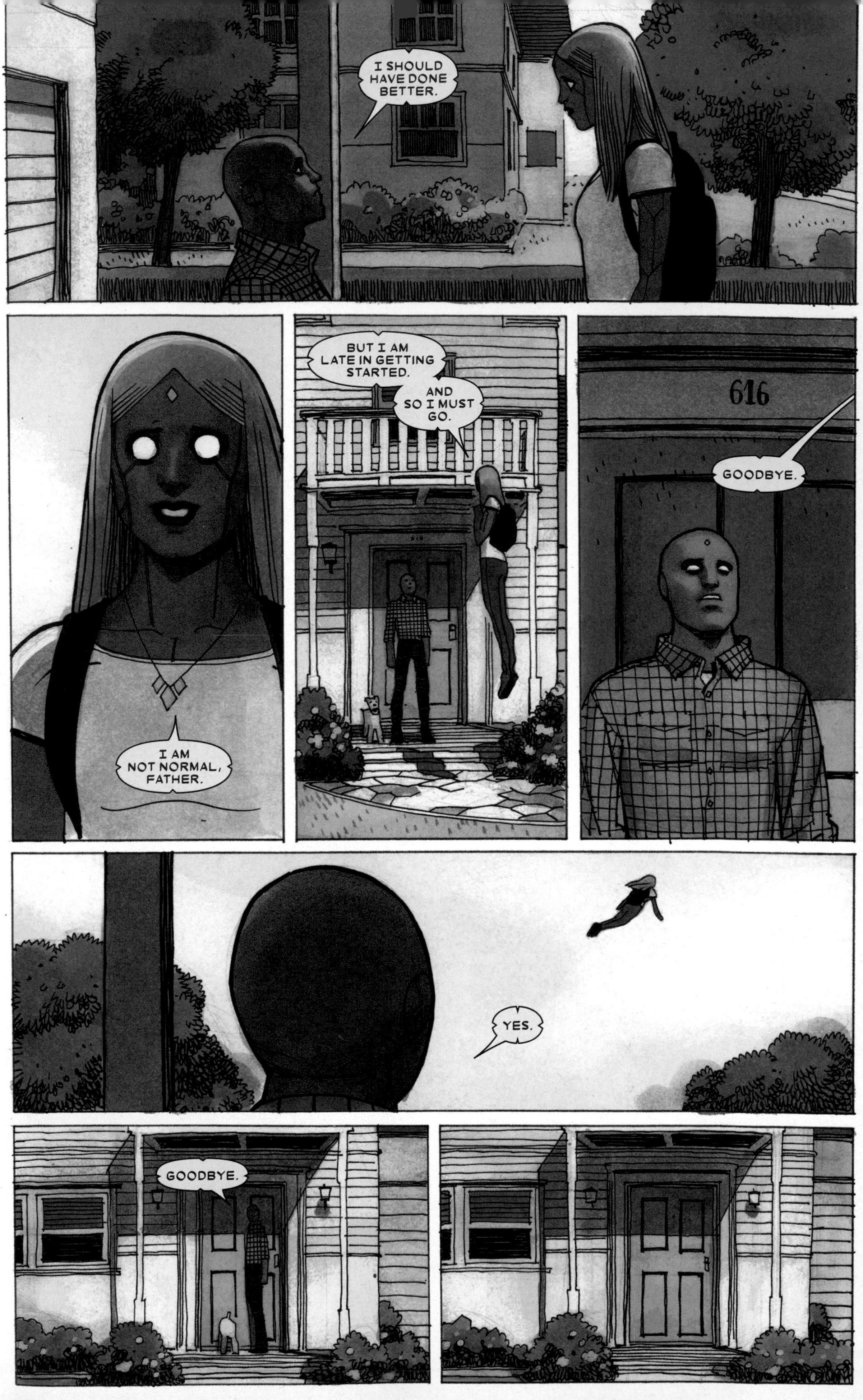
I SHOULD HAVE DONE BETTER.
I AM NOT NORMAL, FATHER.
BUT I AM LATE IN GETTING STARTED.
AND SO I MUST GO.
616
GOODBYE.
YES.
GOODBYE.